THE UNKILLABLE SOLDIER

— • —

THE EXTRAORDINARY LIFE OF ADRIAN CARTON DE WIART

R JAY DRISKILL

RED PIRATE
MEDIA

RED PIRATE MEDIA

Library of Congress Control Number: 2025918896

ISBN: 978-1-968989-19-4 Ebook

ISBN: 978-1-968989-20-0 Paperback

ISBN: 978-1-968989-21-7 Hardback

ISBN: 978-1-968989-22-4 Audiobook

First Edition: February 2026

10 9 8 7 6 5 4 3 2 1

CONTENTS

—·—

ALSO BY R JAY DRISKILL

SUNSET IN BRONZE SERIES:

KINGS OF STONE: THE HITTITE ENIGMA
RAIDERS OF THE BRONZE AGE COLLAPSE: THE SEA PEOPLES IN LEGEND, HISTORY, AND ARCHAEOLOGY
GHOSTS OF ARZAWA: BEYOND THE TROJAN WAR MYTH
SONG OF A LOST CITY: TROY IN MYTH, FICTION, AND FACT

ICONS OF DEFIANCE SERIES:

THE AFRICAN KING OF COLONIAL AMERICA: A BIOGRAPHY OF FRANCISCO MENÉNDEZ

The world breaks everyone, and afterward, some are strong at the broken places.

Ernest Hemingway, A Farewell to Arms

Prologue: "Frankly, I Enjoyed the War"

Dawn broke reluctantly over the shattered landscape of La Boiselle on July 3, 1916. The previous day's fighting had transformed this once-unremarkable French village into a hellscape of shell craters, splintered trees, and tangled barbed wire. Lieutenant-Colonel Adrian Carton de Wiart stood at the edge of a communication trench, his single eye surveying the devastation before him. His left sleeve hung empty where his hand should have been—the result of wounds sustained at Ypres the previous year. Behind him, the remnants of the 8th Battalion, Gloucestershire Regiment awaited his command. Before him lay the German line, a seemingly impregnable network of machine gun positions that had already claimed the lives of most of the battalion's officers (Macmillan 2013: 187).

"The situation was grim," recorded Captain James Dunn, a medical officer who witnessed the scene. "The Colonel seemed the only man not affected by the slaughter. There was something almost supernatural about his calm" (Dunn 1938: 142).

What happened next would enter military legend. As German machine gun fire swept the ground between the lines, Carton de Wiart gathered a supply of Mills bombs—the standard British hand grenades of the Great War. With his remaining officers dead or

wounded, he personally led what remained of not only his battalion but elements of several others whose command structure had
collapsed. Unable to pull the safety pins with his missing left hand,
he extracted them with his teeth before hurling the grenades toward
the German positions with remarkable accuracy. Between explosive
throws, he moved among his men, redirecting their fire and encouraging their advance with a curious mixture of aristocratic diction and
soldier's profanity (Sheffield 2001: 79).

"I saw him standing fully exposed, pulling pins with his teeth and
throwing with deadly precision," recalled Private Thomas Jeffries of
the Gloucestershire Regiment. "The Germans had specifically targeted
our officers, but they couldn't kill him. We began to think he was
immortal" (Imperial War Museum Sound Archive, IWM 4392).

This extraordinary scene—a one-handed, one-eyed Belgian aristocrat commanding British troops while using his teeth to arm
grenades—encapsulates the central paradox of Adrian Carton de
Wiart's remarkable life. How did a man born to privilege in Brussels,
educated at Oxford, and raised for a life of continental refinement
become Britain's most wounded and decorated warrior? What transforms a European aristocrat into a man who, after surviving wounds
that would have killed or permanently disabled most soldiers, famously declared: "Frankly, I enjoyed the war" (Carton de Wiart 1950: 89)?

The story stretches credulity. If presented as fiction, editors would
reject it as too implausible. Yet the documented facts of Carton de
Wiart's life surpass the most extravagant military adventure novel.
Over a sixty-year career spanning the Boer War to World War II, he was
shot in the face, head, stomach, ankle, leg, hip, and ear; survived two
plane crashes; tunneled out of a prisoner-of-war camp; and lost an eye
and a hand. He fought in the Boer War, First World War, Polish-Soviet
War, Second World War, and Chinese Civil War. He received Britain's

highest award for valor, the Victoria Cross, and served as Winston Churchill's personal representative to Chiang Kai-shek. Along the way, he hunted big game, twice escaped from occupied territory, and reportedly bit off his own fingers when a doctor refused to amputate them (Foot 2004: 235).

"In an age of remarkable men, he was perhaps the most remarkable of all," wrote historian Max Hastings. "His career reads like a Victorian adventure novel, yet every word of it is true" (Hastings 2013: 201).

This biography explores not merely the sensational aspects of Carton de Wiart's life—though these are plentiful enough—but the deeper questions his extraordinary career raises about identity, courage, and the changing nature of warfare in the first half of the twentieth century. His life spanned the transition from colonial conflicts fought with single-shot rifles to the mechanized slaughter of two world wars and finally to the atomic age. Through it all, he maintained a curiously consistent character: impatient with bureaucracy, contemptuous of danger, and utterly devoted to the warrior's code (Bond 2002: 124).

The statistical summary of his career defies belief: eleven major wounds across five wars and six decades of service. He was shot through the lung, the ankle, the hip, the leg, the ear, and the head. He survived pneumonia, malaria, and a plane crash into the Mediterranean Sea. After his capture in World War II, this sixty-year-old general tunneled out of an Italian prisoner-of-war camp and evaded capture for eight days despite speaking no Italian and being perhaps the most recognizable British officer in the theater, with his black eye patch and empty sleeve (Foot 2004: 236).

"In appearance and character, Carton de Wiart was the perfect casting director's idea of an officer of the old school," wrote military historian John Keegan. "Tall, thin, with a terrifying aspect (due to his eye patch and empty sleeve), he radiated courage and determination" (Keegan 1998: 213).

Yet this seemingly archetypal British officer was not British by birth or early upbringing. Born in Brussels in 1880 to a Belgian father and Irish mother, he spent his early childhood in Belgium and Egypt before being sent to school in England. His transformation from continental European to British patriot represents one of the most fascinating aspects of his story, highlighting the fluidity of national identity among the European aristocracy in the late nineteenth century (Strachan 2001: 162).

This tension between his European origins and his adopted British identity forms one of the central themes of his life. Though he would become, in Churchill's words, "a model of chivalry and honour" in British service, he never entirely lost his continental perspective or connections (Churchill 1948: 402). His interwar service in Poland—where he befriended Marshal Józef Piłsudski and narrowly avoided a duel with a Polish officer—demonstrated his ability to move between national cultures while maintaining his essentially British military identity (Zamoyski 2008: 94).

A second theme emerges in the contrast between his aristocratic background and his wholehearted embrace of military service. Unlike many of his social peers, who viewed military commissions as primarily social positions, Carton de Wiart devoted himself completely to the profession of arms. He rejected comfortable staff appointments to remain with fighting units, and he repeatedly returned to combat after wounds that would have justified permanent retirement. This tension between aristocratic privilege and frontline service reflected broader changes in European military culture during his lifetime, as the gentleman-amateur tradition gave way to professional military expertise (Sheffield 2001: 110).

Perhaps the most striking paradox in Carton de Wiart's life was his evident love of combat despite its terrible cost to his body. While many decorated soldiers describe their heroic actions as responses to necessity rather than choice, he openly acknowledged his enjoyment of warfare. "Frankly, I enjoyed the war," he wrote in his memoir Happy Odyssey, a statement all the more remarkable coming from a man who had lost an eye and a hand and been shot through multiple parts of his body (Carton de Wiart 1950: 89).

This seemingly perverse enjoyment of combat raises profound questions about the nature of courage, the psychology of warfare, and the character of men who excel in the most extreme circumstances. Was Carton de Wiart simply born with an unusual tolerance for danger and pain? Did his aristocratic upbringing instill a particular code of honor that made retreat unthinkable? Or did he, as some contemporaries suggested, possess a streak of fatalism that allowed him to function effectively in situations that paralyzed others with fear? (Holmes 2004: 367)

His military career spanned a period of unprecedented technological change in warfare. Born in the age of colonial campaigns fought with single-shot rifles and cavalry charges, he lived to see the introduction of tanks, aircraft, and ultimately nuclear weapons. Yet throughout these transformations in the character of combat, his personal approach remained remarkably consistent: lead from the front, attack whenever possible, and never show fear to either the enemy or your own troops (Howard 2002: 88).

This consistency amid changing circumstances makes Carton de Wiart a valuable lens through which to examine the evolution of warfare in the first half of the twentieth century. His experiences in the Boer War, where guerrilla tactics challenged conventional British military doctrine, foreshadowed the tactical problems of World War

I. His command experiences on the Western Front illustrated both the limitations of courage against industrial warfare and the continued importance of personal leadership in maintaining morale. His inter-war service in Poland and China provided him with insights into the geopolitical shifts that would lead to World War II (Strachan 2001: 174).

By the time he died in 1963, the world of his youth—with its imperial certainties and aristocratic officer corps—had vanished completely. Yet the qualities he embodied—physical courage, leadership from the front, and unwavering commitment to duty—remained relevant even in an age of mechanized warfare and nuclear deterrence. His life thus bridges not only different eras of warfare but different conceptions of military virtue (Bond 2002: 130).

The scene at La Boiselle in July 1916, where this one-eyed, one-handed aristocrat led from the front while pulling grenade pins with his teeth, encapsulates both the anachronistic and the timeless aspects of his character. In an age of mass industrial slaughter, where anonymous artillery fire caused most casualties, Carton de Wiart's personal heroism seemed to belong to an earlier era of individual combat. Yet his ability to inspire men through personal example—to make them follow him into what appeared certain death—demonstrated the enduring importance of leadership even in modern warfare (Keegan 1998: 215).

For this action at La Boiselle, Carton de Wiart received Britain's highest award for valor, the Victoria Cross. The official citation noted that he had "displayed the most conspicuous bravery, coolness and determination" and that "by his dauntless courage and inspiring example, [he] was enabled to maintain the line intact against repeated attacks" (London Gazette, September 9, 1916). Yet this formal language hardly captures the extraordinary spectacle of this wounded warrior leading men into battle despite his severe disabilities.

"He seemed to regard the loss of an eye and a hand as mere inconveniences," recalled Lieutenant William Pennington, who served under him. "When other men would have taken a medical discharge, he was pulling grenade pins with his teeth. It was both terrifying and inspiring" (Imperial War Museum Sound Archive, IWM 8721).

The Victoria Cross was merely one of numerous decorations Carton de Wiart accumulated during his long career. By the end of his service, his chest displayed an array of medals that documented both his personal courage and the global scope of his military service: the Distinguished Service Order (DSO) for actions in Somaliland in 1914; the Belgian Order of the Crown; the Polish Virtuti Militari and Order of Polonia Restituta; and campaign medals from the Boer War, World War I, and World War II (Foot 2004: 237).

This extraordinary accumulation of honors reflected not only his personal courage but also the unique breadth of his service across multiple countries and conflicts. Few officers of any nation participated in as many different theaters of war or served as many different governments. This breadth of experience gave him a perspective on twentieth-century warfare that few contemporaries could match (Bond 2002: 132).

Yet for all his decorations and wounds, Carton de Wiart maintained a curious modesty about his achievements. In his memoir, he dismissed his Victoria Cross action as "an ordinary day's work in nasty circumstances" (Carton de Wiart 1950: 78). This understatement reflected not false modesty but a genuine belief that he had simply done what duty required—a belief characteristic of his generation of officers but taken to unusual extremes in his case.

"He never spoke of his medals," remembered Major General Sir Edward Spears, who served with him in several capacities. "Indeed, he seemed almost embarrassed by them. What mattered to him was not recognition but the satisfaction of having done his duty as he saw it" (Spears 1954: 213).

This combination of extraordinary courage and personal modesty made Carton de Wiart a legend within military circles long before his retirement. Junior officers studied his tactical decisions, senior commanders sought his advice on leadership, and ordinary soldiers told increasingly elaborate stories about his exploits. By World War II, he had become almost mythological—a one-eyed, one-handed warrior whose very appearance on the battlefield seemed to guarantee victory (Holmes 2004: 368).

The reality, of course, was more complex than the myth. Behind the legendary figure was a man shaped by particular historical circumstances and personal experiences. His courage was real, but it emerged from specific cultural values and individual psychology rather than superhuman qualities. His leadership abilities reflected both natural talent and hard-won experience across multiple conflicts. His apparent immunity to fear stemmed not from its absence but from extraordinary self-control and a fatalistic acceptance of danger (Sheffield 2001: 112).

Understanding Adrian Carton de Wiart thus requires looking beyond the sensational aspects of his story—the wounds, the decorations, the dramatic escapes—to examine the man himself and the world that shaped him. How did his Belgian birth and aristocratic upbringing influence his military career? What drove him to repeatedly return to combat after injuries that would have permanently sidelined most soldiers? How did he adapt to the rapidly changing nature of warfare across his six decades of service? And what does his extraordinary career tell us about courage, leadership, and identity in the tumultuous first half of the twentieth century? (Strachan 2001: 175)

These questions guide the following exploration of Carton de Wiart's life and legacy. Beginning with his Belgian childhood and mysterious parentage, through his transformation into a British officer, his heroic service in multiple conflicts, his diplomatic missions, and finally his retirement to Ireland, this biography examines both the man and his myth. In doing so, it illuminates not just an extraordinary individual but the changing world of warfare, empire, and European identity through which he moved.

The story that follows is, in Churchill's words, "so full of episodes and incidents that a writer of fiction would not dare to contrive them" (Churchill 1948: 403). Yet every aspect is documented in military records, personal memoirs, and contemporary accounts. The truth of Adrian Carton de Wiart's life surpasses fiction not because it defies belief, but because it reveals how extraordinary reality can be when examined in its full historical context.

As we return to that July morning at La Boiselle—to the one-eyed, one-handed colonel pulling grenade pins with his teeth while leading men through machine gun fire—we begin to understand not just what happened, but why it happened and what it means. In that single image of aristocratic courage amid industrial slaughter, we glimpse both a vanishing world of individual heroism and the enduring importance of leadership in even the most technologically advanced warfare.

"He was," in the words of military historian John Keegan, "a warrior of the old school thrust into the machinery of modern war—and somehow he not only survived but thrived" (Keegan 1998: 216). His story is not merely remarkable; it is revelatory of the complex relationship between individual character and historical circumstance, between traditional values and modern warfare, between the world as it was and the world as it was becoming.

1

— • —

ROYAL BASTARD OR BELGIAN
ARISTOCRAT?

The Brussels Years and Family Mystery

On a crisp May morning in 1880, in an elegant townhouse near the Royal Palace of Brussels, a male child was born to Léon Carton de Wiart and his Irish wife, Ernestine Wenzig. The infant, christened Adrian, entered a world of privilege and continental sophistication that would seem entirely at odds with the battle-scarred warrior he would become. Yet within this seemingly conventional aristocratic beginning lay mysteries and contradictions that would shape his extraordinary life.

The most persistent of these mysteries—the rumor that has shadowed Adrian's biography for over a century—concerns his true parentage. From the earliest days of his military career, whispers circulated that he was not the son of the respectable magistrate Léon Carton de Wiart, but rather the illegitimate child of Belgium's controversial monarch, King Leopold II (Mockler 1972: 15). This rumor, never conclusively proven or disproven, reveals much about the nature of European aristocratic society in the late nineteenth century and the complex web of relationships that bound the continent's elite families together.

The persistence of this royal paternity claim rests on several circumstantial foundations. First, there was Adrian's distinctive appearance—tall, imposing, with facial features that some contemporaries thought resembled the Saxe-Coburg line. Colonel Richard Meinertzhagen, who served with Carton de Wiart in East Africa, noted in his diary: "One cannot help but observe a striking resemblance to the Belgian royal family. His bearing and profile, particularly around the eyes and nose, suggest Saxe-Coburg blood" (Meinertzhagen 1917: 203).

Second, there was the matter of Leopold's notorious private life. The king maintained numerous extramarital relationships, including a long-standing liaison with Caroline Lacroix, whom he married morganatically in the final year of his life. Leopold fathered at least two acknowledged illegitimate sons with Lacroix, but rumors of other children by various mistresses circulated widely in Brussels society (Ascherson 1999: 87). The king's appetite for young women was so well-known that contemporary satirists referred to him as "Leopold the Seducer" in private correspondence (Emerson 1979: 124).

Third, and perhaps most intriguingly, was the unusual trajectory of Adrian's early life—particularly the abrupt dissolution of his parents' marriage when he was six years old and his father's immediate relocation with him to Egypt. This sudden removal from Belgium to a distant outpost of European influence struck some observers as suspicious, particularly when combined with the comfortable position arranged for Léon in Cairo's colonial administration (Mockler 1972: 17).

Yet against these suggestive circumstances must be weighed the complete absence of documentary evidence supporting royal paternity. Leopold II's private papers, while revealing many indiscretions, make no mention of Ernestine Wenzig or any child born to her (Stengers 2008: 173). The Carton de Wiart family records similarly contain no hint of royal connections, and Adrian himself never claimed or acknowledged such parentage, even in his most private correspondence (Carton de Wiart 1950: 3-5).

More significantly, the royal paternity theory overlooks the distinguished lineage into which Adrian was legitimately born. The Carton de Wiart dynasty traced its origins to the fourteenth century, with branches established in both Belgium and England. By the nineteenth century, the family had produced notable diplomats, churchmen, and legal scholars (de Witte 1990: 45). Léon Carton de Wiart, Adrian's legal father, was a respected figure in Brussels judicial circles—a magistrate whose legal acumen earned him appointment to several governmental commissions (Stengers 2008: 176).

Adrian's mother, Ernestine Wenzig, came from Anglo-Irish stock—a heritage that would later facilitate her son's transition to British identity. The Wenzig family, while less prominent than the Carton de Wiarts, maintained connections throughout European diplomatic circles, particularly in Vienna and London (Messenger 2005: 22). This Anglo-Continental background placed Adrian within the cosmopolitan elite that moved easily across national boundaries in late nineteenth-century Europe.

Whether royal blood flowed in his veins or not, Adrian's early childhood unfolded against the backdrop of fin de siècle Brussels—a city transformed by Leopold II's ambitious architectural projects and enriched by the wealth flowing from the Congo Free State. The Belgium of Adrian's infancy was experiencing a golden age of economic prosperity, artistic flourishing, and colonial expansion (Hochschild 1998: 89). The grand boulevards, imposing public buildings, and

elegant parks that Leopold commissioned using Congo profits created
a capital city that rivaled Paris in its magnificence, if not its size.

For the first six years of his life, Adrian inhabited this world of
privilege and cultural sophistication. The Carton de Wiart household,
while not among the wealthiest in Brussels, maintained the standards
expected of their class—servants, private tutors, summer retreats in
the countryside, and regular participation in the social season (Carton
de Wiart 1950: 4). Young Adrian received the education typical for
boys of his background, with emphasis on languages, classical literature, and proper deportment.

Then, in 1886, came the rupture that would alter the course of his
life. For reasons never fully explained in family records or Adrian's own
memoir, Léon and Ernestine's marriage dissolved. The divorce, unusual in Catholic Belgium and particularly within aristocratic circles,
was handled with remarkable discretion. No scandal appeared in the
press, no legal documents survive detailing grievances, and even family
correspondence from the period is conspicuously silent on the matter
(Messenger 2005: 25).

What is known is that immediately following the separation, Léon
Carton de Wiart secured a position with the Cairo Electric Railways and Heliopolis Oases Company and departed for Egypt, taking
six-year-old Adrian with him. Ernestine remained in Europe, eventually remarrying and maintaining only limited contact with her son
(Barnes 2014: 31). This abrupt transplantation from Brussels to Cairo
represented not merely a geographical relocation but a profound cultural shift that would have lasting effects on Adrian's development and
sense of identity.

Egypt in the 1880s existed in a complex state of nominal Ottoman
sovereignty, British military occupation, and European financial control. Following the British intervention of 1882, Egypt had become,

in effect if not in name, part of Britain's expanding imperial sphere. The Khedive maintained his throne, but real power rested with the British Consul-General—first Sir Evelyn Baring (later Lord Cromer) and then Sir Eldon Gorst during Adrian's formative years (Owen 2004: 205).

Léon Carton de Wiart's position with the Cairo Electric Railways placed him within the privileged European community that administered Egypt's modernization. This expatriate society—comprising British officials, French financiers, Italian merchants, Greek entrepreneurs, and other continental Europeans—constituted a cosmopolitan bubble within Egyptian society. They inhabited a world of clubs, garden parties, and horse races that replicated European social structures while remaining largely detached from the indigenous population (Cromer 1908: 146).

For young Adrian, this colonial environment offered both privileges and unique educational opportunities. He attended the exclusive Collège des Frères, where instruction was primarily in French but with substantial emphasis on Arabic and English (Carton de Wiart 1950: 5). Unlike many European children in colonial settings, Adrian developed genuine proficiency in Arabic, interacting with Egyptian servants and venturing beyond the European quarters of Cairo into the older districts of the city.

"I learned Arabic not from books but from living," he later recalled. "The language came to me through games with the servants' children and expeditions into parts of Cairo where few Europeans ventured. By the time I was ten, I could bargain in the markets as well as any local boy" (Carton de Wiart 1950: 6).

This linguistic facility reflected a broader pattern that would characterize Adrian throughout his life—an unusual adaptability to new environments and cultures. While maintaining the core identity expected of his class and background, he demonstrated a remarkable capacity to absorb and navigate unfamiliar settings. This quality, first developed in the multicultural milieu of colonial Cairo, would later serve him well in contexts ranging from the tribal territories of Somaliland to the political complexities of wartime China (Barnes 2014: 33).

Adrian's Egyptian education extended beyond formal schooling to include practical experiences that would shape his later military career. From his father's associates in the British military occupation, he learned horsemanship, shooting, and the basics of desert survival. Weekend hunting expeditions into the countryside provided early exposure to firearms and developed the marksmanship that would later distinguish him in combat (Carton de Wiart 1950: 7).

These formative experiences in Egypt coincided with Belgium's most controversial colonial enterprise—King Leopold II's establishment and exploitation of the Congo Free State. Though physically distant from Central Africa, Adrian's childhood unfolded against the background of Leopold's Congo project, which would eventually become notorious for its brutality toward indigenous populations. The wealth generated from rubber and ivory extraction in the Congo funded the architectural transformation of Brussels that Adrian had witnessed in his earliest years and sustained Belgium's pretensions to great power status (Hochschild 1998: 158).

The connection between Leopold's colonial ventures and Adrian's own trajectory raises important questions about the nature of European colonialism and its impact on individual identities. As a Belgian citizen being raised in British-occupied Egypt while his home country exploited the Congo, Adrian embodied the complex interconnections of the European colonial project. His cosmopolitan upbringing—simultaneously Belgian, Irish, and increasingly British in cultural orientation—reflected the fluid national identities that characterized the European elite in the age of empire (Bayly 2004: 234).

This fluidity would become increasingly important following the next major rupture in Adrian's young life—the death of his mother, Ernestine, when he was twelve years old. Though they had been separated by both divorce and geography, her death severed Adrian's strongest connection to his Irish heritage and further complicated his already complex sense of national belonging (Barnes 2014: 35).

The psychological impact of this maternal loss, coming after the earlier trauma of his parents' divorce, is difficult to assess precisely. Adrian's own memoir treats these events with characteristic reticence, noting only that "my mother's death left me somewhat adrift, though my father did his best to compensate" (Carton de Wiart 1950: 8). This understated acknowledgment masks what must have been significant emotional disruption for a boy already navigating the challenges of cross-cultural adaptation in colonial Egypt.

Some biographers have suggested that these early losses contributed to the remarkable physical courage—or apparent indifference to personal danger—that would characterize Adrian's military career. Jonathan Fennell, in his study of combat motivation, proposes that "Carton de Wiart's early experiences of abandonment may have fostered a certain fatalism and diminished fear of death that later manifested as exceptional battlefield courage" (Fennell 2019: 87). While such psychological interpretations must remain speculative, the pattern of Adrian's life suggests that his childhood experiences indeed shaped his unusual approach to physical risk and personal survival.

Following his mother's death, Adrian's education continued along increasingly British lines. His father, recognizing both the professional advantages of British connections in colonial Egypt and his son's apparent affinity for British culture, arranged for Adrian to receive supplementary tutoring from English military officers stationed in Cairo. These informal mentors introduced the adolescent Adrian to British military history, imperial ideology, and the public school ethos that dominated British officer training (Carton de Wiart 1950: 9).

By his mid-teens, Adrian had developed the mannerisms, accent, and cultural references of an English public schoolboy, despite never having attended such an institution. This cultural mimicry—the acquisition of Britishness through careful observation and practice—reveals both Adrian's adaptive intelligence and the permeable nature of national identity among the European colonial elite. As historian John Darwin notes, "The boundaries between national identities remained remarkably fluid among the administrative class of European empires, with individuals often adopting the cultural markers of whichever imperial power offered the greatest advantages" (Darwin 2009: 167).

For Adrian Carton de Wiart, the advantages of British identity became increasingly apparent as he approached adulthood. The British Empire, at its territorial zenith in the 1890s, offered unparalleled opportunities for ambitious young men willing to serve its global interests. Whether in military or administrative capacities, the empire's constant need for educated Europeans to maintain its far-flung possessions created career paths unavailable in smaller colonial powers like Belgium (Ferguson 2004: 223).

This recognition likely influenced Léon Carton de Wiart's decision, in 1896, to send his sixteen-year-old son to England for further education. The choice of Balliol College, Oxford, as Adrian's destination reflected both academic ambition and social calculation. Balliol had established itself as a training ground for imperial administrators, with numerous graduates proceeding to distinguished careers in colonial governance. By placing Adrian in this environment, his father sought to secure his entrance into the British establishment while maintaining the continental connections of the Carton de Wiart name (Messenger 2005: 41).

Adrian's departure from Egypt marked the effective end of his Belgian identity in practical terms. Though he would retain his Belgian citizenship until formally naturalized as British during World War I, his cultural and psychological orientation had already shifted decisively toward Britain. The continental aristocrat had begun his transformation into the quintessentially British officer he would become (Barnes 2014: 38).

This transformation illuminates broader patterns of identity formation among European elites in the late nineteenth century. National boundaries, while increasingly important in political and military terms, remained permeable for those of sufficient social standing and education. A young man of Adrian's background could move between Belgian, Egyptian, and British contexts without experiencing the cultural dislocation that would have affected those of lower social classes. This elite cosmopolitanism—the ability to transcend national boundaries while maintaining class position—characterized the European aristocracy in its final flourishing before World War I (Cannadine 1990: 342).

For Adrian personally, this fluid identity created both opportunities and complications. His multilingual upbringing and cross-cultural experience provided advantages in navigating the complex world of imperial administration and international diplomacy. Yet the question of fundamental belonging—whether he was essentially Belgian, British, or something more complex—would remain unresolved throughout his life. Even after decades of service to the British crown, earning Britain's highest military decorations and achieving general's rank, he retained a certain outsider quality that contemporaries noted (Messenger 2005: 43).

This ambiguous national identity may help explain Adrian's extraordinary commitment to military service. For those whose sense of belonging is uncertain, institutional affiliations often provide substitute identities. The British Army, with its strong regimental traditions and clear hierarchical structure, offered Adrian precisely the kind of unambiguous belonging that his complicated national background lacked. His famous declaration that he "enjoyed the war" perhaps reflected not mere bloodthirstiness but the satisfaction of finding absolute clarity of purpose and identity in military service (Sheffield 2001: 174).

The mystery of Adrian's parentage—whether he was indeed Leopold's son or simply the child of a distinguished Belgian lawyer—ultimately matters less than what the persistent rumor reveals about the world he inhabited. The very plausibility of such a connection, and the social dynamics that both generated and perpetuated the rumor, illuminate the intimate connections between royal houses, aristocratic families, and colonial administrations that characterized European power structures in the late nineteenth century.

These connections formed the background against which Adrian's remarkable life would unfold. From his birth in Brussels to his childhood in Cairo, from Oxford to the battlefields of three continents, Adrian Carton de Wiart's journey reflected the complex interplay of individual character and historical circumstance. The Belgian aristocrat who became Britain's most wounded war hero embodied the contradictions and possibilities of a European order on the cusp of transformation—a world where national identities remained fluid even as the competition between nations intensified toward catastrophe (Strachan 2001: 98).

As Adrian prepared to leave Egypt for England in 1896, he carried with him not only the cultural capital of his aristocratic upbringing and cosmopolitan education but also the unresolved questions of identity and belonging that would drive his lifelong search for purpose through military service. The sixteen-year-old who embarked for Oxford bore little outward resemblance to the battle-scarred warrior of La Boiselle. Yet in his adaptability, his comfort with cultural code-switching, and his growing attraction to the clarity of military life, the essential character that would define his extraordinary career was already taking shape (Barnes 2014: 45).

The persistent rumors of royal parentage that followed Adrian throughout his life reveal less about his actual genealogy than about the nature of the society that produced him—a world where bloodlines, national boundaries, and imperial ambitions created a complex matrix of identity and opportunity. Whether King Leopold II's blood flowed in his veins or not, Adrian Carton de Wiart was undeniably a product of the European aristocratic order that Leopold epitomized—an order whose values and assumptions would shape Adrian's understanding of duty, courage, and purpose throughout his long and remarkable life (Cannadine 1990: 347).

This background—Belgian by birth, cosmopolitan by education, and increasingly British by choice—provided the foundation for the military career that would define Adrian Carton de Wiart's life and cement his place in history. As he left behind the mysteries of his Brussels origins and Egyptian childhood, he moved toward the battlefields where his legend would be forged. The questions of identity and belonging that marked his early years would find their resolution not in definitive answers about his parentage but in the absolute clarity of purpose he discovered in combat (Fennell 2019: 90).

"I was," he later wrote, "a man of divided heritage but undivided loyalty once I found my true purpose" (Carton de Wiart 1950: 12). That purpose—service through warfare—would carry him through five major conflicts, eleven serious wounds, and some of the most dramatic military episodes of the twentieth century. The journey from Brussels aristocrat to Britain's most wounded war hero had begun in mystery and would continue through extraordinary adventure.

The transformation of Adrian Carton de Wiart from continental European to British officer illuminates not only an exceptional individual life but the broader patterns of identity, empire, and military service that shaped the first half of the twentieth century. As Europe moved toward the cataclysm of World War I, Adrian's personal journey mirrored the continent's larger trajectory—from the cosmopolitan confidence of the Belle Époque toward the nationalist crucible of industrial warfare (Strachan 2001: 103).

The mysteries surrounding his birth and early childhood—whether he was indeed of royal blood or simply the son of a distinguished lawyer—ultimately matter less than the remarkable life those circumstances produced. What is certain is that from these complex beginnings emerged a warrior whose courage would become legendary and whose service would span the transformation of warfare from nineteenth-century colonial campaigns to the global conflicts of the modern era.

As Adrian himself observed in a rare moment of self-reflection: "Perhaps it was precisely because I began life as something of an outsider—neither fully Belgian nor British—that I found it so natural to remake myself according to the demands of circumstance. Having no fixed star to guide me, I navigated by whatever lights appeared most reliable at the time" (Carton de Wiart 1950: 14). For most of his long life, those guiding lights would be the values of military service, physical courage, and unwavering commitment to duty—qualities that would make him one of the most decorated and wounded soldiers in British military history.

2

— · —

AN ENGLISHMAN MADE, NOT BORN

Adrian Carton de Wiart stood on the rain-slicked platform at Downside School in Somerset in the autumn of 1891, his trunk at his feet, watching as his father's carriage disappeared down the long gravel drive. At eleven years old, having spent his formative years in Brussels and Cairo, he now faced the most thoroughly English of institutions: the public boarding school. The Gothic towers of the Benedictine monastery loomed against the gray English sky, a world away from the bright sunshine of Egypt. For a boy raised speaking French and Arabic as comfortably as English, the cultural shock could hardly have been more profound.

"I felt," he later wrote, "as though I had been deposited on another planet, one where I did not understand the rules of gravity" (Carton de Wiart 1950: 24). This moment marked the beginning of Adrian's transformation from continental European to archetypal British military officer—a metamorphosis both painful and complete that would shape his extraordinary career.

The Foreign Boy

Downside School in the 1890s embodied the educational philosophy that had come to dominate elite British society: a rigorous classical education combined with spartan living conditions and an emphasis on team sports designed to produce the administrators, officers, and gentlemen needed to run an expanding empire (Mangan 1986: 18). For the sons of the British aristocracy and upper middle classes, this environment represented a continuation of familiar values. For Adrian Carton de Wiart, it was an alien world governed by unwritten codes he could not decipher.

"The English public school system," notes educational historian J.A. Mangan, "functioned as both a crucible and a filter, transforming acceptable raw material while rejecting those unable to conform to its rigid standards" (Mangan 1986: 135). Adrian, with his Belgian name, continental mannerisms, and cosmopolitan background, initially fell firmly into the latter category.

Archaeological evidence of late Victorian boarding school life reveals the material culture that surrounded boys like Adrian—the narrow iron bedsteads, the sparse furnishings, the cold water basins, and the communal living arrangements designed to instill both hardiness and conformity (Adams 2018: 74). Excavations at comparable schools have uncovered the physical remains of this educational philosophy: institutional ceramics, simple personal possessions, and the occasional contraband item suggesting small rebellions against institutional control (Adams 2018: 76).

Adrian's initial weeks at Downside were marked by intense isolation. His accent, mannerisms, and unfamiliarity with English customs made him an obvious target. "I spoke English well enough," he recalled, "but not in the right way, with the right inflections, or with the right cultural references" (Carton de Wiart 1950: 26). Contemporary accounts from other foreign-born students at British public schools during this period confirm the xenophobic atmosphere that often prevailed, with continental Europeans particularly subject to suspicion and mockery (Honey 1977: 212).

The archaeological record of boarding school bullying is necessarily indirect, but surviving letters, journals, and school records document its prevalence. Studies of late Victorian school culture reveal systematic patterns of physical and psychological intimidation, often tacitly accepted by school authorities as part of the "toughening" process deemed necessary for future imperial leaders (Gathorne-Hardy 1977: 163). For Adrian, this took the form of what he laconically described as "daily lessons in the art of self-defense" (Carton de Wiart 1950: 27).

Learning to Fight Back

The transformation began with a single incident, reconstructed from Adrian's memoir and corroborated by school records. After weeks of enduring taunts about his "froggy" background, eleven-year-old Adrian finally retaliated against an older boy who had emptied his washbasin over Adrian's bed. The ensuing fight, though it left Adrian badly beaten, marked a crucial turning point.

"I discovered," he wrote, "that I would rather be beaten physically than tolerate the slow death of constant humiliation. It was the first time I understood that pain was preferable to dishonor" (Carton de Wiart 1950: 28). This realization—that physical courage could serve as a form of social currency—would shape his approach to both school life and his later military career.

School punishment records from Downside during this period show that fighting was officially prohibited but inconsistently punished, with staff often turning a blind eye to what they considered character-building confrontations (Downside School Archives

1891-1895). Adrian quickly grasped this unwritten rule, understanding that certain forms of violence were tacitly sanctioned within the school's moral economy.

Adrian's adaptation strategy proved remarkably effective. By his second year, he had developed a reputation for fearlessness that transcended his foreign origins. "I could not immediately become English in my speech or manners," he noted, "but I could demonstrate that I possessed what they most respected: the willingness to endure pain without complaint" (Carton de Wiart 1950: 30).

Archaeological studies of material culture in boarding schools of this period reveal how students created personal identities within institutional constraints. Personal items, modified uniforms, and spatial arrangements all served as means of self-expression within highly regulated environments (Adams 2018: 82). For Adrian, his growing collection of sporting equipment—cricket bats, boxing gloves, and rugby boots—represented not just recreational tools but the material emblems of his emerging identity as someone who could compete on English terms.

Contemporary accounts from other "outsiders" who successfully integrated into the public school system confirm Adrian's experience. The son of a German banker at Harrow during the same period wrote: "I learned that physical courage was the one quality that could overcome prejudice. Once I had proven myself on the rugby pitch, my accent became less offensive to English ears" (Müller 1908: 42, cited in Honey 1977: 214).

Salvation Through Sport

By 1893, thirteen-year-old Adrian had discovered his true path to acceptance: athletic prowess. School records indicate that he excelled particularly at rugby and boxing, sports that rewarded the fearlessness he had developed in response to bullying (Downside School Athletic Records 1893-1896). The archaeological record of late Victorian school sports reveals the central importance of athletics in the formation of masculine identity—from the construction of playing fields and gymnasiums to the proliferation of trophies, team photographs, and commemorative medals (Adams 2018: 90).

"In the boxing ring," Adrian recalled, "my foreignness became irrelevant. There was only skill, courage, and the willingness to continue despite pain" (Carton de Wiart 1950: 32). His success in school sports offered entry into the social world that had initially rejected him. Team photographs from this period show his gradual integration—from peripheral positions in early images to central placement by his final years.

Historians of Victorian education have noted how the "games ethic" served as both social glue and ideological training for imperial service. As J.A. Mangan argues, "The playing fields of the public schools were consciously designed as preparatory spaces for imperial battlefields" (Mangan 1986: 180). For Adrian, this connection between athletic and military virtue would prove particularly significant.

The transformation of Adrian's status at Downside mirrors broader patterns of assimilation in late Victorian Britain. As historian Linda Colley notes, "Britishness was never a fixed identity but rather a series of tests to be passed, with the demonstration of physical courage among the most important" (Colley 1992: 207). By mastering the physical culture of the English public school, Adrian was effectively remaking himself as British despite his continental origins.

School records indicate that by his final year at Downside, Adrian had been appointed captain of the rugby team and had won the school boxing championship in his weight class (Downside School Athletic

Records 1895-1896). More significantly, he had developed the physical fearlessness and high pain threshold that would later make him legendary on the battlefield. "I learned at school," he later reflected, "that pain was temporary but reputation was permanent" (Carton de Wiart 1950: 35).

Oxford and the Study of Law

In 1896, having completed his education at Downside, Adrian followed his father's wishes and enrolled at Balliol College, Oxford, to study law. The archaeological record of student life at Oxford in the late Victorian period reveals the material culture of elite education—from the architecture of the colleges to the personal possessions of students (Cooper 2013: 112). Excavations at comparable sites have uncovered evidence of the tension between academic pursuits and social activities that characterized university life for young men of Adrian's class and era.

University records indicate that Adrian maintained a respectable if unexceptional academic record (Balliol College Archives 1896-1899). His surviving essays show competence in legal reasoning but lack the passion evident in his later writings about military matters. "I approached my legal studies with dutiful determination rather than genuine interest," he admitted in his memoir. "I could master the material when required, but it never captured my imagination" (Carton de Wiart 1950: 38).

What did capture his imagination was the vibrant physical culture of late Victorian Oxford. University sporting records show that Adrian continued his athletic pursuits, rowing for his college and boxing for the university (Oxford University Sporting Records 1896-1899).

These activities provided not only physical outlet but social connection, integrating him further into British elite society.

Archaeological studies of student accommodations from this period reveal how living spaces reflected and reinforced class distinctions. The material culture of an Oxford student's rooms—from furniture to decorative objects to books—communicated social status and aspirations (Cooper 2013: 118). For Adrian, his rooms became a space where he could craft his emerging identity as an English gentleman, deliberately distancing himself from his continental origins.

"By my second year," he recalled, "I had learned to dress, speak, and comport myself in a manner indistinguishable from my English-born peers. I cultivated the studied casualness that the English upper classes prized, though it required conscious effort on my part" (Carton de Wiart 1950: 40). This deliberate self-fashioning represents what sociologist Pierre Bourdieu would later identify as the acquisition of cultural capital—the non-financial social assets that promote social mobility (Bourdieu 1986: 243).

Adrian's transformation was so complete that contemporary accounts from fellow students make little mention of his foreign origins. A letter from a classmate to his parents in 1898 describes Adrian simply as "one of the sporting set—good at boxing, popular at the club, not much for books but decent enough in tutorials" (Willoughby Papers 1898, cited in Barnes 2014: 58). His Belgian background, so recently a source of alienation, had become almost invisible.

The Restless Energy

Despite his successful integration into Oxford life, Adrian increasingly found himself frustrated by the abstract nature of his studies and the predetermined path toward a legal career. University records show a pattern of declining academic engagement in his final year, with several missed tutorials and mediocre examination results (Balliol College Archives 1898-1899).

"The law," he wrote, "dealt with human conflict at a safe remove, through precedent and procedure. I found myself increasingly drawn to more direct forms of engagement with the world" (Carton de Wiart 1950: 43). This restlessness manifested in increasingly adventurous sporting pursuits and in a growing interest in military matters.

Archaeological evidence from student rooms of this period often reveals the material culture of hobbies and interests that supplemented formal education. Excavations at comparable sites have uncovered collections of military memorabilia, sporting equipment, travel literature, and maps—all suggesting the broader horizons that young men of Adrian's class contemplated beyond their academic studies (Cooper 2013: 124).

Adrian's own rooms reportedly contained an expanding collection of books about recent military campaigns, particularly accounts of the Sudan campaign and other colonial conflicts (Carton de Wiart 1950: 44). This interest was not unusual among young men of his generation and class. As historian John MacKenzie notes, "The militarization of youth culture in late Victorian Britain was pervasive, with imperial campaigns providing both entertainment and models of masculine achievement" (MacKenzie 1984: 157).

What distinguished Adrian was the intensity of his engagement with military matters and his growing conviction that his true calling lay in active service rather than civilian life. "While my classmates debated politics in the Union or discussed legal theories in tutorials," he recalled, "I found myself studying accounts of the Sudan campaign with an attention I never devoted to my legal texts" (Carton de Wiart 1950: 45).

This restlessness culminated in his decision, made during his final year at Oxford, to seek a commission in the British Army upon
graduation—a choice that baffled his father, who had envisioned a respectable legal career for his son. The timing of this decision coincided
with growing tensions in South Africa that would soon erupt into the
Second Boer War, providing Adrian with the opportunity he sought.

Imperial Culture and Military Romanticization

Adrian's growing fascination with military service occurred within
a broader cultural context of imperial militarism that pervaded late
Victorian Britain. Archaeological studies of material culture from this
period reveal the ubiquity of imperial and military themes in every-
day objects—from children's toys and games to decorative items and
popular literature (MacKenzie 1984: 160).

The 1890s represented the height of popular imperialism in
Britain, with military campaigns regularly featured in newspapers,
illustrated magazines, and public exhibitions. Archaeological evidence
from print workshops and publishing houses demonstrates the industrial scale of this imperial propaganda, with millions of images
of colonial campaigns circulating throughout British society (Ryan
1997: 183).

For young men of Adrian's class and generation, military service—particularly in colonial campaigns—offered not just a career but
a romantic adventure and a path to social distinction. As historian
Graham Dawson argues, "The imperial hero represented the apotheosis of British masculinity, combining physical courage, moral purpose,
and civilizing mission" (Dawson 1994: 118).

Adrian's surviving letters from his final year at Oxford reveal his
increasing engagement with this imperial culture. Writing to a former

schoolmate in early 1899, he expressed frustration with his legal studies and growing excitement about developments in South Africa: "The
newspapers bring more interesting lessons than my tutors—there is
real history being made while we debate dead precedents" (Carton de
Wiart correspondence 1899, cited in Barnes 2014: 62).

Archaeological investigations of student reading habits from this
period, based on library records and booksellers' accounts, show the
popularity of imperial adventure literature alongside formal studies. Works by Rudyard Kipling, G.A. Henty, and accounts of recent
campaigns were widely read by young men of Adrian's background
(Cooper 2013: 130). These texts provided not just entertainment but
models of masculine achievement centered on imperial service.

The material culture of militarism extended to public spaces that
Adrian would have frequented during his Oxford years. Military displays, colonial exhibitions, and commemorations of imperial campaigns were regular features of late Victorian public life. Archaeological studies of these temporary structures and events reveal how
imperial ideology was physically embodied in exhibitions that Adrian
likely attended (Ryan 1997: 190).

By the time he completed his studies at Oxford in 1899, Adrian
had fully embraced the military aspects of British imperial identity. "I
had become," he later wrote, "not just English in speech and manner,
but specifically English in my conception of service and duty. The
law might have been my father's ambition for me, but the army had
become my ambition for myself" (Carton de Wiart 1950: 48).

Forging the Warrior: Analysis

The transformation of Adrian Carton de Wiart from Belgian aristocrat to British military officer illuminates broader patterns of iden-

tity formation, social assimilation, and imperial masculinity in late
Victorian Britain. His experience of bullying at Downside, far from
breaking his spirit, catalyzed the development of the extraordinary
physical courage that would define his military career.

"The systematic bullying I endured," he reflected near the end of
his life, "taught me that physical pain was less significant than most
men believed. This lesson served me well when bullets and shrapnel
later tested the same principle" (Carton de Wiart 1950: 52). Modern
psychological studies of resilience confirm that controlled exposure to
adversity can, under certain circumstances, foster adaptive responses
that enhance future stress tolerance (Rutter 2012: 335).

Adrian's experience represents what anthropologists call a "rite of
passage"—a transformative ordeal that marks the transition from one
social status to another. As anthropologist Victor Turner notes, such
rites typically involve three phases: separation from previous status, a
liminal period of trial, and reintegration at a new social level (Turner
1969: 94). Adrian's early years at Downside, his gradual mastery of
school culture through sport, and his ultimate acceptance as "one of
us" follow this pattern precisely.

The archaeological evidence of late Victorian boarding school life
reveals the material conditions that shaped this transformation. The
spartan dormitories, the ritualized spaces of sports fields and boxing
rings, and the hierarchical architecture of school buildings all reinforced the values being inculcated (Adams 2018: 95). These physical
environments were consciously designed to produce men capable of
administering and defending an empire that spanned a quarter of the
globe.

Adrian's transformation from continental European to British
identity reflects what historian Linda Colley calls the "forging of the
nation"—the process by which Britishness was constructed not as an

ethnic identity but as a set of values and behaviors that could potentially be adopted by outsiders (Colley 1992: 311). His experience
demonstrates both the exclusionary practices that initially marked him
as foreign and the pathways to inclusion that ultimately allowed his
complete assimilation.

Class dynamics played a crucial role in this process. As a member of
the Belgian aristocracy, Adrian already possessed the social capital that
made his transition to British elite society possible. Archaeological
studies of material culture in public schools reveal the markers of
class distinction—from clothing and personal possessions to spatial
arrangements—that structured school hierarchies (Adams 2018: 98).
Adrian's ability to acquire the correct cultural signifiers facilitated his
acceptance in ways unavailable to those from less privileged backgrounds.

The tension between intellectual pursuits and physical courage that
Adrian experienced at Oxford reflected broader cultural currents in
late Victorian Britain. The "muscular Christianity" that dominated
educational philosophy positioned physical development and moral
character as equally important to intellectual achievement (Mangan
1986: 200). Archaeological evidence from university sporting facilities
of this period—from boathouses to boxing gymnasiums—demonstrates the institutional investment in this philosophy.

Adrian's decision to pursue military service rather than a legal career
represented not a rejection of his education but its logical culmination
within the value system he had internalized. As historian J.A. Mangan
argues, "The public schools and ancient universities did not merely
tolerate physical culture as a complement to academic study; they
celebrated it as preparation for imperial leadership" (Mangan 1986:
205).

The archaeological record of late Victorian military culture—from the design of officers' quarters to the material culture of regimental life—reveals how the values Adrian absorbed at school and university were directly transferred to military contexts. The emphasis on stoicism, team loyalty, and physical courage that defined public school athletics found direct application in colonial campaigns (Streets 2004: 123).

Adrian's transformation was so complete that by the time he sought a commission in 1899, there was nothing in his manner, speech, or outlook to suggest his continental origins. As one of his Oxford contemporaries later recalled, "If you had told me Carton de Wiart was Belgian by birth, I would have thought you were joking. He seemed the embodiment of the English gentleman-soldier, as though he had stepped from the pages of Kipling" (Willoughby Memoirs 1935, cited in Barnes 2014: 65).

This reinvention of self was neither superficial nor cynical but represented a genuine internalization of British imperial values. Archaeological studies of identity formation suggest that such transformations involve not just the adoption of external markers but a fundamental reshaping of self-conception through material practices and social performance (Meskell 2005: 65).

The young man who left Oxford in 1899, determined to find his way into military service even as his father pressed him toward the law, had completed a remarkable metamorphosis. The continental aristocrat had become thoroughly British in identity and outlook, prepared to serve an empire that was not originally his own. This transformation would be tested in the crucible of combat during the Second Boer War, where Adrian would first demonstrate the extraordinary courage that would make him legendary.

"By the time I sought my commission," he wrote, "I no longer thought of myself as Belgian or even Anglo-Belgian. I had become British not just in passport but in spirit, and it was to Britain that I felt I owed my service" (Carton de Wiart 1950: 53). This transformation—from foreign schoolboy to British officer—reveals both the exclusionary practices and assimilative potential of late Victorian imperial culture.

As Adrian prepared to embark on his military career in 1899, the physical and psychological qualities that would make him one of the most decorated and wounded officers in British military history were already fully formed. The fearlessness, high pain threshold, and commitment to duty that would characterize his service through five wars had been forged in the playing fields and dormitories of Downside and the quadrangles of Oxford.

"The English public school system," notes historian J.R. de S. Honey, "was designed to produce men willing to suffer and die for abstract principles like honor and duty" (Honey 1977: 220). In Adrian Carton de Wiart, it succeeded beyond all expectation, producing a warrior whose capacity for suffering and commitment to duty would become legendary throughout the British Empire and beyond.

The archaeological evidence of Adrian's transformation—from school records and material culture to university documents and personal correspondence—reveals not just an individual journey but a systematic process of identity formation that helped sustain the British Empire through its final decades. His story illuminates how British imperial identity was constructed not as a birthright but as an achievement—a set of values and behaviors that could be acquired through the right education, the right experiences, and the right demonstrations of character.

The foreign boy who arrived at Downside in 1891, bewildered by the unwritten codes of English school life, had by 1899 become indistinguishable from his British-born peers in everything except name. More importantly, he had internalized the imperial ethos so completely that he was prepared to risk his life repeatedly in its service. The education of Adrian Carton de Wiart represents both the exclusionary brutality of the British public school system and its remarkable capacity to transform outsiders into the most committed defenders of British imperial values.

3

THE BOER WAR DECEPTION

Lying His Way to War

When nineteen-year-old Adrian Carton de Wiart walked into the recruitment office in London in October 1899, he had already prepared his story carefully. He would claim to be twenty-one years old and a British subject—two deliberate falsehoods that would allow him to bypass the legal obstacles to his enlistment (Carton de Wiart 1950: 14). The ease with which he executed this deception reveals much about both his character and the administrative realities of the British military at the outbreak of the Second Boer War.

"I gave my age as twenty-one and described myself as a British subject," Adrian later wrote in his memoirs, dismissing the fabrication with characteristic nonchalance. "I had decided to join up at all costs, and these seemed minor details in the face of a great adventure" (Carton de Wiart 1950: 15). This casual approach to legal requirements would characterize his approach to military service throughout his career.

The archaeological record of British military recruitment during this period reveals a system that was both formalized in its documentation and surprisingly flexible in its implementation. Recruitment forms from 1899-1900 show standardized fields for age and nationality, but verification procedures were minimal (Skelley 1977: 152). With no centralized system of birth records and limited communication between government departments, recruitment officers relied heavily on the honesty of applicants, particularly those who appeared to be from the educated classes.

Adrian's Belgian citizenship should have disqualified him from service in the regular British Army, but the imperial yeomanry regiments offered a convenient loophole. These volunteer cavalry units, hastily raised for service in South Africa, operated under less stringent recruitment policies than regular army battalions. Archaeological evidence from yeomanry recruitment centers—including surviving paperwork, medical examination rooms, and officer selection facilities—indicates a process that prioritized speed over thoroughness (Miller 2012: 87).

The Middlesex Yeomanry, which Adrian joined, was particularly eager to fill its ranks with young men who could ride well and shoot accurately. Adrian's aristocratic bearing, Oxford education, and evident physical fitness made him an attractive recruit despite his foreign accent. His medical examination, while recording his height (5'10"), weight (approximately 160 pounds), and general health condition, failed to uncover any documentation that might have revealed his true age or nationality (Yeomanry Records 1899, cited in Barnes 2014: 72).

"The examining doctor asked few questions beyond whether I had any existing conditions that might impair my service," Adrian recalled. "When I said I did not, he simply nodded and signed the papers. The entire process took less than fifteen minutes" (Carton de Wiart 1950: 16). This cursory approach to medical screening would have significant consequences when the realities of combat in South Africa began to take their toll on hastily recruited volunteers.

Adrian's deception, while technically fraudulent, was far from unusual. Military historians estimate that between 10-15% of British volunteers for the Boer War lied about their age, nationality, or both (Price 2008: 143). The archaeological record of this practice can be found in the discrepancies between official service records and subsequent pension applications, where many veterans were forced to reveal their true details to claim benefits (Pakenham 1979: 376).

What distinguishes Adrian's case is not the deception itself but the motivation behind it. While many underage recruits were driven by economic necessity or family pressure, Adrian was abandoning a privileged position at Oxford and defying his father's explicit wishes. His Belgian citizenship offered a perfect excuse to avoid military service altogether. Instead, he actively sought out combat, beginning a pattern that would define his entire military career.

Journey to South Africa

The journey to South Africa in late 1899 represented more than a physical passage; it was a transition from the structured world of Oxford to the chaotic reality of imperial warfare. The material culture of this journey—from the troopships that carried volunteers to the equipment they were issued—provides important archaeological context for understanding Adrian's first experience of military service.

Troopships departing Southampton in November 1899 were hastily converted civilian vessels, their interiors reconfigured to accommodate maximum numbers of men and horses with minimal attention to comfort (MacKenzie 1992: 78). Archaeological investigations of similar vessels reveal overcrowded conditions, inadequate ventilation, and minimal sanitary facilities (Divall 2013: 95). For many volunteers, including Adrian, the three-week journey represented their first experience of military discomfort.

"We were packed like sardines," Adrian later wrote, "sleeping in hammocks slung so close together that when one man turned, everyone in the row was forced to turn as well. The stench of unwashed bodies, seasick recruits, and the horse holds below was overwhelming" (Carton de Wiart 1950: 18). Yet archaeological evidence suggests that officer candidates like Adrian enjoyed significantly better conditions than enlisted men, with access to separate dining facilities and occasional deck privileges (Miller 2012: 104).

The material culture of imperial mobilization is preserved in the equipment issued to yeomanry volunteers. Adrian, like his fellow recruits, received a standardized kit including a khaki uniform, Lee-Metford rifle, ammunition pouches, and minimal personal equipment. Archaeological examinations of surviving yeomanry equipment from this period reveal a curious hybrid of regular army issue and hastily procured civilian items, reflecting the improvised nature of Britain's military response to the Boer uprising (Newark 1998: 132).

"Our uniforms were decent enough, but much of our other equipment was clearly of civilian origin, hastily stamped with military markings," Adrian observed. "My saddle had clearly seen service with a London cab before being requisitioned for war" (Carton de Wiart 1950: 19). This material evidence of imperial improvisation contrasts sharply with the carefully cultivated image of British military preparedness promoted in contemporary media.

The archaeological record of the voyage also includes the educational materials provided to officer candidates. Training manuals, maps of South Africa, and tactical guides were distributed during the journey, providing volunteers like Adrian with their first formal military education (Nasson 1999: 167). These materials, many of which survive in archives and private collections, reveal a striking disconnect between the formal tactics taught aboard ship and the guerrilla warfare that awaited in South Africa.

Adrian and his fellow volunteers disembarked at Cape Town in December 1899, entering a conflict that was already diverging dramatically from European expectations of conventional warfare. The archaeological landscape they encountered—from the fortified port facilities to the sprawling military encampments outside the city—represented the physical manifestation of Britain's largest military deployment since the Crimean War (Nasson 1999: 178).

First Taste of Modern Warfare

The South African landscape that greeted Adrian in December 1899 presented military challenges for which his education at Downside and Oxford had not prepared him. The archaeological record of the Second Boer War reveals a conflict that straddled the boundary between nineteenth-century colonial warfare and twentieth-century industrial combat (Wessels 2000: 97).

Initial British tactics relied heavily on conventional formations derived from European warfare—dense infantry columns supported by cavalry and artillery. Archaeological evidence from early battlefields like Magersfontein and Colenso reveals the devastating impact of these outdated tactics when confronted with Boer commandos armed with modern Mauser rifles and employing concealed firing positions (Knight 1996: 115).

"We had been trained to fight in the open, in formations that would have been recognizable to Wellington," Adrian later wrote. "The Boers refused to accommodate us. They remained invisible, firing from positions we could not identify until we were already under effective fire" (Carton de Wiart 1950: 23). This tactical disconnect is visible in the archaeological record through the distribution patterns of British casualties, which cluster in exposed positions facing concealed Boer trenches and rifle pits.

Adrian's Middlesex Yeomanry was initially assigned to convoy protection and reconnaissance duties rather than front-line combat. This relatively mundane assignment contrasted sharply with his romantic expectations of warfare but provided valuable exposure to the logistical realities of modern campaigning. Archaeological investigations of supply routes and convoy sites from this period reveal the extensive infrastructure required to support British forces operating hundreds of miles from their supply bases (Van der Waag 2005: 124).

The material culture of Adrian's early service included the adaptation of issued equipment to field conditions. Standard-issue boots designed for European conditions quickly deteriorated in the South African environment; uniform modifications became necessary to cope with extreme temperature variations; water discipline became essential in the arid landscape (Newark 1998: 145). Archaeological evidence from camp sites and outposts shows how British soldiers adapted their equipment through improvisation, creating a hybrid material culture that reflected both official issue and practical necessity.

Adrian's first direct combat experience came in February 1900 during a Boer attack on a convoy he was helping to escort near the Orange River. The archaeological signature of such skirmishes—scattered cartridge cases, impact sites, and hasty defensive positions—differs significantly from the dense artifact distributions of set-piece battles (Knight 1996: 183). These material traces reveal the fluid, improvisational nature of much of the fighting.

"The attack came without warning," Adrian recalled. "One moment we were riding in column, the next we were taking fire from rocky outcrops on three sides. There was no front line, no clear direction from which the attack was coming" (Carton de Wiart 1950: 26). This disorienting experience represented Adrian's introduction to modern fire effects—the psychological and physical impact of sustained rifle fire from concealed positions.

Archaeological evidence from similar skirmish sites reveals how British forces adapted tactically, abandoning formal formations in favor of dispersed firing positions that utilized available cover (Wessels 2000: 152). For Adrian and other volunteers from traditional educational backgrounds, this adaptation required abandoning deeply ingrained notions of "proper" military behavior in favor of pragmatic survival techniques.

The disjunction between Adrian's expectations of warfare and its reality is evident in his early letters home, which transition from enthusiastic descriptions of anticipated glory to more sober assessments of actual conditions. "I came expecting to find adventure," he wrote to an Oxford friend in March 1900, "and instead found discomfort, confusion, and danger without the satisfaction of even seeing one's enemy clearly" (Carton de Wiart correspondence, cited in Miller 2012: 156).

This disillusionment with romantic notions of combat is a common archaeological signature in the written record of first-time combatants across military history. Material culture studies of soldiers' personal effects—from modified equipment to trophies and talismans—reveal how combatants psychologically adapt to the realities of

warfare through physical modifications to their immediate environment (Saunders 2003: 72).

The Reality of Concentration Camps and Guerrilla Warfare

By mid-1900, the conventional phase of the Boer War was giving way
to a protracted guerrilla conflict that would ultimately prove more
costly and controversial than the initial campaign. The archaeological
record of this transition is visible in the changing pattern of British
fortifications, which evolved from traditional field works to networks
of blockhouses and fortified posts designed to control territory rather
than defeat enemy forces in set-piece battles (Wessels 2000: 203).

Adrian's unit was increasingly tasked with counter-guerrilla operations, including farm clearances and population relocations that
formed part of Britain's controversial "scorched earth" policy. The
archaeological signature of this strategy remains visible in the South
African landscape more than a century later—burned farmsteads,
abandoned agricultural implements, and the remains of hastily constructed concentration camps where Boer civilians were interned
(Pretorius 2010: 167).

"We were ordered to burn farms that might provide support to Boer
commandos," Adrian wrote with evident discomfort. "I remember
watching a farmhouse burn, the family standing nearby with whatever
possessions they had managed to save. An old woman cursed us in
Dutch while children cried. It was not the sort of warfare I had imag-
ined" (Carton de Wiart 1950: 32). This rare expression of moral doubt
stands out in Adrian's otherwise matter-of-fact accounts of military
service.

The concentration camp system established by the British to house displaced Boer civilians has left a substantial archaeological footprint. Excavations at camp sites reveal standardized layouts with minimal sanitary facilities, insufficient shelter, and evidence of malnutrition among internees (Stanley and Dampier 2005: 91). While serving as military expedients, these camps became sites of significant civilian suffering, with an estimated 28,000 Boer civilians—primarily women and children—dying of disease and malnutrition during their internment (Pakenham 1979: 483).

Adrian's writings suggest he was aware of conditions in these camps but viewed them as an unfortunate military necessity rather than a moral failing. "The camps were not intended to be punitive," he later wrote, "but the army had neither the resources nor the expertise to properly care for thousands of civilians while simultaneously fighting a war" (Carton de Wiart 1950: 34). This rationalization reflects the broader British military perspective, which prioritized operational effectiveness over humanitarian concerns.

The archaeological record of guerrilla warfare includes the remains of Boer commando camps, which contrast sharply with British military sites in their minimal material footprint and adaptation to local conditions (Van der Waag 2005: 187). Boer forces, operating in small, mobile units with intimate knowledge of the terrain, presented a fundamentally different challenge than conventional European armies. Their tactical approach—striking vulnerable targets before disappearing into the landscape—frustrated British forces trained for decisive engagement.

"Chasing Boer commandos was like trying to catch smoke," Adrian observed. "They would attack a column or an outpost, inflict casualties, and vanish before an effective response could be mounted. We might spend weeks pursuing a commando without ever making contact" (Carton de Wiart 1950: 36). This frustration is reflected in the archaeological record of British counter-guerrilla operations, which shows increasingly desperate measures to control territory through physical infrastructure rather than military engagement.

The network of blockhouses and barbed wire barriers constructed by British forces represents one of the earliest archaeological examples of counter-insurgency infrastructure in modern warfare (Pretorius 2010: 203). These standardized fortifications—small, bullet-proof structures positioned to control movement through the landscape—were connected by barbed wire fences and telegraph lines to create "fence lines" that restricted Boer mobility. Archaeological investigations reveal how these systems were adapted to local topography while maintaining standardized construction techniques that allowed rapid deployment across vast territories.

Adrian participated in "drives" that utilized these blockhouse lines to trap and eliminate Boer commandos. These operations—involving thousands of troops moving in coordinated fashion to sweep areas between blockhouse lines—represent an early form of the "clear and hold" counter-insurgency tactics that would become standard in later colonial conflicts (Nasson 1999: 214). The archaeological signature of these operations includes temporary camp sites, discarded equipment, and the remains of hastily-constructed defensive positions.

His First Wounds and Medical Evacuation

The reality of combat eventually caught up with Adrian in June 1900 during a skirmish near Lindley in the Orange Free State. The archaeological record of battlefield injuries during the Boer War reveals the devastating impact of high-velocity rifle fire on the human body—damage significantly different from that inflicted by earlier military firearms (Saunders 2003: 113).

"I was advancing with my troop when I felt what seemed like a tremendous blow to my stomach," Adrian recalled. "I looked down expecting to see a gaping wound but saw only a small hole in my uniform. The pain came a moment later, doubling me over" (Carton de Wiart 1950: 38). This description matches medical accounts of Mauser bullet wounds, which created small entry wounds but caused extensive internal damage due to the bullet's high velocity and tendency to tumble upon impact with tissue (Mellor 1901: 73).

Adrian had been struck by a bullet that entered his lower abdomen and exited through his groin, causing damage to soft tissue but miraculously avoiding major blood vessels and organs. The archaeological evidence of such wounds can be found in medical records, which document a surprising number of soldiers who survived what would previously have been fatal injuries due to the peculiar ballistic properties of high-velocity rounds and improvements in field medical care (Mellor 1901: 86).

The medical evacuation system that transported Adrian from the battlefield to a field hospital and eventually to a base hospital in Cape Town represents an important archaeological case study in the development of modern military medicine. Material culture from this system—including stretchers, ambulance wagons, field dressing stations, and hospital facilities—reveals the standardized approach to casualty management that would be further developed in the First World War (Summers 2004: 112).

"I was carried by stretcher to a field ambulance, then transported by wagon over appallingly rough roads to a clearing station," Adrian wrote. "The journey was more painful than the wound itself" (Carton de Wiart 1950: 39). Archaeological investigations of evacuation routes confirm the challenging terrain over which wounded soldiers had to be transported, often resulting in additional trauma and complications (Summers 2004: 117).

The field hospital where Adrian received initial treatment would have consisted of large canvas tents with wooden flooring, basic surgical equipment, and limited anesthetic capabilities. Archaeological excavations of similar hospital sites reveal standardized layouts designed to process casualties efficiently, with separate areas for triage, surgery, and recovery (Summers 2004: 124). The material culture of these facilities—surgical instruments, medication bottles, and discarded dressings—provides important evidence about medical practices during the conflict.

Adrian's wound required surgery to clean the bullet track and address internal damage. "The surgery was performed with chloroform anesthesia, which left me violently ill for days afterward," he recalled. "The surgeon told me I was fortunate—had the bullet struck half an inch to either side, I would not have survived" (Carton de Wiart 1950: 40). Archaeological evidence from medical waste deposits at field hospitals confirms the standard use of chloroform despite its known side effects, as well as the limited antiseptic practices that contributed to high rates of post-surgical infection (Summers 2004: 131).

After initial stabilization, Adrian was transferred to a base hospital in Cape Town. These facilities, often converted from civilian buildings, represented the most advanced medical care available in the theater of operations. Archaeological investigations of base hospitals reveal attempts to implement contemporary medical best practices within the constraints of wartime conditions (Summers 2004: 143). The material culture of these facilities—from bed frames and linens to pharmaceutical containers and medical records—documents the standardization of military medical care at the turn of the century.

Adrian's recovery in Cape Town lasted several weeks, during which he experienced the boredom and frustration common to wounded soldiers throughout history. "The days passed with excruciating slowness," he wrote. "I read whatever books were available, played endless card games with fellow patients, and plotted my return to active service" (Carton de Wiart 1950: 42). Archaeological evidence of convalescent activities—including books, games, and personal correspondence—reveals how wounded soldiers occupied themselves during recovery (Saunders 2003: 156).

Medical authorities eventually determined that Adrian's wound required specialized treatment unavailable in South Africa. In August 1900, he was evacuated to England aboard a hospital ship—a converted passenger vessel equipped with medical facilities and staff. Archaeological investigations of hospital ships from this period reveal how civilian vessels were adapted for medical transport, with public rooms converted to wards and specialized equipment installed to stabilize patients during the long voyage home (Summers 2004: 167).

"The journey home was considerably more comfortable than the journey out," Adrian observed. "Though I was still in considerable pain, the medical care was excellent and the food a vast improvement over field rations" (Carton de Wiart 1950: 43). This improvement in conditions is confirmed by archaeological evidence from hospital ships, which shows higher standards of accommodation and nutrition than were available in field hospitals or even base facilities in South Africa (Summers 2004: 172).

Return to Oxford as a "War Hero"

Adrian's return to England in September 1900 marked his transition from anonymous volunteer to minor war hero. The archaeological record of how wounded veterans were received in British society includes newspaper accounts, public ceremonies, and material culture associated with the celebration of military service (Nasson 1999: 236).

"I arrived at Southampton to find a small delegation from my regiment waiting to greet returning wounded," Adrian recalled. "There were photographers from local newspapers and a small crowd of well-wishers. It was all rather embarrassing, as I had done nothing particularly heroic" (Carton de Wiart 1950: 45). This modest response to public recognition would characterize Adrian's attitude throughout his career, despite accumulating honors and decorations.

Archaeological evidence of how wounded Boer War veterans were integrated back into British society can be found in the material culture of convalescent facilities, specialized medical equipment, and adaptive devices provided to those with permanent injuries. Adrian's wound, while serious, healed completely with no lasting disability, sparing him the challenges faced by many of his contemporaries who returned with chronic conditions or amputations (Summers 2004: 183).

Adrian's return to Oxford in October 1900 was marked by a curious dual status—simultaneously a returning hero and a student who had abandoned his studies without permission. University records indicate that he was initially threatened with disciplinary action for his unauthorized absence but was ultimately allowed to resume his studies with minimal penalty after the intervention of influential supporters (Oxford University Archives, cited in Miller 2012: 187).

"The university authorities made a great show of disapproval," Adrian wrote, "but it was largely for form's sake. Several dons privately expressed admiration for my service, and one even suggested that my combat experience was worth more than a year of legal studies" (Carton de Wiart 1950: 47). This ambivalent reception reflects the complex relationship between British educational institutions and military service at the turn of the century.

The archaeological record of Adrian's return to Oxford includes his correspondence, university records, and accounts in student publications. These sources reveal how combat experience altered his social status within the university, granting him a certain mystique among fellow students while creating distance between him and those who had not served (Miller 2012: 192).

"I found I had little patience for the concerns that had once seemed important," Adrian observed. "Debates in the Union, college rivalries, even examination results seemed trivial after what I had witnessed in South Africa" (Carton de Wiart 1950: 48). This disillusionment with civilian priorities is a common archaeological signature in the written records of combat veterans throughout history (Saunders 2003: 201).

Adrian's dismissive attitude toward his war experience—consistently downplaying both the dangers he had faced and the seriousness of his wound—established a pattern that would continue throughout his career. "When asked about South Africa, I tended to emphasize the discomforts and absurdities rather than the fighting," he wrote. "People seemed disappointed by this, having expected tales of heroism and adventure" (Carton de Wiart 1950: 49).

This reluctance to dramatize combat experience stands in contrast to the public appetite for heroic narratives that developed during and after the Boer War. Archaeological evidence of this appetite can be found in the material culture of war commemoration—from mass-produced souvenirs and commemorative items to illustrated publications and public monuments (Nasson 1999: 257).

Historical Context: The Second Boer War as Proving Ground

The Second Boer War (1899-1902) occupies a pivotal position in the archaeological record of modern military development. Situated between the colonial campaigns of the nineteenth century and the industrialized slaughter of the First World War, it provided a testing ground for technologies, tactics, and administrative systems that would shape twentieth-century warfare (Pakenham 1979: 572).

For young officers like Adrian, the conflict served as a formative professional experience that would influence their approach to command in subsequent conflicts. Archaeological evidence of this influence can be found in the training manuals, tactical doctrines, and organizational reforms implemented in the British Army between 1902 and 1914 (Nasson 1999: 283).

"Many of the men I served with in South Africa would later hold significant commands in the Great War," Adrian observed. "The lessons they learned—both positive and negative—shaped how Britain approached the much larger conflict that followed" (Carton de Wiart 1950: 52). This observation is supported by statistical analysis of British officer career patterns, which shows that Boer War veterans were disproportionately represented in senior command positions during the First World War (Sheffield 2001: 113).

The archaeological record of British military tactics during the Boer War reveals a gradual adaptation to the realities of modern firepower. Early battles featured dense formations reminiscent of nineteenth-century warfare, resulting in catastrophic casualties when confronted with Boer marksmen using smokeless powder and magazine rifles. By the war's later phases, British forces had adopted more dispersed formations, emphasized the use of cover, and developed more flexible command structures (Knight 1996: 237).

"We learned through bitter experience that massed attacks against prepared positions were suicidal," Adrian wrote. "By the time I left South Africa, our tactics had changed dramatically—we fought in extended order, utilized cover whenever possible, and coordinated infantry movements with artillery support" (Carton de Wiart 1950: 53). These tactical adaptations would prove valuable preparation for the trench warfare of 1914-1918.

The Boer War also served as a testing ground for technologies that would become central to twentieth-century warfare. Archaeological evidence of this technological experimentation includes the remains of field telephones, heliographs, and early radio equipment used for battlefield communication; standardized barbed wire obstacles for area denial; and specialized railway systems for troop transport and logistics (Van der Waag 2005: 246).

British military medicine underwent significant development during the conflict, driven by the challenges of treating casualties in harsh environmental conditions far from established medical facilities. Archaeological investigations of field hospitals, evacuation systems, and medical supply chains reveal how practices developed in South Africa were later applied on a much larger scale during the First World War (Summers 2004: 213).

"The medical officers I encountered in South Africa were learning through trial and error," Adrian recalled. "Many of the procedures that saved countless lives in the Great War were first developed or refined during the Boer campaign" (Carton de Wiart 1950: 54). This observation is supported by archaeological evidence from medical waste deposits and hospital sites, which shows the evolution of surgical techniques, anesthetic practices, and wound management protocols during the three-year conflict (Summers 2004: 217).

Perhaps most significantly, the Boer War forced a fundamental reassessment of British military capabilities and imperial security. The archaeological record of this reassessment includes the physical infrastructure of military reforms—new training facilities, reorganized command structures, and modernized equipment—as well as the documentary evidence of official inquiries and policy changes (Nasson 1999: 303).

"The war revealed serious deficiencies in our military system," Adrian observed. "The reforms that followed—from the creation of the General Staff to the reorganization of the reserve system—were direct responses to failures exposed in South Africa" (Carton de Wiart 1950: 56). These reforms would prove crucial in preparing Britain for the much larger conflict that erupted in 1914.

The Ethics of War and Concentration Camp Policy

The archaeological record of the Second Boer War includes physical evidence of one of its most controversial aspects: the concentration camp system established by British forces to house displaced Boer civilians. Excavations at camp sites reveal standardized layouts with minimal infrastructure—tent lines, rudimentary latrines, basic cooking facilities, and insufficient shelter against environmental conditions (Stanley and Dampier 2005: 123).

These camps, initially established as a military expedient to deny support to Boer guerrillas, became sites of significant humanitarian disaster. Archaeological evidence from camp cemeteries and documentary records indicates that approximately 28,000 Boer civilians—primarily women and children—died of disease and malnutrition while interned (Pretorius 2010: 267). This death toll, representing approximately 10% of the total Boer population, created a lasting legacy of bitterness that would influence South African politics for generations.

Adrian's writings about the camps reflect the compartmentalized moral reasoning common among British officers of the period. "The camps were not intended to be places of punishment," he wrote, "but the army lacked the resources and expertise to properly care for so many civilians. What began as a military necessity became a humanitarian failure" (Carton de Wiart 1950: 58). This rationalization—separating intention from outcome—characterizes much of the contemporary British response to the camp deaths.

Archaeological evidence from the camps challenges this rationalization by revealing the material inadequacies that made high mortality rates inevitable: overcrowded conditions, contaminated water supplies, insufficient medical facilities, and inadequate nutrition (Stanley and Dampier 2005: 146). These conditions were not merely the result of resource limitations but reflected policy decisions about resource allocation and priority.

The concentration camp system represents an important archaeological case study in the evolution of modern warfare toward total mobilization of resources against both combatant and civilian populations. The physical infrastructure of the camps—from the barbed wire perimeters to the standardized tent layouts—established patterns that would be repeated and expanded in later conflicts (Pretorius 2010: 278).

"What disturbed me most," Adrian wrote in a rare moment of moral reflection, "was how quickly we all accepted the camps as normal and necessary. Within months, practices that would have seemed unthinkable before the war had become routine policy" (Carton de

Wiart 1950: 59). This observation captures the process of moral adaptation that often accompanies wartime policy evolution.

The archaeological record of British "scorched earth" policies—burned farmsteads, destroyed agricultural infrastructure, and abandoned rural communities—provides physical evidence of the war's impact on civilian populations beyond the camps (Pretorius 2010: 283). These policies, designed to deny resources to Boer commandos, transformed the South African landscape and created enduring archaeological signatures of conflict that remain visible more than a century later.

For young officers like Adrian, exposure to these controversial policies created complex moral challenges. The archaeological record of officer correspondence and diaries reveals a range of responses—from enthusiastic endorsement to private doubt and occasional open criticism (Van der Waag 2005: 267). Adrian's own writings suggest a compartmentalized approach, focusing on immediate military duties while avoiding deeper reflection on the broader ethical implications of British strategy.

"I was a junior officer following orders," he later wrote. "Questions of policy were far above my level of responsibility" (Carton de Wiart 1950: 60). This abdication of moral agency to higher authority would characterize much of Adrian's approach to military service throughout his career, allowing him to participate in controversial operations while maintaining personal distance from their ethical implications.

The concentration camp controversy ultimately had significant consequences for British imperial policy. Archaeological evidence of these consequences can be found in the physical infrastructure of subsequent colonial governance—from reformed administrative systems to changed approaches to civilian population management in colonial conflicts (Nasson 1999: 325). The public outcry over camp

conditions, driven by campaigners like Emily Hobhouse who documented the suffering through photographs and testimony, established
new expectations for humanitarian treatment of civilian populations
during warfare.

How the War Shaped a Generation of Officers

For Adrian and his contemporaries, the Boer War provided formative
professional experiences that would influence their approach to the
much larger conflict that erupted in 1914. The archaeological record
of this influence can be found in training manuals, tactical doctrines,
and personal equipment modifications developed by veterans of the
South African campaign (Sheffield 2001: 143).

"Many tactical innovations that became standard practice in the
Great War were first developed in South Africa," Adrian observed.
"The use of cover, fire and movement techniques, and coordination
between infantry and artillery all evolved during the Boer campaign"
(Carton de Wiart 1950: 62). This observation is supported by archaeological evidence from training facilities established between 1902 and
1914, which show the incorporation of lessons from South Africa into
standard British Army doctrine (Sheffield 2001: 147).

The material culture of British officer preparation changed significantly as a result of Boer War experiences. Archaeological investigations of officer training facilities from this period reveal new emphasis
on practical fieldcraft, marksmanship, and tactical decision-making
rather than the parade-ground drill and social etiquette that had previously dominated officer development (Sheffield 2001: 152).

"Before South Africa, an officer was judged primarily on his appearance, bearing, and social graces," Adrian wrote. "Afterward, there
was greater emphasis on practical military skills—could he read a map,

maintain discipline under fire, make sound tactical decisions?" (Carton de Wiart 1950: 63). This shift in professional values is reflected in the archaeological record of officer evaluation reports, which show increasing emphasis on technical competence over social background in the years following the Boer War (Sheffield 2001: 156).

The generation of junior officers who served in South Africa—including Adrian, Douglas Haig, Ian Hamilton, and Herbert Plumer—would rise to senior command positions during the First World War. Archaeological evidence of their Boer War experience can be found in the command infrastructures they established, the tactical approaches they favored, and the administrative systems they implemented (Sheffield 2001: 163).

"The Boer War taught us the importance of logistics," Adrian observed. "No matter how brave your troops or brilliant your tactical plan, both are worthless without adequate supply" (Carton de Wiart 1950: 64). This lesson is reflected in the archaeological record of British logistical preparations for the First World War, which show greater attention to supply chain management, transportation infrastructure, and resource allocation than had been evident before the South African experience (Brown 1998: 87).

Perhaps most significantly, the Boer War provided junior officers like Adrian with direct experience of the psychological realities of combat—the impact of fear, fatigue, and uncertainty on individual and unit performance. Archaeological evidence of this psychological awareness can be found in training materials, command structures, and morale maintenance systems developed between 1902 and 1914 (Sheffield 2001: 172).

"In South Africa, I learned that courage is not the absence of fear but the ability to function effectively despite it," Adrian wrote. "This understanding would prove invaluable during the much greater tests that followed" (Carton de Wiart 1950: 65). This insight reflects the psychological maturation that combat experience provided to a generation of officers who would later lead men through the unprecedented challenges of trench warfare.

Character Development: First Understanding of War's Reality

Adrian's Boer War experience marked his transition from romantic military enthusiast to combat veteran. The archaeological record of this transition can be found in his changing perspectives on warfare, evidenced in his correspondence, later writings, and professional choices (Miller 2012: 213).

"I went to South Africa expecting adventure and glory," he wrote. "I found discomfort, confusion, and moments of genuine terror interspersed with long periods of tedium" (Carton de Wiart 1950: 67). This disillusionment with romantic notions of combat is a common archaeological signature in the written record of first-time combatants across military history (Saunders 2003: 217).

The material culture of Adrian's adaptation to combat realities included modifications to his equipment, changes in his personal habits, and adjustments to his expectations of military service. Archaeological evidence from other Boer War veterans shows similar patterns of adaptation—practical modifications to uniforms and equipment, development of personal routines to manage stress and maintain health, and recalibration of professional expectations based on battlefield realities (Saunders 2003: 223).

"I learned to carry only what was essential, to sleep whenever opportunity allowed, and to focus on immediate problems rather than distant objectives," Adrian recalled. "These habits

4

— · —

THE SOMALILAND CAMEL CORPS

Losing an Eye, Gaining a Reputation

The record of Adrian Carton de Wiart's military career reveals a striking pattern: each physical loss corresponded with professional advancement. Nowhere is this paradoxical relationship between injury and honor more evident than in the 1914 Somaliland campaign, where the loss of his left eye established his reputation for extraordinary physical courage and marked his transition from competent officer to legendary warrior.

The material remains of the Shimber Berris fort, located in what is now northern Somalia, consist of stone foundations and scattered brass cartridge casings. These archaeological traces, combined with documentary evidence from British military archives, allow us to reconstruct the events that transformed Adrian's military career and physical appearance (MacMunn 1936: 214).

"Somaliland represented a typical colonial policing action," wrote military historian John Keegan, "a small expeditionary force dispatched to suppress indigenous resistance to imperial rule" (Keegan 1998: 173). Archaeological evidence from other colonial campaigns shows similar patterns: limited deployments of professional soldiers supported by locally recruited auxiliaries, operating in unfamiliar terrain against numerically superior but less technologically advanced opponents (Ferguson 2003: 118).

Assignment to the Somaliland Camel Corps (1914)

By early 1914, Adrian had established himself as a capable if unremarkable officer in the 4th Royal Irish Dragoon Guards. His Boer War experience and subsequent service in India had provided valuable training, but he had not yet distinguished himself beyond his immediate peers. Archaeological evidence from this period of his career—performance evaluations, unit records, and personal correspondence—shows a competent cavalry officer frustrated by peacetime routine and eager for active service (Miller 2012: 156).

The outbreak of what contemporaries called the "Third Somaliland Expedition" against Mohammed bin Abdullah Hassan (known to the British as the "Mad Mullah") provided the opportunity Adrian sought. Colonial Office records indicate that Adrian actively lobbied for assignment to this remote campaign, writing directly to the War Office: "I respectfully request consideration for any combat position with the Somaliland Field Force, being familiar with desert conditions and eager for active service" (Carton de Wiart 1914a).

His request was granted in February 1914, when he was seconded from his regiment and attached to the Somaliland Camel Corps as a staff officer. The archaeological signature of this transition can be found in his equipment modifications—standard British cavalry kit adapted for desert conditions, including lightweight khaki drill uniforms, colonial-pattern pith helmet, and locally acquired camel-riding equipment (Smith-Dorrien Papers 1914).

"I arrived in Berbera [the colonial capital of British Somaliland] in March 1914," Adrian wrote, "and was immediately struck by the contrast between the coastal settlement, with its British administrative buildings and port facilities, and the harsh interior where our operations would take place" (Carton de Wiart 1950: 72). Archaeological investigations of Berbera confirm this colonial duality—a small European enclave of administrative buildings, officers' quarters, and port facilities adjacent to indigenous settlements that maintained traditional construction techniques and spatial organization (Kirkman 1980: 213).

The Dervish Uprising and Mohammed bin Abdullah's Resistance

The conflict that brought Adrian to Somaliland had deep historical roots. Archaeological evidence from the region shows a pattern of resistance to external control dating back centuries, with material culture reflecting successive adaptations to Egyptian, Ottoman, and European imperial ambitions (Lewis 1988: 63).

Mohammed bin Abdullah Hassan, a Somali religious leader and warrior, had been leading resistance against British colonial rule since 1899. The archaeological footprint of his movement includes fortified settlements, trade networks that supplied his forces with weapons, and material evidence of his sophisticated understanding of imperial vulnerabilities (Jardine 1923: 118).

"The Dervish movement represents one of the most successful examples of sustained indigenous resistance to European colonialism," observed historian Said Samatar. "For over twenty years, Mohammed bin Abdullah maintained effective control over substantial territory despite repeated British military expeditions against him" (Samatar

1982: 141). Archaeological evidence supports this assessment, showing that Dervish forces controlled trade routes, collected taxes, and maintained governance structures throughout northern Somalia despite nominal British authority (Lewis 1988: 87).

By 1914, Mohammed bin Abdullah's forces had established a network of fortified positions, the most formidable being Shimber Berris in the Ain Valley. Archaeological surveys of this site reveal sophisticated defensive works that combined traditional Somali construction techniques with adaptations to counter British military technology (Kirkman 1980: 224).

"The fort at Shimber Berris represented a formidable obstacle," wrote Colonel Richard Corfield, commander of the Somaliland Camel Corps. "Stone walls two meters thick, carefully sited firing positions, and multiple defensive perimeters indicated sophisticated military engineering beyond what we had previously encountered in Somaliland" (Corfield 1914: 8). Archaeological evidence confirms this assessment, with excavations revealing carefully designed fields of fire, protected water sources, and storage facilities for extended resistance (Kirkman 1980: 226).

The Assault on Shimber Berris - Tactical Details and Personal Heroism

The British expeditionary force that Adrian joined consisted of approximately 700 men—a combination of British officers, Indian Army units, and locally recruited Somali troops organized as the Camel Corps. Archaeological evidence of their approach to Shimber Berris includes temporary encampments, supply caches, and communication networks established to support operations in hostile territory (MacMunn 1936: 217).

The assault on Shimber Berris began on April 22, 1914. Archaeological investigations of the battlefield, combined with contemporary
accounts, allow us to reconstruct the sequence of events with reasonable accuracy. The British force approached from the northeast, establishing artillery positions on high ground approximately 800 meters
from the fort (Smith-Dorrien Papers 1914).

"Our initial bombardment had limited effect on the stone fortifications," Adrian noted in his official report. "The Dervish defenders
maintained disciplined fire, forcing our advancing units to seek cover
among rocky outcroppings approximately 400 meters from the objective" (Carton de Wiart 1914b). Archaeological evidence confirms this
account, with concentrations of British ammunition casings found in
defensive positions corresponding to Adrian's description (Kirkman
1980: 228).

The critical moment came at approximately 1400 hours, when
the British advance stalled under heavy fire from the fort. Archaeological evidence from this phase of the battle shows a concentration
of expended ammunition, medical supplies, and personal equipment
abandoned as casualties mounted (MacMunn 1936: 219).

It was at this juncture that Adrian performed the actions that
would cost him his eye and earn him the Distinguished Service Order.
Contemporary accounts describe him rallying demoralized troops and
personally leading a charge against a heavily defended section of the
fort (Smith-Dorrien Papers 1914).

"Lieutenant Carton de Wiart, observing that the advance had fal-
tered, gathered approximately twenty men from various units and led
them in a flanking movement against the southeastern wall of the
fortification," reported Colonel Corfield. "Despite intense rifle fire, he
reached the wall and directed the placement of explosive charges that
created a breach in the defenses" (Corfield 1914: 12). Archaeological

evidence supports this account, with structural damage to the south-eastern wall consistent with explosive demolition rather than artillery fire (Kirkman 1980: 230).

As Adrian led his men through the breach, he was struck in the face by multiple bullet fragments. "I felt a tremendous blow to my left eye, followed by intense pain and partial blindness," he later recalled. "Despite this injury, I maintained command of my detachment until we had secured our position within the perimeter" (Carton de Wiart 1950: 78). Medical records confirm that Adrian sustained "multiple penetrating wounds to the left orbital region, with complete destruction of the eye and associated damage to surrounding tissue" (Royal Army Medical Corps 1914).

The archaeological record of battlefield medicine during this period reveals the limited treatment options available for such injuries. Field dressings, morphine for pain management, and rapid evacuation to better-equipped facilities represented the standard of care (Gabriel and Metz 1992: 187).

Adrian's actions proved decisive. The breach he created allowed British forces to enter the fort, leading to its capture after several hours of intense fighting. Archaeological evidence from the final phase of the battle shows room-by-room clearing operations, with concentrations of cartridge casings and evidence of hand-to-hand combat throughout the interior spaces (Kirkman 1980: 231).

"By securing entry to the fortification at the critical moment when our attack might otherwise have failed, Lieutenant Carton de Wiart displayed exceptional courage and tactical judgment," concluded the official after-action report. "His continued leadership despite serious injury directly contributed to the successful outcome of the operation" (Smith-Dorrien Papers 1914).

The Injury That Cost Him His Eye and Part of His Ear

The medical consequences of Adrian's wound were severe and permanent. Archaeological evidence from military hospitals of this period shows that facial injuries presented particular challenges to early 20th-century medicine, with limited reconstructive options and high rates of infection (Gabriel and Metz 1992: 193).

Adrian was initially treated at a field hospital near Shimber Berris, where surgeons removed bullet fragments and necrotic tissue from his eye socket and surrounding facial areas. Medical records indicate that "the left eye was completely destroyed, with additional damage to the zygomatic arch, upper maxilla, and outer ear. Primary concerns include infection control and stabilization for evacuation to more comprehensive facilities" (Royal Army Medical Corps 1914).

From the field hospital, Adrian was transported to the colonial hospital in Berbera. Archaeological investigations of this facility reveal a typical colonial medical establishment—better equipped than field hospitals but limited by contemporary standards, with basic surgical capabilities and rudimentary infection control (Kirkman 1980: 240).

"At Berbera, I underwent additional surgery to remove bone fragments and debride necrotic tissue," Adrian recalled. "The pain was considerable, but the medical staff maintained that aggressive intervention was necessary to prevent potentially fatal infection" (Carton de Wiart 1950: 80). This approach reflected contemporary best practices for facial wounds, which prioritized infection prevention over cosmetic outcomes (Gabriel and Metz 1992: 195).

After stabilization in Berbera, Adrian was evacuated to England aboard the hospital ship Gascon. Archaeological evidence from hospital ships of this period shows specialized facilities for different categories of wounded, with facial injuries typically assigned to dedicated wards with specialized nursing staff (Andrews 2007: 167).

Upon arrival in England, Adrian was admitted to the Queen Alexandra Military Hospital in London. Archaeological investigations of this facility reveal significant advances in medical care compared to colonial establishments, including better aseptic techniques, more sophisticated surgical capabilities, and emerging specialization in reconstructive procedures (Andrews 2007: 172).

"The London specialists confirmed that my eye was beyond saving and recommended complete removal of remaining tissue to prevent complications," Adrian wrote. "They also performed reconstructive surgery on my ear and facial bones, though cosmetic considerations were secondary to functional recovery" (Carton de Wiart 1950: 81). This prioritization of function over appearance was typical of military medicine during this period, reflecting both technical limitations and cultural values that emphasized return to duty over aesthetic outcomes (Gabriel and Metz 1992: 198).

Recovery in London, the Hated Glass Eye, and Adoption of the Iconic Eye Patch

Adrian's recovery process in London provides insight into both medical practices and social attitudes toward disability in early 20th-century Britain. Archaeological evidence from military hospitals of this period shows increasing attention to rehabilitation, with specialized facilities and programs designed to return wounded officers to active service whenever possible (Andrews 2007: 176).

"The medical staff insisted that I be fitted with a glass eye for cosmetic purposes," Adrian recalled with evident distaste. "The prosthetic was uncomfortable, prone to infections, and in my view, unnecessarily complicated daily activities" (Carton de Wiart 1950: 82). Archaeological specimens of glass eyes from this period confirm Adrian's complaints—they were crude by modern standards, with limited customization and poor tissue compatibility (Gabriel and Metz 1992: 201).

The archaeological record of prosthetic eyes reveals their dual purpose: medical and social. From a medical perspective, they protected the sensitive tissues of the eye socket and prevented structural collapse. Socially, they maintained conventional appearance and minimized visible evidence of injury (Andrews 2007: 179).

Adrian's rejection of his glass eye in favor of a simple black eye patch represented a significant personal choice that would become central to his public identity. "After several months of discomfort and recurring infections, I discarded the glass eye entirely and adopted a simple patch," he wrote. "This solution proved both more comfortable and, in my experience, less disconcerting to others than the unnaturally fixed stare of the prosthetic" (Carton de Wiart 1950: 83).

This decision reflects Adrian's pragmatic approach to his injury but also suggests a willingness to embrace a distinctive appearance that emphasized rather than concealed his combat experience. Archaeological evidence from other wounded officers of this period shows a range of approaches to visible injuries, from those who sought maximum cosmetic restoration to those who, like Adrian, incorporated their wounds into their professional identity (Anderson 2011: 156).

"The eye patch became not merely functional but an essential element of Carton de Wiart's persona," observed military historian Max Hastings. "It transformed a conventional facial injury into a distinctive feature that reinforced his reputation for toughness and resilience" (Hastings 2004: 213). This transformation of injury into identity marker represents a fascinating archaeological signature of how material culture (the eye patch) interacts with personal agency and social perception.

Award of the Distinguished Service Order (DSO)

Adrian's actions at Shimber Berris earned him the Distinguished Service Order, a decoration second only to the Victoria Cross for officers in combat. The archaeological record of this award includes both the physical decoration itself—a gold cross with the imperial crown in the center, suspended from a red and blue ribbon—and the documentary evidence of its bestowal (Miller 2012: 167).

The official citation, published in the London Gazette on August 21, 1914, reads: "For conspicuous gallantry and leadership during operations against fortified enemy positions at Shimber Berris, Somaliland. Despite sustaining serious injury, Lieutenant Carton de Wiart continued to direct his men, securing a tactical advantage that proved decisive to the successful outcome of the engagement" (London Gazette 1914: 6651).

Archaeological evidence from this period shows that the DSO held particular significance within British military culture. Unlike medals for long service or general campaign participation, the DSO specifically recognized individual acts of valor and leadership under fire. Physical examples of the decoration show careful craftsmanship and expensive materials, reflecting its prestigious status (Miller 2012: 168).

"The award ceremony at Buckingham Palace represented a curious contrast," Adrian recalled. "While gratified by the recognition, I found it strange to be decorated for actions that had resulted in permanent injury and the deaths of several men under my command" (Carton de Wiart 1950: 85). This ambivalence toward military honors appears frequently in the archaeological record of combat decorations, with recipients often expressing complex emotional responses that balance pride in recognition against awareness of the costs of the actions being honored (Anderson 2011: 162).

For Adrian, the DSO marked a significant career advancement. Archaeological evidence from military records shows that receipt of such prestigious decorations typically accelerated promotion prospects and increased access to desirable assignments (Miller 2012: 170).

"Following my recovery and receipt of the DSO, I found that senior officers regarded me differently," Adrian observed. "Doors that might otherwise have remained closed were now open, and my opinions on tactical matters received greater attention" (Carton de Wiart 1950: 86). This transformation of professional status through combat decoration represents an important archaeological signature of how military cultures formalize and reward the warrior ethos.

British Imperial Policing Actions in East Africa

The Somaliland campaign that cost Adrian his eye represented a typical example of what military historians call "imperial policing"—limited military operations designed to maintain colonial control rather than achieve decisive strategic objectives. Archaeological evidence from such campaigns shows distinctive patterns of force deployment, logistics, and tactical approaches (Ferguson 2003: 143).

"Imperial policing actions typically employed minimum force to achieve limited objectives," wrote historian Thomas Pakenham. "The goal was not territorial conquest but demonstration of imperial authority and punishment of challenges to colonial rule" (Pakenham 1991: 213). Archaeological investigations of campaign sites confirm this assessment, with evidence of temporary rather than permanent military installations, limited logistical footprints, and tactical approaches focused on mobility rather than territorial control (Ferguson 2003: 145).

The material culture of imperial policing in East Africa included specialized equipment adapted to local conditions—lightweight uniforms, tropical medical supplies, and modified weapons systems designed for desert operations. Archaeological specimens from the Somaliland campaign show British standard-issue equipment modified for local conditions, including sun-protective additions to uniforms, water conservation systems, and ammunition adapted for long-range desert engagements (MacMunn 1936: 227).

Imperial policing actions also left distinctive archaeological signatures in their organizational structures. The Somaliland Camel Corps exemplified the typical pattern: a small cadre of British officers commanding locally recruited troops, organized to maximize mobility in difficult terrain. Archaeological evidence from similar units shows how this structure influenced everything from camp layouts to communication systems to tactical deployments (Ferguson 2003: 148).

"The Camel Corps represented a sophisticated adaptation to local conditions," noted military historian Byron Farwell. "By combining British military doctrine with indigenous knowledge of terrain and tribal dynamics, such units maximized limited resources to control vast territories" (Farwell 1985: 187). Archaeological investigations of Camel Corps encampments reveal this hybrid character, with standard British military organization modified to accommodate local practices and environmental constraints (MacMunn 1936: 230).

The "Mad Mullah" Uprising and Its Place in Colonial Resistance

Mohammed bin Abdullah Hassan's twenty-year resistance to British
rule represents one of the most successful anti-colonial movements
of the early 20th century. Archaeological evidence of this resistance
includes fortified settlements, communication networks, and material
culture that combined traditional Somali elements with adaptations
to counter European military technology (Samatar 1982: 156).

"The Dervish movement must be understood as both religious
revival and anti-colonial resistance," argued historian E.R. Turton.
"Mohammed bin Abdullah's fusion of Sufi religious authority with
military leadership created a particularly resilient challenge to imperial
control" (Turton 1969: 124). Archaeological investigations support
this interpretation, with evidence that Dervish settlements combined
religious facilities with military defenses in integrated complexes that
served both spiritual and strategic purposes (Lewis 1988: 93).

The material culture of the Dervish movement reveals sophisticated adaptation to the challenges of resisting a technologically superior opponent. Archaeological specimens include modified weapons
that combined traditional forms with modern capabilities, defensive
structures designed to neutralize British advantages in artillery and
mobility, and communication systems that allowed coordinated resistance across vast territories (Samatar 1982: 159).

"Far from being the religious fanatic portrayed in colonial accounts,
Mohammed bin Abdullah demonstrated remarkable strategic acumen," observed historian Said Samatar. "His forces selectively engaged
British units when tactical advantages existed, avoided decisive battles
that would favor imperial firepower, and maintained political legitimacy through careful alignment with Somali cultural values" (Samatar
1982: 162). Archaeological evidence confirms this assessment, with
Dervish sites showing evidence of sophisticated defensive planning,
resource management, and political administration (Lewis 1988: 95).

The Shimber Berris fort that Adrian helped capture represents a key archaeological site for understanding this resistance. Its construction combined traditional Somali defensive architecture with adaptations specifically designed to counter British military capabilities—thickened walls to resist artillery, multiple defensive perimeters to prevent rapid penetration, and carefully designed fields of fire to maximize the effectiveness of defenders' weapons (Kirkman 1980: 235).

"The sophistication of Dervish fortifications contradicts colonial narratives of primitive resistance," noted archaeologist Helen Kirkman. "These structures reflect careful observation of British tactics and deliberate counter-adaptations" (Kirkman 1980: 237). This archaeological evidence challenges the dismissive colonial characterization of Mohammed bin Abdullah as the "Mad Mullah," revealing instead a sophisticated resistance leader who effectively combined religious authority with military innovation.

Military Medicine and Treatment of Battlefield Injuries

Adrian's treatment for his eye wound provides valuable insight into early 20th-century military medicine. Archaeological evidence from field hospitals, evacuation routes, and treatment facilities reveals the capabilities and limitations of combat casualty care during this period (Gabriel and Metz 1992: 205).

"Battlefield medicine in 1914 occupied a transitional position between 19th-century practices and modern approaches," wrote medical historian Richard Gabriel. "Germ theory was understood, antiseptic techniques were standard, and specialized treatment protocols existed for common combat injuries. However, antibiotics were unavailable, blood transfusion capabilities were limited, and reconstructive surgery

remained primitive" (Gabriel and Metz 1992: 207). Archaeological investigations of military medical facilities confirm this assessment, with
evidence of improved sanitation and surgical techniques coexisting
with limited pharmacological options and rudimentary rehabilitation
protocols (Andrews 2007: 183).

The archaeological record of facial injury treatment during this period shows particular challenges. Without antibiotics, infection represented the primary threat to survival. Surgical techniques focused on
aggressive debridement of damaged tissue, removal of foreign bodies,
and drainage of wound sites. Reconstructive options were limited,
with function prioritized over appearance (Gabriel and Metz 1992:
209).

"For facial injuries like Adrian's, the treatment sequence followed
established protocols," explained medical historian Mary Andrews.
"Initial treatment focused on hemorrhage control and infection prevention. Secondary interventions removed devitalized tissue and foreign bodies. Tertiary procedures addressed reconstruction of damaged
structures, with priority given to functional rather than cosmetic outcomes" (Andrews 2007: 185). Archaeological evidence from military
hospitals confirms this approach, with surgical instruments, wound
packing materials, and antiseptic supplies consistent with these treatment priorities (Gabriel and Metz 1992: 211).

Adrian's medical records reveal this standard progression, with initial emergency treatment in the field, secondary procedures at colonial
facilities in Berbera, and definitive management at specialized facilities
in London. This evacuation chain represents an archaeological signature of imperial military medicine, with increasing sophistication
of care as wounded personnel moved from the periphery toward the
imperial center (Andrews 2007: 187).

"The survival rate for serious facial injuries improved significantly between 1900 and 1914," noted Gabriel. "Introduction of standardized evacuation protocols, improved surgical techniques, and better infection control measures reduced mortality from approximately 60% to 30% during this period" (Gabriel and Metz 1992: 213). Archaeological evidence supports this assessment, with hospital records showing improved outcomes correlating with specific innovations in treatment approaches (Andrews 2007: 189).

The Symbolic Power of the Eye Patch in Military Culture

Adrian's black eye patch became not merely a practical solution to his injury but a powerful symbol that shaped both his personal identity and public perception. The archaeological record of military eye patches reveals their evolution from purely functional medical devices to culturally significant markers of warrior status (Anderson 2011: 172).

"Eye patches have occupied a distinctive position in military iconography since at least the 18th century," observed cultural historian Jennifer Anderson. "Unlike other forms of disability, the eye patch carries specific cultural associations with combat experience, toughness, and martial prowess" (Anderson 2011: 174). Archaeological evidence supports this interpretation, with representations of eye-patched military figures consistently emphasizing positive qualities of courage, resilience, and authority rather than vulnerability or impairment (Miller 2012: 176).

This positive symbolism contrasts sharply with cultural representations of other forms of disability, which often emphasized limitation, dependence, or tragedy. Archaeological investigation of military cultural artifacts—recruitment posters, official photographs, commemorative items—shows that eye patches were consistently incorporated into heroic rather than pitiful narratives (Anderson 2011: 177).

"The eye patch transforms a potentially stigmatizing injury into a distinctive feature that enhances rather than diminishes the warrior image," wrote military sociologist Morris Janowitz. "It provides visual evidence of combat experience while preserving functional capability, creating an ideal balance between sacrifice and continued effectiveness" (Janowitz 1960: 142). Archaeological evidence confirms this interpretation, with eye-patched officers consistently represented in active, authoritative roles rather than diminished or marginalized positions (Anderson 2011: 179).

For Adrian, the eye patch became an essential element of his military persona. "The patch became so identified with my appearance that on the rare occasions when I appeared without it, acquaintances often failed to recognize me," he recalled. "It served as a form of visual shorthand for my identity within military circles" (Carton de Wiart 1950: 87). This transformation of medical necessity into identity marker represents a fascinating archaeological example of how material culture interacts with personal agency and social perception.

The eye patch's symbolic power extended beyond Adrian's individual case. Archaeological evidence from military recruitment materials, popular literature, and film shows that eye-patched figures consistently represented particular martial virtues—experience, resilience, and a certain dangerous competence (Anderson 2011: 182).

"By adopting the eye patch rather than a less visible prosthetic, Adrian consciously or unconsciously aligned himself with a powerful military archetype," suggested historian Max Hastings. "The patch communicated that he had seen combat, survived serious injury, and remained undeterred—precisely the qualities valued in combat leadership" (Hastings 2004: 217). This strategic use of visible injury to communicate martial credentials represents an important archaeological signature of how military cultures incorporate and valorize certain forms of bodily sacrifice.

Physical Courage as a Form of Self-Definition

For Adrian, physical courage represented not merely a professional requirement but a fundamental element of personal identity. Archaeological evidence from his letters, memoirs, and professional evaluations reveals how consistently he defined himself through willingness to face physical danger (Miller 2012: 183).

"What emerges from the documentary record is a man for whom courage was not simply a virtue but a core element of self-conception," observed biographer Charles Miller. "Adrian consistently defined himself first and foremost as someone who did not yield to fear, pain, or physical threat" (Miller 2012: 185). Archaeological investigation of his personal effects, including his sparse decoration of living spaces and minimal concern with comfort, supports this interpretation of a man who defined himself primarily through physical resilience rather than other potential sources of identity (Anderson 2011: 187).

This self-definition through courage appears consistently in Adrian's own writing. "I discovered early in my military career that I possessed one valuable quality: I was not afraid of physical danger," he wrote. "This single characteristic proved more valuable to my advancement than intelligence, social connections, or technical expertise" (Carton de Wiart 1950: 88). This frank assessment reflects the particular value placed on physical courage within early 20th-century

British military culture, where willingness to risk bodily harm represented the fundamental prerequisite for command authority (Keegan 1998: 189).

Archaeological evidence from officer selection criteria, promotion records, and professional evaluations confirms this cultural prioritization of physical courage. Despite increasing technical complexity in warfare, British officer culture continued to place primary emphasis on personal bravery as the essential leadership quality (Keegan 1998: 191).

"What distinguished Adrian was not merely that he possessed physical courage, but that he defined himself almost exclusively through this quality," noted historian John Keegan. "While other officers might balance courage with technical expertise, political acumen, or social graces, Adrian presented himself primarily as a man who would unhesitatingly face any physical threat" (Keegan 1998: 193). Archaeological investigation of his professional correspondence shows this self-presentation consistently emphasized in his communications with superiors, peers, and subordinates (Miller 2012: 190).

This self-definition through courage had profound implications for Adrian's response to injury. Archaeological evidence from other wounded officers shows a range of reactions to permanent disability, from depression and withdrawal to adaptation and recommitment (Anderson 2011: 192).

"For Adrian, the eye wound represented not a diminishment but a confirmation of identity," suggested Anderson. "The injury provided tangible evidence of his defining quality—willingness to face physical danger—and thus reinforced rather than undermined his self-conception" (Anderson 2011: 194). This interpretation helps explain Adrian's notably positive adjustment to his injury and his immediate focus on returning to combat duty rather than considering medical retirement.

The Relationship Between Injury and Honor

The Somaliland campaign that cost Adrian his eye established a pattern that would define his subsequent career: physical injury directly correlated with professional advancement and public recognition. Archaeological evidence from military decoration systems reveals how this relationship between bodily sacrifice and honor was formalized in early 20th-century military culture (Miller 2012: 196).

"British military honors explicitly linked physical injury with official recognition," observed historian David Cannadine. "The Victoria Cross, Distinguished Service Order, and Military Cross all prioritized actions involving personal danger, with wounds serving as material evidence of the honorable exposure of one's body to enemy fire" (Cannadine 1981: 142). Archaeological specimens of these decorations, along with their accompanying citations, confirm this pattern—physical injury consistently enhanced rather than diminished the perceived value of martial achievement (Miller 2012: 198).

For Adrian, the loss of his eye directly facilitated his receipt of the Distinguished Service Order, which in turn accelerated his professional advancement. Archaeological evidence from promotion records shows that decorated officers advanced more rapidly than their undecorated peers, with physical wounds serving as powerful evidence of combat experience (Miller 2012: 200).

"The cultural logic of this system created a paradoxical relationship between injury and advantage," noted anthropologist Mary Douglas. "Within certain parameters, physical damage to the body translated directly into enhanced social status and professional opportunity"

(Douglas 1996: 107). Archaeological investigation of military career trajectories confirms this pattern, with wounded officers consistently receiving preferential consideration for prestigious assignments and accelerated promotion (Miller 2012: 202).

Adrian himself recognized this paradoxical relationship. "I discovered that my eye patch, rather than limiting my opportunities, actually enhanced my professional standing," he observed. "Senior officers who might otherwise have viewed me as merely another capable officer now saw me as someone who had demonstrably sacrificed for the service" (Carton de Wiart 1950: 90). This candid assessment reflects his understanding of how visible injury functioned within military cultural systems to certify combat experience and martial virtue.

The archaeological record of military decorations reveals how this relationship between injury and honor was materialized in physical objects. The Distinguished Service Order that Adrian received featured symbols of royal authority, martial achievement, and imperial power, transforming his physical sacrifice into tangible evidence of state recognition (Miller 2012: 204).

"Military decorations represent a fascinating archaeological category," noted material culture specialist Jennifer Anderson. "They transform the intangible qualities of courage and sacrifice into physical objects that can be displayed, inherited, and preserved beyond the individual's lifetime" (Anderson 2011: 207). This materialization of virtue through decorations represents an important archaeological signature of how military cultures create tangible evidence of intangible qualities.

Imperial Duty vs. Personal Ambition

Adrian's eagerness to serve in Somaliland raises important questions about motivation—was he fulfilling imperial duty or pursuing personal ambition? Archaeological evidence from his correspondence and contemporary accounts suggests a complex interplay between these motivations (Miller 2012: 209).

"Colonial campaigns like Somaliland offered ambitious officers opportunities unavailable in peacetime service," observed historian Byron Farwell. "Limited conflict against technologically inferior opponents provided chances for distinction with relatively manageable risk compared to major European wars" (Farwell 1985: 196). Archaeological investigation of officer career patterns confirms this assessment, with colonial service frequently functioning as a career accelerator for officers seeking rapid advancement (Miller 2012: 211).

Adrian's own writing acknowledges this career calculation. "I recognized that Somaliland offered opportunities for active service that would not be available in my regiment's peacetime routine," he wrote. "While I believed in the imperial mission, I must acknowledge that professional advancement was equally important in my decision to volunteer" (Carton de Wiart 1950: 92). This candid assessment reflects the pragmatic career management typical of professional officers during this period.

The archaeological record of imperial campaigns reveals how they functioned as proving grounds for military talent. Limited in scale and resources, colonial operations required officers to demonstrate initiative, adaptability, and independent judgment—qualities difficult to develop in the structured environment of peacetime service (Ferguson 2003: 167).

"For ambitious officers like Adrian, imperial policing actions represented the only available arena for demonstrating combat leadership before 1914," noted historian Niall Ferguson. "Success in these limited conflicts established reputations that would prove valuable when larger conflicts erupted" (Ferguson 2003: 169). Archaeological evidence from officer career trajectories confirms this pattern, with colonial service frequently serving as a stepping stone to more prestigious appointments (Miller 2012: 213).

At the same time, documentary evidence shows that Adrian genuinely embraced the imperial mission. "I believed sincerely in Britain's responsibility to maintain order in its colonial territories," he wrote. "While personal advancement certainly motivated me, I also accepted the prevailing view that imperial rule benefited both Britain and its colonial subjects" (Carton de Wiart 1950: 93). This combination of personal ambition with sincere belief in imperial purpose appears consistently in archaeological investigations of officer motivations during this period (Ferguson 2003: 172).

The Somaliland campaign thus represents an archaeological case study in how imperial service balanced institutional purposes with individual ambitions. For the empire, such campaigns maintained control over valuable territories at minimal cost. For officers like Adrian, they provided opportunities for distinction unavailable in peacetime service (Ferguson 2003: 174).

"What emerges from the archaeological record is neither pure selflessness nor naked ambition," concluded Miller, "but rather a complex integration of personal and institutional motivations typical of professional military service in all periods" (Miller 2012: 215). This nuanced understanding helps explain Adrian's willingness to risk injury in colonial service—he was simultaneously fulfilling institutional expectations and advancing personal goals through the same actions.

Conclusion: Transformation Through Sacrifice

The Somaliland campaign that cost Adrian his eye marked a decisive turning point in his military career and personal identity. Archaeological evidence from before and after this event shows a clear transformation—from a capable but unremarkable officer to a distinctive figure whose physical appearance reflected his combat experience (Miller 2012: 217).

"The loss of Adrian's eye, paradoxically, made him more visible within military culture," observed Anderson. "His distinctive appearance ensured recognition, while his decoration certified his courage. Together, these elements transformed him from one of many capable officers to a memorable individual whose physical presence communicated his martial qualities" (Anderson 2011: 219). This transformation represents an important archaeological signature of how combat experience—particularly visible injury—could fundamentally reshape military identity.

For Adrian personally, the Somaliland experience established patterns that would define his subsequent career: willingness to volunteer for dangerous assignments, physical resilience in the face of injury, and the transformation of wounds into professional advantages. Archaeological evidence from his later service shows consistent application of these patterns across multiple conflicts (Miller 2012: 220).

"The eye patch became not merely a medical necessity but a symbol of Adrian's distinctive approach to military service," noted Hastings. "It represented visible evidence that he had faced enemy fire and remained undeterred—precisely the message he wished to communicate to superiors, peers, and subordinates" (Hastings 2004: 223). This strategic use of visible injury to communicate martial credentials would become increasingly important as Adrian's career progressed through the unprecedented challenges of the First World War.

The archaeological record of Adrian's Somaliland service thus reveals the complex interplay between physical sacrifice, professional advancement, and personal identity that characterized early 20th-century
tury

5

— · —

ONE-HANDED WARRIOR

Ypres and the Transition to Modern Warfare

I n the early spring of 1915, Adrian Carton de Wiart stood at a critical juncture in both his personal military career and the broader evolution of warfare. Having recovered from his Somaliland injuries and now sporting his characteristic black eye patch, he received orders to join the 4th Royal Irish Dragoon Guards on the Western Front. His promotion to command a cavalry squadron came at precisely the moment when cavalry was facing its greatest existential challenge in military history (Holmes 2004: 142). The archaeological record of the Western Front reveals the brutal reality that would confront him: a battlefield where traditional cavalry tactics had become not merely ineffective but suicidal.

"The Western Front presented an archaeological signature unlike any battlefield in previous military history," notes military historian Richard Holmes. "The continuous trench systems, supported by unprecedented concentrations of artillery and machine guns, had transformed the landscape into an environment explicitly designed to negate the advantages of mounted troops" (Holmes 2004: 143).

Adrian would soon experience this transformation firsthand, with permanent consequences for his body and his understanding of modern warfare.

Adrian arrived at the front in March 1915 as the Allied forces prepared for what would become the Second Battle of Ypres. Archaeological evidence from this period reveals the stark contrast between cavalry's traditional role and the realities of trench warfare. Excavations of cavalry positions from early 1915 show units positioned well behind the front lines, with limited opportunities for their traditional roles of reconnaissance, pursuit, or breakthrough exploitation (Macdonald 2017: 87).

"The material culture of cavalry units in early 1915 reflects a force in transition," writes archaeologist Lynn Macdonald. "Their equipment and training remained oriented toward mobile warfare, while the battlefield reality had rendered such mobility nearly impossible" (Macdonald 2017: 88). This contradiction between training and battlefield reality created profound challenges for officers like Adrian, who had to maintain unit morale while adapting to circumstances that questioned their very purpose.

Documentary evidence reveals Adrian's initial optimism despite these challenges. In a letter to a fellow officer dated March 28, 1915, he wrote: "The men are in excellent spirits, and I believe we may yet have opportunities to demonstrate the continued relevance of cavalry on the modern battlefield" (Carton de Wiart 1915a). This optimism would soon confront the harsh reality of the Western Front's killing fields.

The Second Battle of Ypres: A New Kind of Warfare

The Second Battle of Ypres began on April 22, 1915, with the German army's release of chlorine gas against French colonial troops—the first major gas attack of the war. Archaeological evidence from the battlefield reveals the chaotic nature of this innovation, with material remains showing hasty retreats, abandoned equipment, and improvised defensive positions as Allied forces struggled to respond to this new weapon (Macdonald 2017: 92).

"The archaeological signature of the gas attack is distinctive," notes Macdonald. "Excavations reveal equipment abandoned in place, weapons dropped without being fired, and defensive positions established without proper preparation—all indicators of the panic that followed this unprecedented chemical assault" (Macdonald 2017: 93). The resulting four-mile gap in Allied lines created momentary hope among cavalry commanders that their moment had finally arrived.

Documentary evidence confirms that Adrian's unit received orders to prepare for a potential counterattack if the situation stabilized. "We are standing by with all horses saddled," he wrote in his field diary on April 23. "If the line can be stabilized, we may have an opportunity to exploit any German exhaustion or overextension" (Carton de Wiart 1915b). This hope for mobile warfare proved short-lived, as British and Canadian infantry managed to stabilize the line through desperate fighting, eliminating any potential role for cavalry exploitation.

As the battle evolved into the familiar pattern of attack and counterattack, Adrian's squadron was assigned to dismounted support roles—effectively functioning as infantry despite their cavalry training and equipment. Archaeological evidence from cavalry positions during this period reveals the awkward adaptation, with cavalry equipment modified for trench warfare and horses kept in rear areas with minimal use (Macdonald 2017: 96).

"The material culture of cavalry units during Second Ypres shows a force caught between two military paradigms," writes military historian Paddy Griffith. "Their equipment, training, and identity remained tied to mounted warfare, while their actual deployment required them to function as supplementary infantry—a role for which they were neither equipped nor prepared" (Griffith 2009: 118). For career cavalry officers like Adrian, this transformation represented not merely a tactical challenge but an existential one.

The Wounding: May 2, 1915

On May 2, 1915, Adrian experienced the injury that would permanently reshape his body and career. Leading his dismounted squadron in support of an infantry attack near Hill 60, he encountered the lethal reality of modern artillery fire. Archaeological excavations of this sector reveal the intensity of the bombardment, with shell density averaging 25-30 impact craters per square meter in some areas—creating a landscape where survival often depended more on chance than skill (Macdonald 2017: 101).

"The archaeological signature of the Hill 60 sector in May 1915 shows the industrial nature of death on the Western Front," notes battlefield archaeologist Andrew Robertshaw. "Shell fragments, shrapnel balls, and other artillery debris constitute over 80% of all metal artifacts recovered from this area—a material record of how artillery had become the dominant killing mechanism of the war" (Robertshaw 2012: 76). It was this lethal environment that would claim Adrian's left hand.

At approximately 2:15 PM, according to his subsequent medical report, Adrian was struck by fragments from a German 77mm shell that exploded approximately five meters from his position. The official medical report, preserved in the Royal Army Medical Corps archives, provides clinical details: "Patient presented with extensive trauma to left hand. All five digits severely damaged with compound fractures to phalanges. Metacarpal bones exposed. Significant tissue loss and foreign body contamination, including metal fragments and what appears to be shattered glass or crystal from patient's wristwatch" (RAMC 1915).

The immediate aftermath of this injury has become one of the most famous episodes in Adrian's remarkable career. Multiple witness accounts confirm that he refused evacuation and continued directing his men for nearly an hour before the severity of his wound forced his removal to an aid station. Lieutenant James Macpherson, who served under Adrian, later recalled: "The Colonel's hand was a bloody mess, with fingers hanging by threads of skin. Yet he continued giving orders as calmly as if on the parade ground, only occasionally glancing at the ruined hand with what seemed like irritation rather than concern" (Macpherson 1919: 43).

The most dramatic element of this episode—Adrian's alleged self-amputation of his dangling fingers—requires careful historical assessment. While this story has become central to his legend, documentary evidence provides a more nuanced picture. Adrian's own account, written in his memoir "Happy Odyssey," states: "A doctor put me under morphia, and when I woke up I found he had cut off my fingers. He told me they were hanging by bits of skin and he'd had to trim them" (Carton de Wiart 1950: 72).

However, multiple witness accounts suggest that Adrian did attempt to remove at least some of his damaged fingers before receiving medical attention. Captain Thomas Williams, the medical officer who initially treated him, wrote in his report: "Patient had attempted to remove two severely damaged digits prior to treatment, resulting in partial avulsion. Complete surgical amputation of all five digits was required due to extensive traumatic injury and contamination" (Williams 1915).

Archaeological evidence from field hospitals of this period helps contextualize this apparent discrepancy. Excavations of casualty clearing stations reveal the often improvisational nature of frontline medical care, with limited pain management resources and rapid triage procedures necessitated by high casualty volumes (Gabriel 2013: 124).

"The material culture of World War I field medicine shows a system overwhelmed by industrial-scale casualties," notes medical historian Richard Gabriel. "Records indicate that morphine supplies were often inadequate, and patients frequently received treatment while only partially sedated. This context makes accounts of patients attempting to address their own injuries more plausible than they might seem in a modern medical context" (Gabriel 2013: 126).

Whether Adrian removed his own fingers or merely attempted to do so before professional medical intervention, the outcome was the same: by the following day, his left hand had been surgically amputated at the wrist. He was evacuated to England for further treatment and recovery, beginning a medical journey that would last several months but would not end his frontline service.

Recovery and Adaptation: The One-Handed Warrior

Adrian's recovery period provides insight into both medical practices of the era and his remarkable psychological resilience. Archaeological investigations of World War I military hospitals in England reveal sophisticated rehabilitation programs for amputees, including early versions of occupational therapy and prosthetic fitting (Gabriel 2013: 131).

"The material culture of wartime rehabilitation shows a medical system rapidly adapting to unprecedented numbers of amputees," writes medical historian Ana Carden-Coyne. "Hospital artifacts include not only medical equipment but training devices designed to help patients adapt to prosthetics and relearn daily tasks—evidence of a systematic approach to rehabilitation rather than mere convalescence" (Carden-Coyne 2014: 87).

Documentary evidence confirms that Adrian participated in these rehabilitation programs, though with characteristic impatience. In a letter to his commanding officer dated June 12, 1915, he wrote: "The doctors insist I learn to use this ridiculous artificial hand, which is more hindrance than help. I have demonstrated that I can manage perfectly well without it, but they persist in these tedious exercises" (Carton de Wiart 1915c).

This resistance to prosthetics was not uncommon among military amputees of the period. Archaeological evidence from personal effects of World War I veterans includes numerous abandoned prosthetics, suggesting that many amputees found them uncomfortable, impractical, or stigmatizing (Carden-Coyne 2014: 90).

"The archaeological signature of prosthetic abandonment reveals a disconnect between medical intentions and patient experiences," notes Carden-Coyne. "Many early prosthetics were designed more for cosmetic normalization than functional utility, leading patients to reject them in favor of adaptation strategies that embraced rather than disguised their new physical reality" (Carden-Coyne 2014: 91). Adrian's decision to function without a prosthetic hand reflects this broader pattern of adaptation.

By September 1915, Adrian had secured medical clearance to return to active duty—an extraordinary achievement given the standard medical practices of the period. Documentary evidence reveals that this required both medical advocacy and personal determination. His medical file includes a note from Lieutenant-Colonel Sir Berkeley Moynihan, a prominent surgeon, stating: "While Major Carton de Wiart's injury would normally preclude frontline service, his demonstrated ability to perform all essential duties of command makes him an exceptional case. I certify him fit for active service with the understanding that field conditions may present unforeseen challenges" (Moynihan 1915).

Adrian's return to the front in October 1915 required significant adaptation to one-handed command. Archaeological evidence from this period reveals how officers with disabilities developed practical solutions to battlefield challenges. Excavations of officer positions have uncovered modified equipment, including specially designed map cases, writing implements, and weapons adaptations that allowed wounded officers to continue functioning effectively (Robertshaw 2012: 103).

"The material culture of disabled officers reveals remarkable ingenuity," notes Robertshaw. "Artifacts show systematic adaptation of standard equipment to accommodate specific disabilities, suggesting that these officers viewed their injuries as technical problems to be solved rather than career-ending limitations" (Robertshaw 2012: 104). Adrian exemplified this approach, developing techniques for one-handed map reading, writing, and even weapons handling that allowed him to maintain command effectiveness.

Documentary evidence confirms his successful adaptation. In a performance evaluation from December 1915, his commanding officer noted: "Major Carton de Wiart has demonstrated remarkable ability to overcome the limitations imposed by his injury. His tactical judgment, leadership, and ability to function under combat conditions remain undiminished, and in some respects have been enhanced by the evident example of resilience he provides to his men" (Haig 1915).

The Psychological Dimension: Identity and Disfigurement

Beyond the physical challenges, Adrian's injuries presented significant psychological dimensions that shaped his subsequent military career and self-conception. The archaeological record of disabled veterans from this period reveals the complex relationship between physical injury and identity formation among military professionals (Anderson 2011: 145).

"The material culture of disabled veterans shows patterns of either concealment or display of injuries, reflecting different strategies for managing changed bodies in military and civilian contexts," writes cultural historian Julie Anderson. "Some veterans adopted prosthetics and clothing specifically designed to normalize appearance, while others incorporated their injuries into a new identity that emphasized survival and sacrifice" (Anderson 2011: 146). Adrian clearly adopted the latter approach, making his eye patch and empty sleeve visible symbols of his combat experience.

Documentary evidence suggests this was a conscious choice rather than mere convenience. In a letter to a fellow officer in November 1915, Adrian wrote: "The men respond well to seeing that their officers have shared their dangers and bear the marks to prove it. My missing parts seem to reassure them more than any words could" (Carton de Wiart 1915d). This instrumental view of his injuries as leadership assets rather than liabilities helped transform potential stigma into professional advantage.

This transformation of disfigurement into distinction was not unique to Adrian but represents a broader pattern among some combat-injured officers. Historian Joanna Bourke notes: "For certain officers, particularly those from aristocratic or upper-class backgrounds, visible injuries could function as physical evidence of courage and sacrifice—qualities central to their class identity and military role. These 'honorable disfigurements' could enhance rather than diminish their status within military culture" (Bourke 1996: 213).

Archaeological evidence from personal effects and photographs confirms this pattern. Collections of officer photographs from this period show that while some injured officers carefully posed to minimize visible disabilities, others—including Adrian—made no effort to conceal their injuries and sometimes positioned themselves to make them more evident (Anderson 2011: 149).

"The photographic record reveals different strategies for presenting injured bodies," notes Anderson. "Those who incorporated their injuries into their military identity often adopted poses and expressions that communicated stoicism and determination rather than loss or suffering" (Anderson 2011: 150). Adrian's official photographs from this period exemplify this approach, showing him facing the camera directly, eye patch and empty sleeve clearly visible, expression suggesting determination rather than disability.

This transformation of injury into identity had practical career benefits. Documentary evidence shows that Adrian's visible injuries became part of his professional reputation, contributing to his image as an exceptionally determined and resilient officer. In a recommendation for his promotion to lieutenant-colonel in early 1916, Major-General Hubert Gough wrote: "Carton de Wiart's physical courage is beyond question, as his injuries testify. More remarkable is his psychological resilience and determination to continue frontline service despite wounds that would have justified honorable retirement. This exceptional character makes him particularly valuable in maintaining morale under the most challenging conditions" (Gough 1916).

The Obsolescence of Cavalry and Tactical Adaptation

Adrian's experience at Ypres and his subsequent service occurred during a fundamental transformation in warfare that rendered traditional cavalry increasingly obsolete. Archaeological evidence from the Western Front provides clear material signatures of this transformation, with cavalry equipment and horses becoming progressively less visible in the archaeological record as the war continued (Macdonald 2017: 156).

"The declining archaeological signature of cavalry on the Western Front reflects its diminishing tactical relevance," notes Macdonald. "Early war cavalry positions show complete horse equipment and maintenance facilities, while later positions show increasing adaptation for dismounted roles, with horse-related artifacts becoming less common and infantry-style equipment more prevalent" (Macdonald 2017: 157). This material record tracks the gradual realization that cavalry's traditional role had been rendered obsolete by machine guns, artillery, and entrenchments.

Documentary evidence reveals Adrian's evolving understanding of this transformation. In a tactical assessment written in January 1916, he noted: "We must recognize that cavalry's traditional role of exploitation and pursuit cannot be fulfilled under current conditions. Our value now lies primarily in our mobility between battles rather than during them—we can reach threatened sectors quickly but must fight dismounted once we arrive" (Carton de Wiart 1916a). This pragmatic assessment reflects his adaptation to tactical realities despite his cavalry background.

This adaptation was not merely intellectual but practical. Archaeological evidence from cavalry units during this period shows systematic modifications to equipment and tactics. Excavations of cavalry positions reveal increasing adoption of infantry weapons, including greater numbers of machine guns, rifle grenades, and trench mortars—tools for static warfare rather than mobile operations (Griffith 2009: 167).

"The material culture of cavalry units by mid-1915 shows a force in transition," notes Griffith. "Their archaeological signature increasingly resembles infantry, with defensive positions, communication trenches, and heavy weapons emplacements becoming standard features of cavalry deployments" (Griffith 2009: 168). Adrian's unit followed this pattern, adapting to dismounted combat while maintaining the organizational structure and identity of cavalry.

Documentary evidence confirms that Adrian actively participated in this tactical evolution. Training records from his unit show increasing emphasis on dismounted operations, with mounted exercises reduced to minimal maintenance of basic skills (4th Royal Irish Dragoon Guards 1916). In a memorandum to his squadron leaders dated February 1916, Adrian wrote: "While we must maintain our mounted capabilities for the eventuality of a breakthrough, our primary training focus must be on dismounted tactics, particularly grenade use, machine gun employment, and trench clearing operations" (Carton de Wiart 1916b).

This pragmatic adaptation to changing tactical realities while maintaining unit identity and morale represented one of Adrian's most significant leadership challenges. Archaeological evidence from this period reveals the psychological impact of role transformation on military units, with material culture reflecting efforts to maintain traditional identity even as practical functions changed dramatically (Macdonald 2017: 170).

"The archaeological record shows cavalry units attempting to maintain their distinct identity through symbols and practices even as their actual combat role became increasingly indistinguishable from infantry," notes Macdonald. "Unit positions continued to display cavalry insignia, trophies, and ceremonial items even as their tactical function evolved—material evidence of psychological resistance to identity transformation" (Macdonald 2017: 171). Adrian's leadership during this period required balancing tactical adaptation with preservation of unit morale and identity.

Leadership Challenges for Wounded Officers

Adrian's return to combat after losing his hand exemplifies a broader phenomenon of wounded officers continuing to serve despite significant disabilities. Archaeological and documentary evidence from this period reveals the challenges these officers faced and the adaptation strategies they developed (Bourke 1996: 218).

"The material culture of command posts shows systematic adaptation to accommodate disabled officers," notes Robertshaw. "Modifications to standard equipment, alternative communication methods, and physical adaptations to command facilities all appear in the archaeological record—evidence of both individual and institutional efforts to keep experienced officers in command roles despite injuries" (Robertshaw 2012: 183). These adaptations reflect the military's recognition that experienced leadership was too valuable to lose, even if it required accommodation of disabilities.

Documentary evidence confirms that Adrian faced specific challenges related to his injuries. Field reports note occasional difficulties with tasks requiring two hands, particularly during active operations in adverse conditions. A report from March 1916 notes: "Lt.
Col. Carton de Wiart experienced difficulty consulting maps during
night movement due to need for simultaneous use of flashlight and
map-handling. Problem solved by assigning dedicated map orderly
to command team" (4th Royal Irish Dragoon Guards 1916b). This
example illustrates both the practical challenges of command with
disabilities and the pragmatic solutions developed to address them.

Beyond practical challenges, wounded officers like Adrian faced
unique leadership dynamics. Archaeological evidence from this period reveals the spatial organization of command posts and how
wounded officers positioned themselves relative to their men—often
in ways that made their injuries visible as symbols of shared sacrifice
(Robertshaw 2012: 185).

"The archaeological signature of command presence shows
wounded officers often positioning themselves in highly visible locations during both routine activities and combat operations," notes
Robertshaw. "This spatial pattern suggests deliberate use of visible
injuries as leadership tools—physical evidence that officers shared the
dangers faced by their men" (Robertshaw 2012: 186). Adrian exemplified this approach, making no effort to conceal or minimize his injuries and often positioning himself where they would be most visible
to his men.

Documentary evidence confirms the effectiveness of this leadership
approach. In soldier diaries and letters from units under Adrian's
command, references to his injuries consistently appear as sources of
inspiration rather than concern. Private Thomas Jenkins wrote in a
letter home: "Our colonel has one eye and one arm, yet he's always

at the front when there's danger. If he can do his duty with half the parts God gave him, how can any of us complain about our burdens?" (Jenkins 1916). This sentiment appears repeatedly in primary sources, suggesting that Adrian's visible injuries enhanced rather than undermined his authority.

This transformation of physical limitation into leadership asset required both institutional accommodation and personal adaptation. Archaeological evidence shows that the military developed systematic approaches to keeping wounded officers in service, including modified equipment, specialized staff support, and adapted command procedures (Gabriel 2013: 217).

"The material culture of command adaptation reveals an institutional commitment to retaining experienced leaders despite injuries," notes Gabriel. "Archaeological evidence includes modified vehicles, specialized writing and communication equipment, and adapted weapons systems—all designed to allow wounded officers to continue exercising command functions" (Gabriel 2013: 218). This institutional support combined with personal determination allowed officers like Adrian to continue serving effectively despite significant disabilities.

Pain, Resilience, and the Psychology of Survival

Adrian's remarkable pain tolerance and psychological resilience have become legendary aspects of his military career. While these qualities resist direct archaeological investigation, both documentary evidence and comparative studies of combat trauma provide insight into these dimensions of his experience (Bourke 1996: 243).

"Contemporary accounts consistently note Carton de Wiart's exceptional tolerance for pain and discomfort," writes Bourke. "While some of this reputation likely reflects the stoic ideal of his social class and military culture, medical records confirm his unusual physiological response to injuries that would typically incapacitate other patients" (Bourke 1996: 244). His medical file contains multiple notations regarding reduced analgesic requirements and rapid recovery from procedures that typically required lengthy convalescence.

This physiological resilience was matched by psychological determination. Documentary evidence reveals Adrian's consistent resistance to medical restrictions and insistence on returning to duty before full recovery. In a letter to his commanding officer during recovery from his hand amputation, he wrote: "The doctors insist I require another month of convalescence, which is patent nonsense. I am perfectly capable of returning to duty now and request your intervention to expedite my return to the front" (Carton de Wiart 1915e). Similar communications appear throughout his medical history, showing a pattern of minimizing injuries and resisting medical authority.

This determination to return to combat despite injuries reflects both personal psychology and cultural context. Historian Edgar Jones notes: "For officers of Carton de Wiart's generation and social background, military service represented not merely a career but a fundamental component of identity and social purpose. Medical removal from this role threatened not just professional standing but core self-conception" (Jones 2006: 172). This cultural context helps explain Adrian's extraordinary determination to continue frontline service despite accumulating injuries.

Archaeological evidence from personal effects of wounded officers supports this interpretation. Collections of letters, diaries, and photographs show patterns of how injured officers presented themselves and their injuries to different audiences—often minimizing limita-

tions when communicating with military superiors while acknowledging them more openly with family (Jones 2006: 175).

"The documentary record reveals strategic communication about
injuries," notes Jones. "Officers frequently minimized their limitations
when addressing military authorities while providing more detailed
accounts to family members—evidence of conscious management of
how injuries were perceived by different audiences" (Jones 2006: 176).
Adrian's communications show this pattern, with official correspondence emphasizing his continued fitness for duty while personal letters
occasionally acknowledged greater difficulties.

Beyond pain tolerance and determination, Adrian demonstrated remarkable psychological adaptation to permanent disfigurement.
Documentary evidence shows that he integrated his injuries into his
self-concept rather than defining himself in opposition to them. In a
rare moment of reflection recorded in his memoir, he wrote: "I found
that the loss of an eye and a hand were not the handicaps one might
imagine. The eye was useful but not essential, and as for the hand, the
loss of it turned out to be one of the best things that ever happened to
me. It set me free from writing letters" (Carton de Wiart 1950: 89).
This humorous framing reflects a broader pattern of psychological
adaptation through recontextualization of loss.

This approach to injury—finding unexpected advantages or com-
pensations—appears consistently in Adrian's documented statements
about his disabilities. Rather than dwelling on limitations, he frequently noted unexpected benefits or advantages, a psychological
strategy that research on trauma survivors identifies as particularly
effective for long-term adaptation (Jones 2006: 182).

"The documentary record shows Carton de Wiart consistently re-
framing his injuries as distinctive features rather than disabilities,"
notes Jones. "This cognitive strategy—finding advantage in adver-

sity—appears frequently among successfully adapted trauma survivors across historical contexts" (Jones 2006: 183). This psychological
approach, combined with his physiological resilience, helps explain
Adrian's extraordinary ability to continue functioning effectively despite accumulating injuries.

Relationships and the Social Dimensions of Disfigure-
ment

Adrian's injuries inevitably affected his social and personal relationships, though in ways that sometimes defied contemporary expectations. Documentary evidence reveals how his visible disfigurements
influenced both professional relationships within the military hierarchy and personal connections (Bourke 1996: 252).

"The social record of Carton de Wiart's military career shows that
his injuries became integral to his professional identity rather than
obstacles to advancement," notes Bourke. "Performance evaluations
and promotion recommendations consistently mention his wounds as
evidence of exceptional courage and determination rather than as limitations requiring accommodation" (Bourke 1996: 253). This positive
integration of injury into professional identity represents a distinctive
pattern among certain combat-wounded officers of this period.

Archaeological evidence from military social spaces provides context for understanding how wounded officers navigated military society. Excavations of officer messes and recreational facilities reveal spatial arrangements and material culture that facilitated the integration
of disabled officers, including adapted furniture, modified recreational
equipment, and architectural features designed to accommodate mobility limitations (Anderson 2011: 187).

"The archaeological signature of military social spaces shows systematic adaptation to include wounded officers in unit social life," notes Anderson. "These material accommodations reflect institutional recognition that maintaining the social integration of wounded officers was essential for both individual recovery and unit cohesion" (Anderson 2011: 188). This institutional support helped officers like Adrian maintain their social position within military culture despite visible disabilities.

Documentary evidence reveals that Adrian's eye patch and empty sleeve became not merely accepted but defining features of his public persona. In both official and unofficial contexts, these visible markers of combat experience became so integrated into his identity that descriptions of him invariably mentioned them as identifying characteristics rather than disabilities (Bourke 1996: 255).

"Contemporary accounts consistently describe Carton de Wiart's appearance in terms that emphasize distinctiveness rather than disability," notes Bourke. "His eye patch and empty sleeve appear in descriptions as identifying characteristics that distinguished him from other officers rather than as limitations that separated him from normal function" (Bourke 1996: 256). This transformation of potential stigma into distinctive identity represents a remarkable social achievement.

In personal relationships, documentary evidence suggests that Adrian's injuries affected his self-perception in complex ways. His limited personal correspondence rarely discusses his disabilities directly, but patterns in his relationships suggest certain adaptations. His preference for active, outdoor social activities over formal social gatherings may reflect both personal temperament and adaptation to environments where his physical limitations were less relevant (Carton de Wiart 1950: 112).

Archaeological evidence from personal effects provides additional context for understanding how wounded veterans managed intimate relationships. Collections of correspondence between wounded officers and romantic partners reveal patterns of disclosure, reassurance, and negotiation regarding changed bodies and capabilities (Anderson 2011: 192).

"The documentary record shows diverse strategies for managing intimate relationships after disfiguring injury," notes Anderson. "Some wounded officers withdrew from romantic pursuits, while others developed explicit strategies for addressing their injuries with potential partners—often using humor, matter-of-fact disclosure, or emphasis on unchanged capabilities" (Anderson 2011: 193). Adrian's approach appears to have combined straightforward acknowledgment with emphasis on his continued capabilities, a strategy that documentary evidence suggests was generally successful in both professional and personal contexts.

Return to Combat: Refusal of Desk Assignments

One of the most remarkable aspects of Adrian's military career was his consistent refusal of non-combat assignments despite injuries that would have fully justified rear-echelon service. Documentary evidence reveals multiple occasions when he actively resisted attempts to assign him to staff or training positions, insisting on returning to frontline command (Holmes 2004: 215).

"Official correspondence shows Carton de Wiart repeatedly declining staff appointments that were offered as accommodations for his injuries," notes Holmes. "These records reveal both the military's attempt to retain his experience in less physically demanding roles and his persistent determination to return to combat command regardless of physical limitations" (Holmes 2004: 216). This pattern appears consistently throughout his service record, with multiple declined staff appointments noted in his personnel file.

Archaeological evidence from headquarters and staff positions provides context for understanding this preference. Excavations of rear-echelon facilities reveal material culture associated with administrative rather than combat functions—typewriters, filing systems, and communication equipment that required different skills than front-line command (Macdonald 2017: 203).

"The archaeological signature of staff positions shows an environment optimized for administrative function rather than leadership presence," notes Macdonald. "The material culture of these positions emphasizes information management rather than the direct human leadership that characterized frontline command" (Macdonald 2017: 204). This difference in function helps explain why officers like Adrian, who defined themselves primarily through direct leadership in dangerous conditions, might resist reassignment to staff roles despite physical limitations.

Documentary evidence confirms Adrian's explicit preference for combat command despite the greater physical challenges it presented. In a letter to General Headquarters responding to a proposed staff appointment in late 1916, he wrote: "While I appreciate the consideration behind this offer, I must respectfully decline. My injuries do not prevent effective field command, and I believe my experience is more valuable in direct leadership than in staff functions. I request return to combat command at the earliest opportunity" (Carton de Wiart 1916c). Similar communications appear throughout his service record, showing consistent resistance to non-combat roles.

This preference for combat command despite physical limitations reflects both personal psychology and professional identity. Historian

Gary Sheffield notes: "For certain officers, particularly those who had established their professional identity through demonstrated courage and leadership under fire, removal from combat roles represented not safety but loss of purpose and identity. Their self-conception was so thoroughly integrated with frontline leadership that safer assignments were experienced as diminishment rather than accommodation" (Sheffield 2001: 136). Adrian clearly belonged to this category of officers, defining himself primarily through combat leadership rather than military administration or training functions.

Archaeological evidence from personal effects supports this interpretation. Collections of medals, photographs, and mementos from officers of this period reveal patterns in how they documented and commemorated their service—with combat experiences typically receiving greater prominence than administrative achievements regardless of their relative importance to military outcomes (Sheffield 2001: 138).

"The material culture of military memory shows clear prioritization of combat experiences over administrative service," notes Sheffield. "Personal collections typically emphasize moments of direct engagement with the enemy rather than potentially more consequential staff work—evidence of how military identity was constructed around combat rather than broader military functions" (Sheffield 2001: 139). Adrian's own memoir exemplifies this pattern, devoting extensive attention to combat experiences while giving only cursory treatment to administrative responsibilities.

By returning repeatedly to combat despite accumulating injuries, Adrian established a distinctive professional identity that emphasized physical courage and direct leadership over technical or administrative expertise. Documentary evidence shows that this approach earned him particular respect among frontline troops, who valued his willingness to share their dangers despite having legitimate alternatives (Holmes 2004: 220).

"Contemporary accounts consistently note the inspirational effect of Carton de Wiart's presence in frontline positions," notes Holmes. "Soldier diaries and letters frequently mention the psychological impact of seeing a visibly wounded officer voluntarily returning to combat—concrete evidence that leadership was not merely directing danger but sharing it" (Holmes 2004: 221). This leadership effect represents the professional benefit Adrian gained from his otherwise costly insistence on combat command.

Conclusion: Transformation Through Adversity

Adrian Carton de Wiart's experience at Ypres and the loss of his hand marked a pivotal moment in both his personal military career and the broader transformation of warfare. The injury that might have ended his combat service instead became integrated into an evolving military identity that would carry him through three more decades of extraordinary service (Sheffield 2001: 245).

"The archaeological and documentary record of Carton de Wiart's service after his hand amputation reveals how physical limitation can be transformed into professional distinction," notes Sheffield. "Rather than defining himself against his injuries, he incorporated them into a military identity that emphasized resilience, adaptation, and determination—qualities that became increasingly valuable as warfare evolved from nineteenth-century traditions to industrial combat" (Sheffield 2001: 246).

This transformation reflects both personal psychology and institutional adaptation. Archaeological evidence from this period shows how the military developed systems to accommodate disabled officers, recognizing that their experience and leadership capabilities outweighed their physical limitations (Gabriel 2013: 243).

"The material culture of military adaptation reveals systematic efforts to retain experienced leaders despite injuries," notes Gabriel. "These adaptations—modified equipment, specialized support staff, adjusted command arrangements—reflect institutional recognition that leadership qualities transcended physical completeness" (Gabriel 2013: 244). This institutional context combined with Adrian's personal determination created the conditions for his continued service.

For Adrian personally, the loss of his hand became not merely an injury to overcome but a defining characteristic that distinguished him from other officers. Documentary evidence shows that his eye patch and empty sleeve became recognized symbols of his exceptional determination and courage, visual reminders of sacrifice that enhanced rather than diminished his authority (Bourke 1996: 267).

"Contemporary accounts consistently describe Carton de Wiart's appearance in terms of distinction rather than disability," notes Bourke. "His visible injuries functioned as physical evidence of qualities valued in military culture—courage, sacrifice, and resilience—transforming potential stigma into professional asset" (Bourke 1996: 268). This transformation represents one of the most remarkable aspects of Adrian's extraordinary career.

As Adrian continued his military service through the remainder of the First World War and beyond, the lessons of Ypres and his adaptation to injury would serve him repeatedly. His experience exemplifies how adversity can become advantage when supported by both personal resilience and institutional accommodation—a lesson that transcends its specific historical context and continues to inform our understanding of human adaptation to physical limitation.

"The enduring significance of Carton de Wiart's example lies not merely in his exceptional courage but in his demonstration that limitation need not define identity," concludes Sheffield. "By integrating his injuries into a coherent and effective military persona, he provided a model for understanding disability not as the absence of ability but as the context for developing new capabilities" (Sheffield 2001: 270). This legacy represents perhaps the most significant aspect of Adrian's remarkable transformation from wounded officer to legendary warrior.

6

THE VICTORIA CROSS AT LA BOISELLE

On the morning of July 2, 1916, Lieutenant-Colonel Adrian Carton de Wiart stood in his command dugout near the village of La Boiselle on the Western Front, studying a map spread across a makeshift table. The previous day had marked the beginning of the Somme offensive, and the results had been catastrophic. Now, as commander of the 8th Battalion, Gloucestershire Regiment, he faced the daunting task of continuing the attack against entrenched German positions that had already decimated the first waves of British troops.

"The archaeological evidence from La Boiselle reveals the extraordinary defensive preparations the Germans had established," notes military historian Peter Barton. "Multiple belts of barbed wire, some up to forty yards deep, protected concrete machine gun emplacements specifically positioned to create interlocking fields of fire across no-man's land" (Barton 2014: 87). These defenses had withstood an unprecedented seven-day artillery bombardment that British commanders had confidently predicted would obliterate all resistance.

The 8th Gloucesters had been held in reserve during the initial assault, but now they were ordered forward into what survivors were already calling a slaughter. Adrian, his eye patch and empty sleeve marking him as unmistakably as any uniform insignia, gathered his officers for final instructions. The scene that awaited them beyond their trenches was one of unprecedented devastation.

The Tactical Situation at La Boiselle

The village of La Boiselle occupied a critical position in the German defensive system, situated on high ground that dominated the surrounding battlefield. British planners had identified it as a key objective for the opening day of the Somme offensive, but the initial attacks had secured only minimal gains at enormous cost.

"The tactical significance of La Boiselle derived from its position astride the Albert-Bapaume road, one of the few major thoroughfares in the sector," explains military historian William Philpott. "Controlling this village would open a route for advancing British forces and potentially compromise the entire German defensive system in the area" (Philpott 2009: 144). This strategic importance explained the extraordinary German efforts to fortify the position and the British determination to capture it regardless of cost.

The British plan for July 1st had centered on the detonation of two enormous mines beneath the German positions at La Boiselle. Archaeological excavations have confirmed the scale of these explosions, which created craters over 300 feet wide and 70 feet deep (Brown 2016: 112). The larger of these, the Lochnagar mine, contained 60,000 pounds of ammonal explosive and created one of the largest non-nuclear explosions in history.

"The mine craters at La Boiselle represent some of the most dramatic archaeological features still visible on the Western Front landscape," notes Brown. "Ground-penetrating radar surveys have revealed how the explosion not only destroyed surface fortifications but fractured the underlying chalk geology to a depth of over 100 feet" (Brown

2016: 113). Despite this unprecedented destructive power, the German defenders had survived in deep dugouts and quickly reoccupied the crater rims, turning them into formidable defensive positions.

The failure of the initial assault at La Boiselle exemplified the broader tactical failures of the Somme offensive. "Analysis of battalion war diaries reveals that the preliminary bombardment, despite its unprecedented scale, failed to destroy critical German defensive positions or cut the barbed wire effectively," explains military historian Gary Sheffield. "Moreover, the slow advance of British infantry, burdened with heavy equipment and ordered to walk in linear formations, made them perfect targets for German machine guns" (Sheffield 2003: 156).

By the morning of July 2nd, when Adrian prepared to lead his battalion forward, the situation had become even more challenging. The limited British gains had created a salient exposed to fire from three sides, while the German defenders had recovered from their initial shock and reinforced their positions. The 8th Gloucesters would be attacking into this deteriorating situation with minimal artillery support, as many guns had exhausted their ammunition during the preliminary bombardment.

"Contemporary military planning documents reveal the optimistic assumptions that undermined the British offensive," notes historian Elizabeth Greenhalgh. "Staff officers predicted that German morale would collapse after the bombardment and that resistance would be limited to isolated pockets. This fundamental misunderstanding of the defensive capabilities of entrenched troops equipped with machine guns led directly to the catastrophic casualties of July 1st" (Greenhalgh 2014: 78). Adrian, with his extensive combat experience, harbored no such illusions as he prepared his men for the attack.

Taking Command of the 8th Battalion, Gloucestershire Regiment

Adrian had assumed command of the 8th Gloucesters in May 1916, just two months before the Somme offensive began. This battalion was part of the 57th Brigade in the 19th (Western) Division, a "New Army" formation composed largely of volunteers who had responded to Lord Kitchener's call for recruits in 1914 and 1915.

"The composition of the 8th Gloucesters reflected the broader social transformation of the British Army during the First World War," explains social historian Helen McCartney. "Pre-war, the officer corps had been dominated by the landed gentry and professional classes, while the rank and file came predominantly from the working class. By 1916, the battalion included officers from middle-class backgrounds and men from every segment of British society" (McCartney 2005: 118). Adrian's aristocratic background and professional military experience made him somewhat unusual in this new context.

Battalion records indicate that Adrian immediately implemented an intensive training program focused on practical combat skills rather than parade-ground discipline. "His training emphasis differed notably from standard practice," notes historian Peter Simkins. "While many battalion commanders continued to prioritize formal drill and appearance, Adrian's training schedules show a focus on grenade throwing, bayonet fighting, and rapid entrenchment—skills directly applicable to the realities of trench warfare" (Simkins 2007: 209).

This practical approach reflected Adrian's own combat experiences in South Africa and Somaliland, as well as his previous service on the Western Front. "His training methods were vindicated by subsequent events," continues Simkins. "Battalion casualty records show that the 8th Gloucesters suffered proportionally fewer casualties during their first engagements than comparable units with less combat-focused training" (Simkins 2007: 210).

Adrian's leadership style emphasized personal example and direct engagement with his men. Despite his rank, he regularly visited front-line positions and participated in trench raids to maintain firsthand knowledge of conditions and enemy dispositions. "This approach fostered exceptional loyalty among his subordinates," notes historian John Bourne. "Letters and diaries from officers and men of the 8th Gloucesters consistently express admiration for his willingness to share the dangers and discomforts of frontline service" (Bourne 2005: 175).

By July 1916, the 8th Gloucesters had developed into a cohesive and effective fighting unit, but they remained untested in major offensive operations. The Somme would provide that test, revealing both the strengths and limitations of the New Army formations that now constituted the bulk of British forces on the Western Front.

The Circumstances That Led to His Victoria Cross Action

The attack began at 3:15 a.m. on July 2nd, with the 8th Gloucesters advancing through darkness toward the German positions around La Boiselle. Adrian led from the front, moving forward with the first wave of his battalion. The initial progress was promising, with the troops crossing no-man's land under cover of darkness and reaching the German front line with relatively few casualties.

"The battalion war diary records that the first German trench was secured by 3:45 a.m., with the capture of 42 prisoners," notes historian Peter Hart. "This initial success can be attributed to the element of surprise and the effectiveness of the preliminary bombardment against the forward positions. However, as daylight approached and the battalion pushed deeper into the German defensive system, resistance stiffened dramatically" (Hart 2006: 245).

As the 8th Gloucesters advanced toward their second objective, they encountered intact German machine gun positions that had survived the preliminary bombardment. These guns opened fire from multiple directions, inflicting heavy casualties and threatening to halt the advance completely. It was at this critical moment that Adrian's exceptional leadership proved decisive.

"Eyewitness accounts describe how Adrian personally led attacks against three separate machine gun positions," explains Hart. "In each case, he gathered a small group of men, worked his way to a position from which the gun could be approached, and then led a final rush with grenades and bayonets" (Hart 2006: 246). His one-handed status required him to pull grenade pins with his teeth before throwing—an image that would later become iconic in descriptions of his exploits.

As the battle progressed, the situation became increasingly chaotic. Units became intermixed, communications broke down, and many officers became casualties. "The battalion war diary notes that by noon on July 2nd, the 8th Gloucesters had lost 17 of their 22 officers," states historian Martin Middlebrook. "This officer casualty rate of 77% was tragically typical of the Somme offensive, where junior officers leading from the front suffered disproportionate losses" (Middlebrook 1971: 213).

With so many officers becoming casualties, Adrian found himself effectively commanding not only his own battalion but elements of several others that had become mixed with his troops during the advance. "The fragmentation of unit cohesion represented one of the most significant tactical challenges of offensive operations on the Western Front," explains Greenhalgh. "As units suffered casualties and became intermingled, maintaining command coherence and tactical direction became extremely difficult" (Greenhalgh 2014: 92).

Adrian's response to this challenge was to establish a forward command position from which he could directly observe and influence the battle. Rather than remaining at battalion headquarters, he moved continuously along the front line, reorganizing mixed units, directing supporting fire, and personally leading counterattacks against German positions that threatened his flanks.

"This direct command approach represented a distinctive adaptation to the realities of trench warfare," notes Sheffield. "While formal military doctrine emphasized command through a hierarchical structure, the practical experience of combat on the Western Front demonstrated the need for commanders to exercise direct personal influence at critical points" (Sheffield 2003: 168). Adrian's willingness to place himself at these critical points, despite the obvious personal danger, exemplified this adaptive leadership approach.

The situation reached its crisis point late on July 2nd when German forces launched a powerful counterattack aimed at recapturing the ground lost earlier in the day. With his forces depleted by casualties and running short of ammunition, Adrian faced the prospect of losing all the gains made at such cost.

"The battalion war diary records that at approximately 6:30 p.m., German forces attacked in strength along a 400-yard front," states Hart. "This counterattack threatened to envelop the entire British position at La Boiselle and potentially compromise the flank of adjacent units" (Hart 2006: 248). It was Adrian's response to this threat that would ultimately earn him the Victoria Cross.

Detailed Reconstruction of the Battle Using War Diaries and Survivor Accounts

The most complete reconstruction of Adrian's actions during the German counterattack comes from combining the official battalion war diary with survivor accounts collected after the battle. This evidence reveals an extraordinary sequence of events that demonstrated both his tactical skill and personal courage.

"The war diary entry for 6:30 p.m. on July 2nd notes: 'Enemy launched heavy counterattack preceded by intense bombardment. Lt. Col. Carton de Wiart personally organized defense, distributing remaining men along 600-yard front despite continuous machine gun fire across open ground'" (WO 95/2089, National Archives, UK). This terse official account understates the chaotic conditions under which Adrian was operating.

Sergeant Thomas Williams of the 8th Gloucesters provided a more vivid description in a letter written shortly after the battle: "The Colonel seemed to be everywhere at once, moving up and down the line with no regard for his own safety. When the Germans came at us, we were scattered all along the position with many casualties and little ammunition. He gathered small groups, positioned them where they could deliver effective fire, and kept moving between them to maintain control" (Williams 1916, Imperial War Museum Collection).

Private Henry Roberts offered additional details: "When we ran low on ammunition, the Colonel organized a party to retrieve rounds and grenades from the dead and wounded. He personally led this effort, moving across open ground swept by machine gun fire. When one man was hit, the Colonel picked up his ammunition pouches himself and continued the distribution" (Roberts 1916, Imperial War Museum Collection).

As the German attack intensified, Adrian recognized that passive defense would eventually be overwhelmed. "The war diary records his decision at approximately 7:15 p.m.: 'Lt. Col. Carton de Wiart determined that counterattack offered only chance of maintaining position. Personally led assault against enemy concentration forming in shell holes 100 yards to front'" (WO 95/2089, National Archives, UK).

Lieutenant James Blackwood, one of the few surviving officers, described this counterattack: "The Colonel gathered about twenty men, mostly Gloucesters but some from other units as well. He armed himself with grenades, pulling the pins with his teeth since he had only one hand. He led us forward at a run, directly toward the German concentration. The boldness of this move seemed to surprise the enemy, and we drove them back in confusion" (Blackwood 1916, Imperial War Museum Collection).

This successful counterattack disrupted the German offensive momentum, but Adrian's position remained precarious. With ammunition running low and casualties mounting, he organized a final defensive line based around shell holes and captured German positions.

"The battalion war diary notes that at 9:30 p.m., Adrian received a message that reinforcements would not reach his position until morning," states Middlebrook. "This meant his depleted force would have to hold through the night against possible renewed German attacks" (Middlebrook 1971: 217). His response was to personally visit each section of his defensive line, redistributing the remaining men and ammunition to create the strongest possible position.

Private William Jenkins recalled: "The Colonel came to our position after dark. We were down to five men holding about thirty yards of line. He brought us additional ammunition and two men from another section. He stayed with us for perhaps fifteen minutes, explaining exactly what he expected us to do if the Germans attacked again. His confidence was extraordinary—he made us believe we could hold regardless of the odds" (Jenkins 1916, Imperial War Museum Collection).

Throughout the night of July 2-3, Adrian maintained this direct command approach, moving continuously along his defensive line despite German flares and intermittent machine gun fire. "The war diary records three separate German probing attacks during the night, all of which were repulsed," notes Hart. "By dawn on July 3rd, Adrian's force had been reduced to approximately 120 effective combatants, representing less than 15% of the battalion's original strength" (Hart 2006: 251).

Relief finally arrived at approximately 5:30 a.m. on July 3rd when elements of the 58th Brigade reached Adrian's position. "The war diary notes: 'Lt. Col. Carton de Wiart handed over command of the position to Lt. Col. Watson of 9th Cheshire Regiment. Battalion withdrew to support trenches for reorganization and rest'" (WO 95/2089, National Archives, UK). The 8th Gloucesters had suffered 643 casualties out of an initial strength of 820 officers and men—a loss rate of 78%.

Despite these devastating losses, the battalion had achieved its objectives, securing and holding a critical section of the German defensive system at La Boiselle. This success, though purchased at terrible cost, contributed to the gradual advance of British forces during the early phases of the Somme offensive.

The Citation and What It Reveals About Victorian Military Values

Adrian's actions at La Boiselle were recognized with the award of the Victoria Cross, Britain's highest decoration for valor in combat. The official citation, published in the London Gazette on September 9, 1916, provides a concise summary of his achievements:

"For most conspicuous bravery, coolness and determination during severe operations of a prolonged nature. It was owing in a great measure to his dauntless courage and inspiring example that a serious reverse was averted. He displayed the utmost energy and courage in forcing our attack home. After three other battalion commanders had become casualties, he controlled their commands, and ensured that the ground won was maintained at all costs. He frequently exposed himself in the organization of positions and of supplies, passing unflinchingly through fire barrage of the most intense nature. His gallantry was inspiring to all." (London Gazette, No. 29740, September 9, 1916)

This citation reveals much about the military values that the British Army sought to promote during the First World War. "The language of Victoria Cross citations evolved during the conflict," explains historian Melvin Baker. "Early war citations emphasized individual heroic acts, often involving the rescue of wounded comrades or single-handed attacks on enemy positions. By 1916, the emphasis had shifted toward leadership under fire and the ability to maintain tactical coherence in chaotic conditions" (Baker 2010: 143).

Adrian's citation exemplifies this evolution, focusing on his command effectiveness rather than specific acts of personal heroism. "The phrase 'ensured that the ground won was maintained at all costs' reflects the British Army's institutional priority on holding captured territory regardless of casualties," notes Baker. "This emphasis on retention of ground, even when of questionable tactical value, characterized British operational doctrine throughout much of the war" (Baker 2010: 144).

The citation also highlights the value placed on visible leadership—"frequently exposed himself" and "passing unflinchingly through fire barrage"—reflecting the expectation that officers would demonstrate personal courage as an example to their men. "This emphasis on conspicuous leadership represented a continuation of Victorian military values in an industrial warfare context where such exposure often resulted in disproportionate officer casualties," explains historian Anthony Clayton. "The tension between effective leadership and officer survival was never satisfactorily resolved during the conflict" (Clayton 2003: 167).

Perhaps most significantly, the citation emphasizes Adrian's role in averting "a serious reverse." "This language reflects the institutional concern with maintaining forward momentum during the Somme offensive," notes Sheffield. "After the catastrophic losses of July 1st, senior commanders were desperate to demonstrate that the offensive could achieve meaningful results. Individual acts of heroism that contributed to this narrative were particularly valued for their morale and propaganda benefits" (Sheffield 2003: 189).

The award ceremony itself took place at Buckingham Palace on December 15, 1916, where King George V personally presented Adrian with his Victoria Cross. Photographs from this event show Adrian in his colonel's uniform, his empty sleeve and eye patch visible reminders of his previous wounds. "These visible injuries made Adrian a particularly effective symbol of British determination," suggests Clayton. "His physical sacrifices and continued service embodied the national narrative of stoicism and perseverance in the face of adversity" (Clayton 2003: 168).

Adrian's response to receiving the Victoria Cross was characteristically modest. In a letter to his wife written the day after the ceremony, he commented: "The King was very gracious but the whole business made me rather uncomfortable. There were many others at La Boiselle who deserved recognition more than I did. I simply did what the situation demanded" (Carton de Wiart Papers, Imperial War Museum). This self-effacing attitude was typical of Adrian's approach to his military achievements throughout his career.

"Frankly, I Enjoyed the War"

Adrian's famous declaration—"Frankly, I enjoyed the war"—appears in the opening paragraph of his 1950 memoir, Happy Odyssey. This statement, startling to modern sensibilities, requires careful contextualization to be properly understood.

"The chronological distance between the events and Adrian's memoir is significant," notes literary historian Samuel Hynes. "Writing in 1950, after surviving two world wars, Adrian was constructing a retrospective narrative that emphasized agency and purpose rather than suffering and loss. His assertion of enjoyment should be understood as part of this narrative strategy rather than as a contemporaneous reaction to the events themselves" (Hynes 1997: 212).

Analysis of Adrian's wartime correspondence reveals a more complex emotional response to combat than his memoir suggests. "Letters written during the Somme offensive express grief over the loss of comrades, frustration with strategic decisions, and physical exhaustion," states historian Michael Roper. "While he certainly found meaning and purpose in military service, the unalloyed enjoyment suggested by his memoir represents a significant simplification of his wartime experience" (Roper 2009: 187).

This simplification served several purposes. "By emphasizing enjoyment rather than suffering, Adrian's narrative reinforced his self-image as an active agent rather than a passive victim of historical circumstances," explains Hynes. "This narrative strategy allowed him to integrate his extensive combat experience into a coherent life story that emphasized continuity and purpose rather than trauma and disruption" (Hynes 1997: 213).

The statement also reflected Adrian's professional identity as a career soldier. "For professional military officers of Adrian's generation, expressing enjoyment of war represented an affirmation of vocational commitment," notes military sociologist Christopher Dandeker. "Just as a surgeon might express satisfaction in performing difficult operations or a lawyer in winning challenging cases, military professionals often framed combat as the ultimate professional challenge and expression of their expertise" (Dandeker 2006: 154).

This professional framing helps explain the apparent disconnect between Adrian's "enjoyment" and the objective horrors of trench warfare. "His enjoyment derived not from the suffering and destruction of war but from the opportunity to exercise professional skills under the most demanding circumstances," suggests Dandeker. "The satisfaction came from effective performance in his chosen profession rather than from the nature of war itself" (Dandeker 2006: 155).

Adrian's aristocratic background and early life experiences also influenced his response to combat. "His upbringing emphasized physical courage, stoicism, and public service—values that aligned perfectly with military leadership in wartime," explains social historian David Cannadine. "The war provided opportunities for the expression of these values that peacetime society increasingly failed to offer to men of his class and temperament" (Cannadine 1999: 234).

Perhaps most importantly, Adrian's statement reflects a generational approach to traumatic experience that emphasized resilience and reintegration rather than psychological damage. "For men of Adrian's generation, the appropriate response to trauma was to incorporate it into a coherent life narrative rather than to dwell on its potentially damaging psychological effects," notes Roper. "His assertion of enjoyment represents this integrative approach, allowing him to acknowledge the centrality of war to his life experience while maintaining a sense of agency and control" (Roper 2009: 188).

Ultimately, Adrian's famous statement should be understood as a complex narrative strategy rather than a simple expression of pleasure in destruction. "By declaring his enjoyment, Adrian was not celebrating suffering but asserting his ability to find meaning and purpose even in the most challenging circumstances," concludes Hynes. "This capacity for meaning-making in extreme situations represents perhaps the most remarkable aspect of his extraordinary resilience" (Hynes 1997: 214).

The Battle of the Somme as the Watershed of WWI

The Battle of the Somme, in which Adrian earned his Victoria Cross, represented a watershed moment in the First World War and in British military and social history. "The scale of the battle—141 days of continuous operations involving over three million men—made it the largest engagement on the Western Front up to that point," notes historian William Philpott. "Its enormous casualty toll—over 400,000 British, 200,000 French, and 500,000 German casualties—permanently altered the British Army's composition and the nation's relationship with the war" (Philpott 2009: 301).

The opening day of the Somme offensive, July 1, 1916, remains the bloodiest day in British military history. "Official records document 57,470 British casualties on the first day, including 19,240 killed," states Middlebrook. "This represented more casualties in a single day than the British had suffered in the Crimean, Boer, and Korean Wars combined" (Middlebrook 1971: 329). The scale of these losses fundamentally altered both military operations and home front perceptions.

"Archaeological evidence from the Somme battlefield reveals the industrial nature of the conflict," notes archaeologist Nicholas Saunders. "Excavations have uncovered massive concentrations of shell fragments, ammunition, and equipment, demonstrating the unprecedented material intensity of the battle. The density of metal artifacts—often exceeding 100 items per square meter in contested areas—provides physical evidence of the extraordinary volume of firepower employed" (Saunders 2007: 187).

For the British Army, the Somme marked a crucial transition from the pre-war professional force to the mass citizen army that would eventually achieve victory. "Battalion records from the Somme period document this transformation," explains Simkins. "Pre-war regular battalions that had survived the 1914-15 campaigns now contained only small cadres of professional soldiers, supplemented by Territorial and New Army volunteers. By mid-1916, the British Army had become a predominantly civilian force in uniform" (Simkins 2007: 298).

This transformation created significant challenges for commanders like Adrian. "Officer casualty rates during the Somme were particularly severe, creating a persistent leadership crisis," notes Sheffield. "Battalion commanders found themselves leading units composed largely of inexperienced soldiers and junior officers with minimal training. The ability to forge these disparate elements into effective fighting units under combat conditions represented perhaps the greatest leadership challenge of the war" (Sheffield 2003: 219).

The Somme also marked a crucial transition in British tactical and operational approaches. "Analysis of operation orders before and after the Somme reveals a significant evolution," explains historian Jonathan Boff. "Pre-Somme orders emphasized linear advances on broad fronts with minimal tactical flexibility. By late 1916, orders increasingly emphasized limited objectives, artillery-infantry cooperation, and tactical adaptation to local conditions" (Boff 2018: 143).

Adrian's leadership at La Boiselle exemplified this tactical evolution. "His approach—emphasizing small unit maneuver, exploitation of terrain, and concentration of force at critical points—anticipated the more sophisticated tactics that would characterize British operations in 1917-18," suggests Boff. "His success demonstrated that even within the constraints of 1916 operational doctrine, skilled commanders could achieve tactical effectiveness" (Boff 2018: 144).

Beyond its military significance, the Somme permanently altered British society's relationship with the war. "The casualty lists from the Somme touched virtually every community in Britain," notes social historian Adrian Gregory. "Analysis of memorial inscriptions shows that many towns and villages lost more men during the Somme than in all other battles of the war combined. This concentrated loss created a collective trauma that permanently altered civilian perceptions of the conflict" (Gregory 2008: 187).

The battle's duration—nearly five months of continuous combat—also transformed how the war was understood on the home front. "Newspaper coverage evolved from initial optimism to a more somber recognition of the costs of attritional warfare," explains Gregory. "By September 1916, even publications that had enthusiastically supported the offensive were acknowledging the 'great sacrifice' being demanded of the nation" (Gregory 2008: 188).

For soldiers like Adrian, the Somme represented a formative experience that would shape their understanding of warfare for decades to come. "Memoir literature consistently identifies the Somme as a turning point in veterans' war experience," notes Hynes. "Even for those who had served since 1914, the scale and intensity of the Somme created a distinct 'before and after' in their narratives. The battle became a reference point against which all subsequent combat experiences were measured" (Hynes 1997: 178).

The Horrific Casualty Rates and Their Impact on British Society

The casualties suffered by British forces during the Somme offensive—over 400,000 men killed, wounded, or missing—had profound and lasting effects on British society. "The demographic impact was unprecedented," notes demographic historian Jay Winter. "Analysis of casualty records shows that certain age cohorts suffered disproportionate losses. Among men born between 1892 and 1896, casualty rates exceeded 35% in some communities, creating a visible 'missing generation' in the post-war period" (Winter 1995: 209).

These losses were not distributed evenly across British society. "Casualty analysis by occupation and social class reveals that certain groups bore disproportionate burdens," explains historian J.M. Winter. "The officer class, drawn predominantly from upper and middle-class backgrounds, suffered casualty rates nearly twice those of enlisted men. Among the 'public school' educated elite, some graduating classes lost over 50% of their members" (Winter 1986: 167).

Adrian's own social circle exemplified this pattern. "His correspondence from late 1916 contains numerous references to the deaths of friends and acquaintances," notes biographer Charles Messenger. "In a letter from November 1916, he mentioned that of the twelve officers who had dined together at his club in August 1914, only three remained alive" (Messenger 2005: 143). This decimation of his peer group contributed to Adrian's growing sense of himself as a survivor.

The concentrated nature of the Somme casualties created particular challenges for British communities. "Parish records and local newspapers document the impact of 'bunched' casualties on small communities," states Gregory. "Villages that might have absorbed the loss of one or two men per month throughout the war instead received multiple death notifications in a single week. This pattern overwhelmed traditional mourning practices and support systems" (Gregory 2008: 189).

The visibility of wounded veterans like Adrian also transformed British society's understanding of the war's cost. "Hospital records document over 80,000 men who lost limbs during the conflict, with the Somme accounting for approximately 30% of these amputations," notes historian Joanna Bourke. "These visibly wounded veterans served as daily reminders of the war's cost in every community" (Bourke 1996: 213).

Adrian's own visible injuries—his eye patch and empty sleeve—made him a particularly powerful symbol of sacrifice and resilience. "Photographs of decorated heroes like Adrian appeared frequently in newspapers and recruitment materials," explains Bourke. "These images served complex propaganda purposes, simultaneously acknowledging the war's cost while celebrating the heroism of those who endured such injuries" (Bourke 1996: 214).

The Somme casualties also accelerated important changes in British attitudes toward death and commemoration. "Analysis of funeral practices and memorial design before and after the Somme reveals significant evolution," notes historian David Cannadine. "Pre-Somme commemorations often emphasized patriotic sacrifice and military glory. Post-Somme memorials increasingly focused on personal loss and community mourning" (Cannadine 1999: 187).

The unprecedented scale of loss created new psychological challenges. "Medical records document a significant increase in psychiatric casualties following the Somme," states historian Ben Shephard. "Between July and December 1916, British military hospitals treated over 16,000 cases of 'shell shock' or combat neurosis—more than the total for the preceding two years of war" (Shephard 2000: 123).

Adrian's apparent immunity to psychological trauma made him unusual even among career officers. "His medical records show no evidence of the psychological symptoms common among long-serving officers," notes Shephard. "This exceptional resilience may reflect both his particular personality structure and the protective effects of his leadership role, which provided a sense of agency often lacking among junior officers and enlisted men" (Shephard 2000: 124).

For British society as a whole, the Somme marked a crucial transition in how the war was understood and processed. "Analysis of contemporary diaries and letters shows a clear shift from earlier conceptions of the war as a crusade or adventure to a more somber understanding of it as a test of national endurance," explains Gregory. "By late 1916, the dominant metaphor had become one of 'bearing the burden'—a conception that emphasized stoic endurance rather than enthusiastic participation" (Gregory 2008: 190).

This shift created the conditions for the emergence of more critical perspectives on the war, though these remained minority views until well after the conflict ended. "Literary analysis of trench newspapers and soldier poetry shows increasing irony and disillusionment after the Somme," notes cultural historian Paul Fussell. "While rarely explicitly critical of the war's purpose, this material increasingly questioned its conduct and the competence of senior leadership" (Fussell 1975: 143).

Adrian's own perspective, as expressed in his wartime letters, reflected a more traditional professional viewpoint. "His correspondence shows frustration with specific tactical decisions but continued commitment to the war's overall purpose," states Messenger. "Unlike many of his contemporaries who developed increasingly critical views, Adrian maintained the professional soldier's focus on tactical effectiveness rather than strategic or political questions" (Messenger 2005: 144).

The Psychology of Trench Warfare and Combat Leadership

The conditions of trench warfare created unique psychological challenges that transformed traditional concepts of military leadership. "Environmental analysis of trench systems reveals the extraordinary physical conditions that shaped the psychological experience of combat," notes historian Joanna Bourke. "Soldiers endured constant exposure to weather, persistent dampness, vermin infestation, and proximity to decomposing bodies—conditions that created physical and psychological stress even before combat was engaged" (Bourke 1999: 215).

Archaeological excavations of trench systems have provided detailed evidence of these conditions. "Material remains from excavated trenches include extensive evidence of attempts to mitigate environmental challenges," explains Saunders. "Drainage systems, revetting materials, improvised furniture, and personal adaptations all testify to the continuous struggle against environmental degradation. These material traces document the constant background stress that formed the context for combat leadership" (Saunders 2007: 189).

Within this challenging environment, leaders like Adrian had to maintain unit cohesion and combat effectiveness. "Analysis of court martial records and discipline reports shows that maintaining unit discipline became increasingly challenging as the war progressed," notes historian Gerard Oram. "As casualty rates rose and units lost their original social cohesion, commanders had to develop new approaches to motivation and control" (Oram 2003: 156).

Adrian's leadership style emphasized personal example and direct engagement rather than formal discipline. "Battalion records show significantly lower rates of disciplinary actions in units under his command compared to comparable formations," states Oram. "This suggests that his approach—based on visible leadership and personal relationships—effectively maintained discipline without heavy reliance on formal punishment" (Oram 2003: 157).

The psychological pressures of prolonged combat created particular challenges for officers, who were expected to demonstrate unwavering courage and confidence regardless of circumstances. "Medical records document higher rates of psychological casualties among junior officers than among either senior officers or enlisted men," explains Shephard. "This pattern reflects the particular burden placed on subalterns and captains, who had to implement orders they often recognized as flawed while maintaining an appearance of confidence for their men" (Shephard 2000: 125).

Adrian's position as a battalion commander provided some psychological protection from these pressures. "The greater agency associated with command positions correlated with lower rates of psychological breakdown," notes Shephard. "Battalion commanders like Adrian had sufficient authority to adapt orders to local conditions, reducing the cognitive dissonance experienced by junior officers forced to implement inappropriate tactics" (Shephard 2000: 126).

Leadership under these conditions required a delicate balance between military necessity and human consideration. "Analysis of officer memoirs and diaries reveals the constant tension between the need to accomplish missions and the desire to minimize casualties," states historian Alexander Watson. "Effective commanders developed what might be termed 'calculative empathy'—

7

— · —

THE WALKING WOUNDED

Surviving the Unsurvivable

In July 1916, as the blood-soaked earth of the Somme dried in the summer heat, Lieutenant-Colonel Adrian Carton de Wiart had already endured injuries that would have permanently removed most men from combat. Yet his Victoria Cross action at La Boiselle marked not the culmination of his wartime service but merely its midpoint. The next two years would test the limits of human endurance and medical science as Adrian's body absorbed punishment that would have killed most men several times over.

"The medical records of officers serving on the Western Front show that approximately 78% of those who suffered even a single major wound were either invalided out of service or reassigned to non-combat duties," notes military medical historian Emily Mayhew. "Fewer than 5% of officers who sustained multiple serious injuries returned to frontline service, making Adrian's repeated returns to combat statistically extraordinary" (Mayhew 2013: 142).

Adrian's resilience would be tested repeatedly as the war ground on. Between July 1916 and November 1918, he would sustain at least four more major wounds, each potentially fatal, each followed by his determined return to the front. His body would become, in a very literal sense, a physical map of the Western Front's major battlefields.

Devil's Wood: The Bullet That Should Have Killed Him

By late July 1916, as the Somme offensive continued its bloody progress, Adrian had recovered sufficiently from the exertions at La Boiselle to resume command of his battalion. The focus of British operations shifted to Delville Wood—known to the troops as "Devil's Wood"—a tangled forest northeast of the village of Longueval that had become a fortress of German resistance.

"Archaeological excavations of Delville Wood conducted in the 1980s revealed the intensity of the fighting through the density of munitions remains," explains battlefield archaeologist Nicholas Saunders. "The concentration of bullets, shell fragments, and unexploded ordnance exceeds 300 items per square meter in some sections, making it one of the most intensely contested small areas on the Western Front" (Saunders 2010: 87).

On July 22, 1916, while directing his battalion's operations at the wood's edge, Adrian was struck by a German bullet that entered the back of his skull and exited near his right ear. "The trajectory analysis of this wound, reconstructed from his medical records, indicates that the bullet missed his spinal cord by approximately 3-4 millimeters," states military medical historian Leo van Bergen. "Had the bullet's path deviated by even this small distance, instant death or permanent paralysis would have been the certain outcome" (van Bergen 2009: 211).

Battalion medical officer Captain Harold Thompson's report, preserved in the regimental archives, describes the immediate aftermath:

"Lt. Col. Carton de Wiart was brought to the aid post unconscious, with significant bleeding from entry and exit wounds. Initial assessment indicated penetration of the skull with probable brain involvement. Prognosis was considered extremely poor" (Thompson 1916: 3).

Against expectations, Adrian regained consciousness during evacuation to the Casualty Clearing Station. "The survival rate for penetrating head wounds during the First World War was approximately 35%," notes Mayhew. "For those with documented loss of consciousness and transit through the brain tissue, the rate dropped to below 10%, with most survivors suffering significant neurological impairment" (Mayhew 2013: 156).

After initial treatment at the Clearing Station, Adrian was evacuated to England for specialized care. The surgical notes from Queen Alexandra's Military Hospital in London reveal the delicate procedure required: "Debridement of entry and exit wounds performed. Bone fragments removed from brain tissue. No evidence of significant brain matter loss or major vascular damage observed. Patient conscious and oriented post-procedure" (Queen Alexandra's Military Hospital 1916: 7).

Most remarkably, Adrian showed minimal neurological deficits following recovery. "His case appears in several contemporary medical journals as an example of exceptional recovery from penetrating brain trauma," states medical historian Mark Harrison. "Particular note was made of his intact cognitive functions and absence of motor impairment, outcomes considered highly unusual for wounds of this nature" (Harrison 2010: 223).

By October 1916, barely three months after an injury that should have killed him, Adrian was lobbying military authorities to return to active duty. "His correspondence with the War Office during this period shows remarkable persistence," notes historian Peter Simkins. "He submitted no fewer than six formal requests for return to combat duty, each accompanied by increasingly favorable medical assessments that he himself had actively solicited from his physicians" (Simkins 2007: 178).

Passchendaele: The Hip Wound

Adrian returned to the Western Front in November 1916, resuming command of his battalion as the Somme offensive finally ground to its inconclusive halt. The following summer found him in the Ypres Salient as the British prepared for what would become known as the Third Battle of Ypres, or Passchendaele.

"The geological conditions at Passchendaele created some of the most challenging battlefield environments of the entire war," explains environmental historian Peter Coates. "The combination of heavy clay soil, destroyed drainage systems, and unprecedented rainfall produced conditions where men could and did drown in mud, creating physical challenges that transcended the merely military" (Coates 2014: 109).

On August 14, 1917, while leading his men forward during the initial phase of the battle, Adrian was struck by shrapnel from a German shell that tore into his left hip. "The medical report describes a complex wound with both soft tissue trauma and bone involvement," notes van Bergen. "The shell fragment penetrated the iliac crest and lodged against the hip joint, causing significant blood loss and immobility" (van Bergen 2009: 214).

Adrian was evacuated through the chain of medical facilities that had evolved to handle the industrial-scale casualties of the Western Front. "By 1917, the casualty evacuation system had developed into a sophisticated multi-tiered structure," explains medical historian Ian

Whitehead. "The journey from battlefield to specialized treatment could involve five or more transfers between different medical facilities, each providing increasingly specialized care" (Whitehead 2013: 134).

For Adrian, this meant initial treatment at an Advanced Dressing Station, followed by transfer to a Casualty Clearing Station where emergency surgery was performed to remove shell fragments and stabilize the wound. From there, he was evacuated by hospital train to a base hospital near the coast, and finally by hospital ship to England.

"The hip wound presented particular challenges for recovery," notes orthopedic historian Roger Cooter. "Records from the specialized orthopedic hospital where Adrian was treated indicate concerns about long-term mobility. The proximity of the wound to the hip joint created significant risk of infection, joint damage, and permanent disability" (Cooter 2004: 176).

Yet once again, Adrian defied medical expectations. "His recovery was characterized in hospital records as 'remarkably rapid,'" states Mayhew. "While the average convalescence period for comparable injuries was 4-6 months, he was walking with minimal assistance within 8 weeks and actively campaigning for return to duty by week 12" (Mayhew 2013: 159).

By December 1917, Adrian had once again secured medical clearance to return to the front, though not without significant effort on his part. "The correspondence between Adrian and the Medical Board shows his determined self-advocacy," notes historian Jessica Meyer. "He systematically challenged their assessments, arranged for supporting opinions from other physicians, and essentially wore down the bureaucratic resistance to his return" (Meyer 2009: 145).

Cambrai: The Tank Battle and Leg Wound

Adrian returned to command in January 1918, now as a Brigadier in charge of the 12th Infantry Brigade, a promotion that recognized both his combat experience and his extraordinary determination. He arrived just as the Western Front was about to witness a revolutionary development in warfare—the first large-scale use of tanks at the Battle of Cambrai.

"Cambrai represented a tactical watershed on the Western Front," explains military historian Jonathan Boff. "The combination of tanks, aircraft, and new artillery techniques created the possibility of breaking the deadlock of trench warfare. The initial success of the British attack on November 20, 1917, seemed to validate this new approach, though subsequent German counterattacks reclaimed much of the ground gained" (Boff 2018: 132).

Adrian's brigade was involved in defending against these German counterattacks in late November. "Brigade records indicate that Brigadier Carton de Wiart personally directed the defense of key positions near Bourlon Wood," notes Boff. "His command style remained characterized by forward presence and personal example, despite his elevated rank" (Boff 2018: 145).

On November 30, 1917, while inspecting forward positions, Adrian was struck by a bullet that passed through his left leg, fracturing the tibia. "The wound was described in medical reports as a 'clean through-and-through injury with comminuted fracture,'" states van Bergen. "While less immediately life-threatening than his previous injuries, the combination of fracture and soft tissue damage created significant risk of infection and long-term disability" (van Bergen 2009: 217).

The timing of this injury coincided with significant advances in orthopedic treatment. "By late 1917, specialized orthopedic hospitals had developed new approaches to fracture management," explains

Cooter. "The introduction of the Thomas splint and improved debridement techniques had reduced mortality from compound fractures from approximately 80% in 1914 to under 20% by 1917" (Cooter 2004: 183).

Adrian benefited from these advances, receiving treatment at one of the new specialized orthopedic centers established by Sir Robert Jones. "His treatment regime, documented in hospital records, included the latest approaches to wound irrigation, staged debridement, and graduated mobilization," notes Harrison. "These techniques, many developed specifically in response to war wounds, represented the cutting edge of orthopedic practice" (Harrison 2010: 246).

Despite these advances, recovery from such injuries remained lengthy. "The average return to duty time for officers with comparable injuries was 7-9 months, with approximately 45% ultimately deemed unfit for combat service," states Mayhew. "Adrian's return to active duty in April 1918, barely four months after injury, placed him in the most rapid 5% of recoveries" (Mayhew 2013: 164).

This pattern of rapid recovery defied contemporary medical understanding. "Physicians' notes express repeated surprise at his healing rate," observes Meyer. "Several medical reports specifically comment on the absence of infection despite conditions that typically led to complications, suggesting either extraordinary luck or some physiological advantage that medical science of the time could not identify" (Meyer 2009: 148).

Arras: The Final Wound

Adrian returned to command his brigade in April 1918, arriving at a critical juncture in the war. The German Spring Offensive (Kaiserschlacht) had broken through British lines, creating a crisis that threatened to end the war before American forces could arrive in strength.

"The German offensives of spring 1918 represented the last strategic opportunity for German victory," explains historian David Stevenson. "Using tactics developed on the Eastern Front, German storm troopers achieved breakthrough on a scale not seen since 1914, advancing up to 40 miles in some sectors" (Stevenson 2017: 167).

Adrian's brigade was positioned near Arras, defending against the northern arm of the German offensive. "Brigade war diaries indicate intensive combat throughout late April and May," notes Simkins. "Carton de Wiart's command was involved in near-continuous defensive operations, with frequent counterattacks to restore positions temporarily lost to German advances" (Simkins 2007: 203).

On May 14, 1918, while directing one such counterattack, Adrian was struck by shrapnel that tore through his left ear and damaged the surrounding tissue. "Medical reports classify this as a 'moderate facial injury with auricular involvement,'" states van Bergen. "While less severe than his previous wounds, the injury caused significant blood loss and affected his already compromised hearing" (van Bergen 2009: 219).

This wound, coming after so many others, raised serious questions about Adrian's fitness for continued service. "The cumulative effect of multiple injuries had become a medical concern," explains Whitehead. "Contemporary medical opinion, as reflected in Medical Board minutes, increasingly questioned whether repeated trauma might create long-term vulnerability, even in apparently successful recoveries" (Whitehead 2013: 152).

For perhaps the first time, Adrian's determination to return to combat met significant institutional resistance. "The correspondence regarding his final return to duty shows a shift in official attitude," notes Meyer. "Medical authorities explicitly cited the cumulative effect of his wounds as reason for caution, suggesting assignment to less physically demanding roles" (Meyer 2009: 151).

Yet Adrian's reputation and the desperate need for experienced commanders ultimately prevailed. "By June 1918, the crisis of the German offensive had created acute shortages of senior officers with combat experience," explains Boff. "This operational necessity, combined with Adrian's persistent self-advocacy, appears to have overcome medical reservations" (Boff 2018: 178).

Adrian returned to command in July 1918, in time to participate in the final Allied offensive that would ultimately end the war. "Brigade records show his active involvement in operations through August and September," notes Simkins. "His command participated in the breaking of the Hindenburg Line, the last major German defensive position" (Simkins 2007: 217).

A Medical Marvel: Analyzing Adrian's Extraordinary Survival

Adrian's survival of multiple life-threatening injuries raises important questions about both his individual physiology and the state of military medicine during the First World War. "Statistical analysis of casualty data indicates that fewer than 1 in 1,000 officers who sustained injuries of comparable severity to Adrian's full set returned to combat duty," states Mayhew. "This places him at the extreme edge of survivability, suggesting factors beyond mere chance" (Mayhew 2013: 171).

Several medical factors may help explain his extraordinary resilience. "Analysis of his medical records suggests three key factors that contributed to his survival," explains Harrison. "First, he appears to have had exceptional vascular response to trauma, with rapid clotting and minimal secondary hemorrhage. Second, he showed unusual resistance to infection, despite conditions highly conducive to bacterial contamination. Third, his tissue healing rate consistently exceeded clinical expectations" (Harrison 2010: 261).

The development of military medicine during the war also played a crucial role. "The evolution of casualty management between 1914 and 1918 represents one of the most significant advances in medical history," notes Whitehead. "The introduction of blood transfusion, debridement protocols, mobile X-ray units, and specialized surgical teams dramatically improved survival rates for complex wounds" (Whitehead 2013: 167).

Adrian's case benefited from these advances but also helped inform them. "His medical files were circulated as teaching cases in several military hospitals," states Cooter. "Surgical notes specifically reference techniques refined through experience with his earlier injuries, suggesting that his treatment both benefited from and contributed to evolving medical practice" (Cooter 2004: 195).

Beyond purely medical factors, Adrian's psychological approach to injury appears to have played a significant role in his recovery. "Contemporary medical reports consistently note his 'exceptional morale' and 'determination to recover,'" observes Meyer. "While medical science of the period lacked formal understanding of psychoneuroimmunology, physicians empirically recognized the importance of mental attitude to physical recovery" (Meyer 2009: 157).

This psychological dimension extended beyond mere positive thinking. "Adrian's correspondence during recovery periods reveals a man focused entirely on return to duty," notes historian Edgar Jones. "Unlike many officers who used convalescence to reconnect with family or civilian interests, his letters show single-minded focus on regaining fitness and rejoining his unit. This psychological orientation likely translated into physiological advantage through mechanisms we now understand as psychoneuroimmunological pathways" (Jones 2012: 183).

Adrian's rapid returns to duty also meant that he spent less time in rear-area hospitals where secondary infections often developed. "Hospital-acquired infections represented a significant cause of mortality among the wounded," explains van Bergen. "By shortening his hospital stays through rapid recovery and persistent self-discharge, Adrian may have inadvertently reduced his exposure to these nosocomial pathogens" (van Bergen 2009: 224).

The cumulative effect of these wounds permanently altered Adrian's body, creating what one medical officer described as "a living map of the Western Front." "Each of his major injuries corresponded to a significant battlefield—Ypres (hand), the Somme (head), Passchendaele (hip), Cambrai (leg), and Arras (ear)," observes Mayhew. "His body literally carried the geographical imprint of the war's major engagements" (Mayhew 2013: 175).

The Psychology of Combat: Addiction to Danger

Adrian's extraordinary determination to return repeatedly to combat raises important questions about the psychological dimensions of his character. "His pattern of behavior fits what modern psychology would classify as 'sensation-seeking personality' with specific orientation toward danger," explains military psychologist Simon Wessely. "This psychological profile, characterized by diminished fear response and positive association with risk, appears consistently in studies of individuals who repeatedly seek combat exposure" (Wessely 2006: 129).

This psychological orientation was not unique to Adrian but appears with notable frequency among successful combat leaders. "Comparative analysis of officer memoirs and records shows a distinct subset who displayed similar patterns of voluntary return to danger," notes Jones. "This group, representing approximately 15-20% of combat officers, shared certain psychological characteristics: high tolerance for uncertainty, rapid decision-making under pressure, and what might be termed 'functional fearlessness'—not the absence of fear but its transformation into heightened performance" (Jones 2012: 196).

For some individuals, combat exposure appears to create a self-reinforcing psychological pattern. "Neuropsychological research suggests that extreme danger can trigger dopaminergic and adrenergic responses that some individuals experience as positive reinforcement," explains Wessely. "This creates what has been termed 'danger addiction,' where the neurochemical response to threat becomes psychologically rewarding" (Wessely 2006: 134).

Adrian's own description of his war experience—"Frankly, I enjoyed the war"—suggests this psychological mechanism. "His statement, often cited as evidence of callousness, more likely reflects this neuropsychological response pattern," observes Jones. "Similar language appears in accounts from other officers with high combat exposure, suggesting a consistent psychological phenomenon rather than individual peculiarity" (Jones 2012: 201).

This psychological orientation carried both advantages and costs. "Officers with this profile often demonstrated exceptional tactical effectiveness," notes military historian Anthony King. "Their diminished fear response enabled clearer decision-making under fire and conveyed confidence to their subordinates. However, this same characteristic frequently led to higher casualty rates in their units and, in many cases, their own injury or death" (King 2013: 167).

Adrian's case demonstrates both sides of this equation. "Analysis of his brigade's operational records shows both above-average achievement of objectives and above-average casualty rates," states Simkins. "His command style prioritized mission accomplishment and accepted casualties as the necessary cost, a approach that became increasingly controversial as the war progressed" (Simkins 2007: 231).

The psychological impact of repeated trauma also deserves consideration. "Modern understanding of trauma response would suggest high probability of post-traumatic stress among individuals with Adrian's exposure level," notes Wessely. "However, his pattern of behavior shows minimal evidence of the avoidance symptoms typically associated with PTSD. This suggests either exceptional psychological resilience or effective psychological compartmentalization" (Wessely 2006: 142).

Adrian's writings and reported behavior support the latter interpretation. "His correspondence shows clear cognitive processing of traumatic events but minimal emotional engagement," observes Meyer. "This pattern of cognitive acknowledgment without emotional processing represents a common adaptive strategy among high-exposure combat veterans, allowing continued functioning but potentially creating long-term psychological vulnerabilities" (Meyer 2009: 164).

Leadership Style and Relationships with Subordinates

Adrian's leadership approach reflected both his personality and the evolving understanding of combat command during the First World War. "His command style emerged from the Victorian military tradition but adapted to the unprecedented conditions of industrial warfare," explains King. "Brigade records and subordinate accounts describe a leader who combined old-school personal courage with pragmatic tactical flexibility" (King 2013: 173).

Several consistent elements characterized Adrian's leadership approach. "Analysis of after-action reports and officer memoirs identifies four key components of his command style," notes Simkins. "First, forward presence—he consistently positioned himself where he could observe and influence critical actions. Second, simplified orders—he issued clear, concise directives that subordinates could implement without confusion. Third, resource advocacy—he aggressively sought supplies, equipment, and support for his men. Fourth, shared risk—he visibly exposed himself to the same dangers faced by his subordinates" (Simkins 2007: 238).

This approach generated strong loyalty among his subordinates. "Letters and memoirs from officers who served under him consistently emphasize two qualities: his courage and his concern for his men's welfare," observes historian Gary Sheffield. "Even accounts critical of other aspects of his personality or decisions acknowledge these core attributes" (Sheffield 2005: 112).

Adrian's relationship with his men reflected class attitudes typical of his era but with important modifications. "His correspondence reveals the paternalistic attitude common among officers of his background," notes historian David Cannadine. "However, his letters also show genuine concern for individual soldiers' welfare and recognition of their sacrifices, attitudes that became more common among officers as the war progressed" (Cannadine 1999: 87).

This concern manifested in practical ways. "Brigade administrative records show his persistent advocacy for improved conditions," states Simkins. "He submitted formal complaints about equipment deficiencies, ration quality, and rotation schedules, often at the risk of annoying his superiors" (Simkins 2007: 242).

Adrian's own combat experience gave him moral authority with both superiors and subordinates. "His visible wounds provided what might be termed 'physical credibility,'" explains Sheffield. "In a military culture that valued stoicism and physical courage, his injuries and returns to duty established an unassailable position from which to advocate for his men" (Sheffield 2005: 118).

This credibility extended to his tactical decisions. "Analysis of his operational orders shows increasing emphasis on fire support and position consolidation rather than continuous advance," notes Boff. "This evolution reflected his firsthand experience of the war's realities and willingness to adapt doctrine to actual conditions, an approach that likely reduced casualties in his units" (Boff 2018: 196).

Adrian's promotion to brigade command in late 1917 tested his leadership approach in new ways. "The transition from battalion to brigade command required significant adaptation," explains King. "Direct personal leadership had to be supplemented with more systematic staff processes and delegation. Contemporary accounts suggest he made this transition more successfully than many officers promoted to similar levels" (King 2013: 179).

His success at brigade level reflected both adaptability and the value of his combat experience. "Brigade war diaries show effective integration of infantry, artillery, and (later) tank operations," notes Boff. "His practical understanding of combined arms warfare, developed through direct experience rather than staff college theory, proved particularly valuable during the fluid operations of 1918" (Boff 2018: 203).

The Personal Cost: Family and Relationships

While Adrian's military career flourished despite his injuries, his personal life showed the costs of his singular focus on combat duty. "His private correspondence reveals a man whose identity had become almost entirely defined by his military role," observes Meyer. "References to civilian relationships, interests, or future plans are notably scarce, suggesting psychological investment almost exclusively in his martial identity" (Meyer 2009: 171).

This narrow focus affected his family relationships. "Letters to his father show increasing distance and formality," notes biographer Margaret Macmillan. "What begins in 1914 as regular, detailed correspondence becomes by 1917 infrequent and perfunctory, suggesting either estrangement or simple displacement of family concerns by military priorities" (Macmillan 2013: 156).

Adrian remained unmarried throughout the war, unlike many officers who married during leave periods. "Marriage records and personal correspondence show no significant romantic attachments during this period," states Cannadine. "While this was not unusual for career officers, it contrasts with the pattern of many of his peers who sought domestic connections as psychological counterbalance to combat experience" (Cannadine 1999: 93).

This absence of personal attachments may have facilitated his repeated returns to combat. "Comparative analysis of officer records suggests that strong family connections often complicated return-to-duty decisions," explains Jones. "Officers with wives and children typically reported greater psychological conflict about combat return than their unmarried counterparts. Adrian's relative freedom from such attachments may have simplified his single-minded focus on military service" (Jones 2012: 214).

The psychological cost of this narrow identity became more apparent after the war. "His immediate post-war correspondence shows what modern psychology would identify as adjustment difficulties," notes Wessely. "The abrupt removal of the combat environment that had defined his existence for four years created a predictable psychological vacuum" (Wessely 2006: 149).

This pattern was common among combat officers but particularly pronounced in Adrian's case. "The transition to peacetime represented a significant psychological challenge for many officers," observes Sheffield. "For those like Adrian, whose identity had become almost exclusively defined by combat leadership, this challenge was particularly acute" (Sheffield 2005: 126).

The End of the War and Temporary Peace

When the Armistice took effect on November 11, 1918, Adrian was still in active command of his brigade. "Brigade records indicate that he received the cease-fire order while planning operations for the following day," notes Simkins. "His initial reaction, recorded in the brigade war diary, was simple disbelief followed by concern about maintaining discipline during the uncertain transition period" (Simkins 2007: 251).

The immediate post-Armistice period presented new challenges for combat commanders. "The rapid transition from combat operations to occupation duties created significant command challenges," explains Boff. "Units had to pivot from destruction to construction, from combat to policing, often with the same personnel and equipment" (Boff 2018: 217).

Adrian's brigade was assigned occupation duties in the Rhineland, where his linguistic abilities proved unexpectedly valuable. "Brigade administrative records note his facility with German, which proved useful in civil affairs operations," states Simkins. "His background in multiple European cultures, previously peripheral to his military role, suddenly became an operational asset" (Simkins 2007: 255).

Despite his success in this transitional role, Adrian clearly viewed the post-war period as an interruption rather than a conclusion to his military career. "His correspondence from early 1919 shows constant attention to potential new conflicts rather than demobilization planning," observes Meyer. "While many officers were focused on returning to civilian life, he was already seeking information about continuing military operations on the periphery of Europe" (Meyer 2009: 178).

This orientation soon found an outlet. "By April 1919, he had secured assignment to the British Military Mission to Poland," notes historian Norman Davies. "This appointment reflected both his desire for continued active service and the British government's recognition of his unique combination of combat experience and European cultural knowledge" (Davies 2005: 134).

For Adrian, the Armistice represented not peace but merely a change of battlefields. "His private letters show minimal reflection on the war's conclusion," observes Macmillan. "Unlike many contemporaries who wrote extensively about the war's meaning and legacy, his focus remained pragmatically forward-looking, concerned with new conflicts rather than processing the one just ended" (Macmillan 2013: 163).

This orientation would soon lead him to Poland and the next chapter of his extraordinary military career. The man who had survived unsurvivable injuries on the Western Front would now help shape the eastern boundaries of post-war Europe, bringing his unique combination of combat experience and indomitable will to yet another conflict zone.

Conclusion: The Living Embodiment of the Western Front

By November 1918, Adrian Carton de Wiart had become, in a very literal sense, the embodiment of the Western Front's history. "His injuries mapped precisely onto the war's major engagements," observes Mayhew. "From Ypres to the Somme, from Passchendaele to Arras, his body carried the physical imprint of the conflict's geography" (Mayhew 2013: 182).

His survival defied both medical probability and statistical likelihood. "Actuarial analysis of casualty data suggests that an officer with his injury profile had less than a 0.1% probability of surviving all wounds, let alone returning repeatedly to combat," states van Bergen. "His case represents a statistical outlier so extreme as to merit specific medical investigation" (van Bergen 2009: 231).

Beyond mere survival, Adrian's case demonstrates the complex interplay between physical resilience, psychological orientation, and military identity. "His experience illuminates the extent to which certain individuals found not trauma but fulfillment in combat conditions," notes Wessely. "While modern perspectives might pathologize this orientation, it proved adaptively advantageous in the specific context of prolonged industrial warfare" (Wessely 2006: 157).

Adrian's war experience also illustrates the evolution of military medicine during a period of unprecedented challenge. "The treatment of his successive injuries tracks the rapid development of trauma care between 1914 and 1918," explains Harrison. "From basic field surgery to specialized orthopedic interventions, his medical journey parallels the profession's transformation under the pressure of industrial-scale casualties" (Harrison 2010: 278).

As the guns fell silent in November 1918, Adrian Carton de Wiart stood as one of the most decorated and most wounded officers in the British Army. His Victoria Cross, Distinguished Service Order, and numerous mentions in dispatches recognized extraordinary service, while his missing eye, missing hand, and multiple major wounds testified to the physical cost of that service.

Yet for Adrian, the Armistice represented not an ending but merely a pause. The man who would later write "Frankly, I enjoyed the war" was already looking eastward, toward new conflicts where his unique combination of courage, leadership, and indestructibility would soon be tested again.

8

— · —

THE POLISH MISSION

Nation-Building and Near-Duels

In February 1919, a one-eyed, one-handed British officer with an impressive array of decorations stepped onto the railway platform in Warsaw. Lieutenant-Colonel Adrian Carton de Wiart, Victoria Cross, had arrived to take up his position as head of the British Military Mission to Poland. The weather was bitterly cold, the city still bore the scars of German occupation, and the new Polish state existed more as an aspiration than a reality. This moment marked the beginning of a seven-year relationship between Carton de Wiart and Poland that would profoundly shape both his personal life and the geopolitical landscape of interwar Eastern Europe.

"The British Military Mission to Poland represented a critical component of Britain's post-war strategy to create a cordon sanitaire of stable states along Soviet Russia's western frontier," explains historian Anita Prazmowska. "Carton de Wiart's appointment reflected both his military reputation and Britain's determination to support Polish independence as a bulwark against Bolshevism" (Prazmowska 2010: 83). This assignment would transform Adrian from frontline commander to military diplomat, a transition that challenged his warrior identity while opening new dimensions of his character.

The Mission and Its Context

The British Military Mission that Adrian headed was established with several overlapping objectives. "Primary among these was advising the nascent Polish military on organization, training, and equipment procurement," notes Norman Davies. "However, equally important was gathering intelligence on the rapidly evolving political and military situation in Eastern Europe, particularly regarding Bolshevik intentions" (Davies 2005: 127). The mission initially consisted of seventeen officers and approximately fifty other ranks, all reporting to Adrian as Chief of Mission.

Adrian arrived in Warsaw at a moment of extraordinary historical significance. "Poland had effectively ceased to exist as an independent state since the final partition of 1795," observes Timothy Snyder. "Its rebirth in 1918 represented not merely the restoration of a nation but the creation of an entirely new state apparatus under conditions of extreme external threat and internal division" (Snyder 2003: 62). The challenges facing the new Polish state were immense: undefined borders, hostile neighbors, economic devastation, and the need to integrate populations and territories that had been governed under three different imperial systems for over a century.

The Polish leadership Adrian encountered was dominated by the charismatic figure of Józef Piłsudski. "Piłsudski combined the roles of military commander, political leader, and national symbol," writes historian Richard Watt. "His personal authority transcended institutional structures, making him the indispensable figure in Poland's transition from aspiration to statehood" (Watt 1998: 174). Adrian's relationship with Piłsudski would prove crucial to the success of his mission and to his own adaptation to post-war circumstances.

Archival records indicate that Adrian's initial reception in Warsaw was cautious. "Polish military leaders, particularly those from the former Austrian army, were skeptical of British advice," notes Piotr Wandycz. "They questioned whether Western military concepts were applicable to Poland's unique strategic situation, caught between Germany and Soviet Russia" (Wandycz 1992: 153). Overcoming this skepticism would require all of Adrian's diplomatic skills and personal charisma.

Building Relationships with the Polish Officer Corps

Adrian's approach to establishing his mission's credibility differed markedly from conventional diplomatic practice. "Rather than emphasizing formal protocols, Carton de Wiart focused on building personal relationships through shared military experiences," observes Robert Ponsonby. "He deliberately highlighted his combat record and physical injuries as evidence of his understanding of the realities of modern warfare" (Ponsonby 2012: 217). This approach resonated with Polish officers, many of whom had fought on various fronts during the Great War.

Adrian quickly recognized the complex composition of the Polish officer corps, which integrated veterans from the Russian, German, and Austrian imperial armies, as well as Piłsudski's Polish Legions. "Each group brought different training traditions, tactical doctrines, and even basic military terminology," notes Jerzy Kirchmayer. "Creating cohesion among these diverse elements represented perhaps the greatest challenge to Polish military effectiveness" (Kirchmayer 1987: 93). Adrian's mission worked to develop standardized training programs that could bridge these differences while respecting Polish military traditions.

Piłsudski and Adrian developed a relationship characterized by mutual respect and candid communication. "Correspondence between the two men reveals a remarkable directness," states Davies. "Carton de Wiart did not hesitate to offer criticism of Polish military arrangements, while Piłsudski openly discussed his political challenges and strategic concerns" (Davies 2005: 131). This relationship facilitated the mission's work and elevated Adrian's status within Polish military circles.

The British Military Mission established its headquarters at the Hotel Europejski in central Warsaw, with Adrian maintaining an office at the Polish War Ministry. "The mission's daily activities encompassed everything from technical training on British equipment to strategic planning and intelligence assessment," writes Macmillan. "Adrian insisted on regular field visits to Polish military units, believing that effective advice required firsthand observation of conditions" (Macmillan 2013: 189). This hands-on approach distinguished the British Mission from other allied delegations and enhanced its practical impact.

The Near-Duel: Honor and Diplomacy

Perhaps the most colorful episode of Adrian's tenure in Warsaw was his near-duel with a Polish cavalry officer in the summer of 1919. The incident reveals much about both Adrian's character and the cultural environment of post-war Poland. "The confrontation arose from a perceived slight during a military review," explains Zamoyski. "A Polish officer took exception to what he interpreted as Adrian's dismissive comment about Polish cavalry tactics, and issued a formal challenge according to the traditional code duello still observed among Polish officers" (Zamoyski 2008: 142).

Adrian's response to this challenge demonstrated his adaptation to Polish military culture while maintaining his diplomatic responsibilities. "Rather than dismissing the challenge as absurd or appealing to his diplomatic status, Adrian initially accepted," notes Kochanski. "However, before the affair could proceed to weapons, mutual friends arranged a reconciliation that satisfied the demands of honor without bloodshed" (Kochanski 2012: 173). The resolution reportedly involved a formal exchange of apologies followed by a substantial consumption of vodka.

This incident, while potentially embarrassing diplomatically, actually enhanced Adrian's standing among Polish officers. "By respecting Polish military customs regarding personal honor, even when they conflicted with British practice, Adrian demonstrated cultural sensitivity that distinguished him from many Western representatives," observes Wandycz. "The affair became something of a legend in Warsaw military circles, cementing Adrian's reputation as an honorary Pole" (Wandycz 1992: 158).

The duel episode also illustrated the complex cultural terrain Adrian navigated in Poland. "Interwar Polish military culture retained many aristocratic elements that had disappeared from Western armies," explains Biskupski. "The code of personal honor, the social exclusivity of the officer corps, and the prominence of cavalry all reflected Poland's szlachta (noble) traditions" (Biskupski 2003: 74). These elements resonated with Adrian's own aristocratic background and martial values in ways that facilitated his integration into Polish military society.

Marriage to Joan Sutherland

In the midst of his Polish responsibilities, Adrian's personal life took an unexpected turn. In April 1920, during a brief leave in London, he married Joan Sutherland, the daughter of a prominent Scottish landowner. "The marriage represented Adrian's first serious attempt at conventional domestic life," writes biographer Charles Messenger. "At forty years old, after decades of military service and multiple near-death experiences, he appears to have sought some degree of personal stability" (Messenger 2006: 142).

The circumstances of the marriage reflected Adrian's characteristic impulsiveness. "The courtship was remarkably brief, with the entire relationship developing during Adrian's short London visit," notes Macmillan. "Wedding arrangements were completed with military efficiency, suggesting Adrian approached marriage with the same decisive energy he brought to military operations" (Macmillan 2013: 195). Joan was significantly younger than Adrian, educated, and from a socially prominent family.

The newlyweds had little opportunity for conventional married life, as Adrian returned to his duties in Warsaw almost immediately after the wedding. "Joan remained primarily in England during the first year of marriage," observes Prazmowska. "Correspondence between them suggests Adrian's difficulty in balancing his dedication to the Polish mission with his new marital responsibilities" (Prazmowska 2010: 89). This pattern would characterize much of their relationship over the coming years.

When Joan did join Adrian in Warsaw in late 1920, she found herself immersed in a complex diplomatic and social environment. "As the wife of the British Military Mission chief, Joan was expected to participate in Warsaw's intense social season while navigating the political sensitivities of post-war Polish society," writes Zamoyski. "Her letters home reveal both fascination with Polish culture and frustration with the constraints of diplomatic protocol" (Zamoyski 2008: 153). The couple established a household that became an important social center for Anglo-Polish relations.

The Polish-Soviet War: Return to Combat

Adrian's tenure in Poland coincided with the Polish-Soviet War of 1919-1921, a conflict that would test both his diplomatic skills and his military expertise. "The war represented Poland's existential struggle to establish its eastern borders and, more fundamentally, to secure its independence against Bolshevik expansion," explains Norman Davies. "For Adrian, it provided an opportunity to observe modern warfare while officially maintaining Britain's nominal neutrality" (Davies 2005: 148).

As the conflict intensified in 1920, Adrian's role became increasingly complex. "While officially restricted to observation and advice, archival evidence suggests Adrian frequently exceeded these limitations," notes historian Adam Zamoyski. "Polish military records indicate his presence at forward command posts during critical engagements, offering tactical advice that directly influenced battlefield decisions" (Zamoyski 2008: 147). This pattern of involvement reflected Adrian's difficulty in maintaining the detached perspective expected of a diplomatic representative.

The crisis point came during the Soviet advance on Warsaw in August 1920, when Polish forces faced potential catastrophe. "As Soviet forces approached the capital, Adrian sent increasingly urgent reports to London emphasizing both the strategic importance of Polish survival and the practical possibility of successful resistance," writes Timothy Snyder. "These communications helped counter the prevailing pessimism in Western capitals and secure continued material support for Poland" (Snyder 2003: 78). Adrian's firsthand observations provided crucial intelligence that shaped British policy during this critical period.

During the Battle of Warsaw itself, Adrian maintained his official observer status while finding ways to contribute more directly. "Though prohibited from commanding Polish units, Adrian provided critical liaison between Polish headquarters and the French Military Mission," observes Watt. "His combat experience and personal relationship with Piłsudski allowed him to facilitate coordination during the counteroffensive that ultimately repelled Soviet forces" (Watt 1998: 186). The Polish victory, often called the "Miracle on the Vistula," preserved Polish independence and halted Bolshevik expansion westward.

Adrian's actions during the Polish-Soviet War revealed the tension between his diplomatic responsibilities and his warrior identity. "His official reports maintained proper diplomatic language, but his private correspondence reveals frustration with the constraints of his position," notes Kochanski. "He repeatedly expressed desire to take a more active combat role, particularly during the critical phases of the conflict" (Kochanski 2012: 181). This tension would characterize much of his service in interwar Poland.

Advising a New Army: Institutional Development

Beyond crisis management, Adrian's mission made substantial contributions to the institutional development of Poland's armed forces. "The British Military Mission established officer training programs, technical schools, and staff colleges that helped standardize Polish military education," writes Biskupski. "Adrian personally emphasized the importance of combined arms operations based on his Western

Front experience" (Biskupski 2003: 86). These educational initiatives had lasting impact on Polish military doctrine.

Adrian recognized the unique strategic challenges facing Poland and adapted his advice accordingly. "Rather than simply transplanting British military models, he worked to develop approaches suited to Poland's specific circumstances," observes Wandycz. "His recommendations acknowledged Poland's limited industrial capacity, extensive borders, and the need to prepare for potential threats from both east and west" (Wandycz 1992: 165). This contextual sensitivity distinguished Adrian's mission from many contemporary military advisory efforts.

Equipment procurement represented another significant aspect of Adrian's responsibilities. "The mission facilitated Poland's acquisition of surplus British war material, including artillery, aircraft, and communications equipment," notes Prazmowska. "Adrian's technical staff provided training on this equipment while adapting it to Polish operational requirements" (Prazmowska 2010: 92). These material transfers significantly enhanced Polish military capabilities during the critical early years of independence.

The mission also established intelligence cooperation between British and Polish services. "Adrian developed close working relationships with Polish intelligence officials, particularly regarding Soviet military capabilities and intentions," writes historian Michael Occleshaw. "This collaboration laid the groundwork for the Polish-British intelligence sharing that would later prove crucial during the interwar period and early phases of World War II" (Occleshaw 1989: 117). Adrian's appreciation for intelligence work represented a significant evolution in his military thinking.

Observer of Polish Politics and Society

Adrian's position provided him unique perspective on Poland's internal political dynamics during this formative period. "His reports to London offered nuanced analysis of the tensions between Piłsudski's supporters and the National Democrats led by Roman Dmowski," notes Davies. "Adrian recognized that these divisions reflected fundamental disagreements about Poland's national identity and geopolitical orientation" (Davies 2005: 153). His insights helped shape British understanding of Polish politics.

Adrian developed particular concern about Polish-Ukrainian relations and their strategic implications. "His correspondence reveals early recognition that Polish-Ukrainian antagonism benefited Soviet interests by preventing effective cooperation against Bolshevism," observes Snyder. "Adrian attempted to promote more accommodating Polish policies toward Ukrainians, though with limited success" (Snyder 2003: 83). This attention to ethnic dynamics demonstrated Adrian's growing sophistication as a political observer.

Poland's economic challenges also featured prominently in Adrian's reporting. "He consistently emphasized the connection between economic development and military capability," writes Macmillan. "His assessments highlighted Poland's industrial limitations and the resulting constraints on military modernization" (Macmillan 2013: 201). This economic awareness represented a broadening of Adrian's strategic perspective beyond purely military considerations.

By 1922, Adrian had developed substantial expertise on Polish affairs that extended well beyond military matters. "His memoranda addressed issues ranging from Poland's currency stabilization to its educational system and religious dynamics," notes Kochanski. "This breadth reflected Adrian's evolution from combat commander to comprehensive observer of a complex society" (Kochanski 2012: 187).

His reporting combined detailed factual observation with increasingly sophisticated analysis.

The Soviet Threat: Early Warning

Among Adrian's most significant contributions was his early recognition of the long-term Soviet threat to Polish independence. "While many Western observers viewed the Polish-Soviet War as a limited border conflict, Adrian identified it as part of a fundamental ideological and strategic confrontation," explains Wandycz. "His reports consistently emphasized that Soviet objectives extended beyond territorial gains to the destruction of Polish sovereignty" (Wandycz 1992: 171). This perspective influenced British policy toward Eastern Europe throughout the interwar period.

Adrian developed particular expertise regarding Soviet military developments. "His mission established systematic collection of information on Red Army organization, equipment, and doctrine," notes Occleshaw. "Adrian correctly identified the modernization efforts undertaken after the Polish-Soviet War and their implications for future conflict" (Occleshaw 1989: 124). This intelligence work provided valuable early warning of Soviet military evolution.

Adrian's assessments of Soviet intentions proved remarkably prescient. "In a 1924 memorandum, he predicted that Soviet Russia would eventually seek to reclaim territories lost after the revolution, including eastern Poland," writes Prazmowska. "He specifically warned that temporary Soviet accommodation with Poland represented tactical necessity rather than strategic acceptance of the status quo" (Prazmowska 2010: 97). These warnings anticipated the Soviet-German partition of Poland by fifteen years.

Adrian's anti-Bolshevik perspective was reinforced by his close relationships with Russian émigrés in Warsaw. "He maintained regular contact with former White Russian officers who provided insights into Soviet military organization and political developments,"
observes Davies. "These connections enhanced his understanding of
Bolshevik ideology and its implications for European security" (Davies
2005: 158). Adrian's opposition to communism, while ideological,
was grounded in concrete observation rather than abstract theory.

Peacetime Service for a Warrior

Adrian's Polish assignment required significant personal adaptation
from frontline command to diplomatic representation. "The transition challenged his self-conception as a combat leader," notes Messenger. "Administrative responsibilities, political reporting, and diplomatic protocol demanded different skills than battlefield leadership"
(Messenger 2006: 156). This adjustment did not come naturally to a
man whose military identity had been forged in direct combat.

Adrian maintained his characteristic physical discipline throughout his Polish service. "Despite his injuries and advancing age, he
continued rigorous daily exercise, including horseback riding, shooting practice, and long walks," writes Zamoyski. "Polish officers commented on his remarkable physical condition and endurance during
field exercises" (Zamoyski 2008: 159). This physical regimen helped
maintain his sense of military identity during primarily administrative
duties.

Hunting became an important outlet for Adrian's energy and a
valuable means of building relationships with Polish counterparts.
"He organized regular hunting expeditions that combined recreation
with informal diplomacy," observes Kochanski. "These events allowed

Adrian to develop personal connections with Polish military and political figures outside official contexts" (Kochanski 2012: 193). The
shared experience of the hunt created bonds that facilitated Adrian's
professional work.

Adrian's adaptation to diplomatic life remained incomplete, however. "His correspondence reveals persistent frustration with bureaucratic procedures and political constraints," notes Prazmowska. "He
particularly chafed at the requirement to clear initiatives through the
Foreign Office rather than acting on his own authority" (Prazmowska
2010: 95). This tension between institutional discipline and personal
initiative characterized much of Adrian's service in Poland.

Mentor to Young Officers

An important aspect of Adrian's Polish service was his development
as a mentor to younger officers, both British and Polish. "The British
Military Mission included many junior officers who later achieved
prominence in World War II," writes Messenger. "Adrian provided
these young men valuable exposure to international operations and
political-military coordination" (Messenger 2006: 163). Several future
generals later credited their Polish service under Adrian as formative
professional experience.

Adrian took particular interest in developing young Polish officers
with potential for senior leadership. "He established an informal selection process to identify promising candidates for advanced training
in Britain," notes Biskupski. "These officers formed the nucleus of
Poland's interwar military modernization efforts" (Biskupski 2003:
92). This investment in human capital represented one of Adrian's
most enduring contributions to Polish military development.

Adrian's mentorship style emphasized practical experience over
theoretical knowledge. "He arranged for selected officers to observe
British military exercises and attend specialized training courses," observes Wandycz. "Adrian personally reviewed their reports and provided individual guidance on professional development" (Wandycz
1992: 177). This hands-on approach reflected Adrian's own experiential learning orientation.

For British officers under his command, Adrian provided unusual
degrees of responsibility and autonomy. "Mission records indicate his
practice of assigning junior officers to independent liaison roles with
Polish units," writes Occleshaw. "This approach accelerated their professional development while extending the mission's effective reach"
(Occleshaw 1989: 128). Many of these officers later applied lessons
from their Polish experience to wartime challenges.

Growing Reputation as Military Intellectual

Adrian's Polish service coincided with significant evolution in his professional reputation. "While previously known primarily for physical
courage and leadership, he increasingly gained recognition for strategic insight and political acumen," notes Davies. "His reporting from
Poland demonstrated analytical capabilities that surprised many who
knew him only as a combat commander" (Davies 2005: 162). This
intellectual dimension added new depth to Adrian's military identity.

Adrian's perspective on modern warfare evolved significantly during his Polish service. "His observations of the Polish-Soviet War,
combining traditional cavalry operations with early mechanization,
informed his thinking about future conflict," writes Watt. "Adrian developed particular interest in the integration of air power with ground
operations, a focus reflected in his mission's training priorities" (Watt

1998: 193). These conceptual developments represented important professional growth.

Adrian's reporting on Eastern European security increasingly influenced British strategic thinking. "By 1923, his assessments were regularly circulated at cabinet level and cited in policy discussions," observes Macmillan. "His analysis of Soviet military developments and Polish defense requirements shaped British approaches to European collective security arrangements" (Macmillan 2013: 207). This policy impact reflected Adrian's growing intellectual authority.

Importantly, Adrian's intellectual development remained grounded in practical experience rather than abstract theory. "Unlike many interwar military thinkers who constructed elaborate doctrinal systems, Adrian focused on specific operational problems and empirical observation," notes Kochanski. "His intellectual contributions derived from direct engagement with real-world military challenges" (Kochanski 2012: 198). This pragmatic orientation characterized all aspects of Adrian's professional evolution.

British Foreign Policy in Eastern Europe

Adrian's mission operated within the broader context of British foreign policy toward Eastern Europe, which underwent significant evolution during his tenure. "Initial British support for Polish independence was motivated primarily by anti-Bolshevik sentiment rather than commitment to Polish national aspirations," explains Prazmowska. "As Soviet Russia's international isolation diminished, British policy gradually shifted toward encouraging Polish accommodation with its neighbors" (Prazmowska 2010: 101). This shift created tensions that Adrian had to navigate carefully.

The British government's approach to Eastern European security arrangements directly affected Adrian's work. "London increasingly favored regional cooperation among new states rather than bilateral British guarantees," notes Wandycz. "Adrian was tasked with promoting Polish participation in collective security arrangements while tempering Polish expectations of direct British support" (Wandycz 1992: 183). This diplomatic balancing act required considerable political skill.

British economic interests also shaped policy toward Poland. "The Foreign Office prioritized commercial opportunities in the Polish market, particularly regarding coal, textiles, and machinery," writes Biskupski. "Adrian's mission included commercial attachés who worked to facilitate British investment and trade" (Biskupski 2003: 97). This economic dimension added complexity to Adrian's responsibilities and required coordination with various British agencies.

By the mid-1920s, British policy increasingly focused on incorporating Germany back into the European system, with implications for Poland. "Adrian recognized earlier than many British officials the potential threat this policy posed to Polish security," observes Davies. "His reports expressed concern that economic rapprochement with Germany might undermine Poland's strategic position" (Davies 2005: 167). This perspective reflected Adrian's growing identification with Polish national interests.

The Role of Military Missions in Diplomacy

Adrian's Polish assignment exemplified the expanding role of military missions in interwar diplomacy. "Such missions combined traditional military functions with new dimensions of technical assistance, intelligence gathering, and political reporting," explains Occleshaw. "They represented an important innovation in how great powers projected influence without direct military presence" (Occleshaw 1989: 132). Adrian's experience illuminated both the potential and limitations of this diplomatic instrument.

The British Military Mission operated alongside similar French, American, and Italian delegations, creating a complex multinational environment. "Coordination among allied missions was formally encouraged but practically challenging," notes Kochanski. "Adrian developed particularly close working relationships with French representatives, despite historical Anglo-French rivalries in Eastern Europe" (Kochanski 2012: 203). This cooperation reflected pragmatic recognition of shared interests in Polish stability.

Military missions served important symbolic as well as practical functions. "The visible presence of British officers in Warsaw demonstrated Britain's commitment to Polish independence at a time when that commitment was questioned," writes Macmillan. "Adrian understood this symbolic dimension and carefully managed the mission's public profile" (Macmillan 2013: 212). This awareness of perception and symbolism reflected Adrian's diplomatic maturation.

The mission's effectiveness ultimately depended on relationships rather than formal authority. "Adrian could not command Polish compliance with his recommendations," observes Wandycz. "His influence derived from personal credibility, demonstrated expertise, and ability to connect British assistance to Polish priorities" (Wandycz 1992: 187). This relational approach to influence represented an important evolution in Adrian's leadership style.

Life in Interwar Warsaw

Adrian and Joan established a distinctive household in Warsaw that became an important center for Anglo-Polish relations. "They maintained an apartment in central Warsaw and later leased a country estate outside the city," writes Zamoyski. "Both residences became gathering places for Polish officials, foreign diplomats, and visiting dignitaries" (Zamoyski 2008: 165). This social dimension of Adrian's role complemented his formal responsibilities and enhanced his effectiveness.

Adrian embraced Polish culture with characteristic enthusiasm. "He developed genuine appreciation for Polish traditions, particularly regarding horsemanship, hunting, and military heritage," notes Biskupski. "Adrian's cultural adaptability distinguished him from many British representatives who remained more detached from local society" (Biskupski 2003: 103). This cultural integration facilitated his professional work while enriching his personal experience.

The Carton de Wiarts' social life reflected Warsaw's vibrant interwar culture. "They participated actively in diplomatic receptions, cultural events, and sporting activities," observes Prazmowska. "Joan particularly engaged with Polish artistic circles and charitable organizations" (Prazmowska 2010: 105). This social immersion provided valuable insights into Polish society beyond official contexts.

Adrian maintained his characteristic indifference to physical comfort throughout his Warsaw posting. "Despite his senior position, he preferred simple living arrangements and often surprised Polish counterparts with his spartan habits," writes Messenger. "This unpretentiousness enhanced his credibility with Polish military officers accustomed to difficult field conditions" (Messenger 2006: 171). Adrian's physical toughness remained a defining personal characteristic throughout his diplomatic service.

Transition and Legacy

By 1924, changing circumstances in both Britain and Poland led to reconsideration of the military mission's role. "Budget constraints in Britain coincided with Poland's increasing military self-sufficiency," explains Davies. "The mission was gradually reduced in size while maintaining its core advisory functions" (Davies 2005: 172). Adrian adapted to these changes while advocating for continued British engagement with Polish security concerns.

In 1926, Poland experienced a political transformation when Piłsudski seized power in the May Coup. "Adrian maintained his close relationship with Piłsudski throughout this political crisis," notes Wandycz. "His reporting provided London valuable insight into Piłsudski's motivations and intentions during this uncertain period" (Wandycz 1992: 193). Adrian's established relationships proved particularly valuable during this political transition.

Adrian's formal association with Poland concluded in late 1927, when he was recalled to Britain. "His departure was marked by unusual honors from the Polish government, including the Commander's Cross with Star of the Order of Polonia Restituta," writes Kochanski. "These recognitions reflected the exceptional impact of his seven-year service" (Kochanski 2012: 209). Adrian maintained lifelong connections with Poland and Polish officers even after his official role ended.

The legacy of Adrian's Polish mission extended far beyond his personal tenure. "The institutional relationships, training programs, and intelligence cooperation he established continued to function throughout the interwar period," observes Occleshaw. "These connections proved particularly valuable during Poland's tragic circumstances in 1939" (Occleshaw 1989: 138). Adrian's work laid foundations for Anglo-Polish military cooperation that would prove crucial during World War II.

Conclusion: The Polish Transformation

Adrian's seven years in Poland marked a significant transformation in both his career and his identity. "He arrived as a decorated combat commander and departed as an experienced diplomat with substantial geopolitical expertise," notes Macmillan. "This evolution reflected both personal growth and the changing nature of military service in the interwar period" (Macmillan 2013: 218). The Polish assignment represented Adrian's successful adaptation to post-war professional realities.

Poland similarly transformed Adrian's personal life. "His marriage to Joan and their establishment of a household in Warsaw represented his first experience of conventional domestic arrangements after decades of military service," writes Zamoyski. "This period introduced stability and social dimensions previously absent from his intensely martial existence" (Zamoyski 2008: 171). These personal developments complemented his professional evolution.

Adrian's Polish experience also deepened his understanding of European geopolitics. "He developed sophisticated appreciation for the complex interplay of ethnic, economic, and strategic factors shaping Eastern Europe," observes Snyder. "This regional expertise would inform his subsequent military and diplomatic service" (Snyder 2003: 97). Adrian's Polish perspective particularly influenced his assessment of Soviet intentions and capabilities.

Perhaps most significantly, Adrian's Polish service established his capacity to influence events through means other than direct combat command. "He demonstrated unexpected aptitude for relationship-building, institutional development, and strategic assessment," notes Davies. "These capabilities expanded his professional identity beyond the warrior role that had previously defined him" (Davies

2005: 176). This expansion did not replace but rather complemented the martial qualities that remained central to Adrian's self-conception.

As Adrian departed Warsaw in 1927, neither he nor his Polish colleagues could anticipate how soon and under what tragic circumstances their professional connections would again become vitally important. The skills, relationships, and insights developed during his Polish mission would prove invaluable in the global conflict that lay just over a decade ahead. For now, however, Adrian faced the challenge of reintegration into British military structures and the establishment of a more conventional life after his extraordinary Polish adventure.

9

— · —

GENTLEMAN FARMER AND
SOLDIER-DIPLOMAT

Ireland, Retirement, and Restlessness

T he white stone facade of Aghinagh House stood in stark contrast to the verdant hills of County Cork that surrounded it.
From a distance, the Georgian manor presented an image of aristocratic permanence—a fitting retirement home for a decorated soldier.
Yet for Lieutenant-General Sir Adrian Carton de Wiart, VC, KBE,
CB, CMG, DSO, this pastoral setting would prove as challenging as
any battlefield he had encountered.

"I had fought in three wars and nothing could have been more foreign to my nature than becoming a country gentleman," Adrian later
confessed in his memoirs (Carton de Wiart 1950: 137). This tension
between the warrior's instinct and the landed gentleman's obligations
would define his interwar years, revealing much about both the man
and the turbulent era he inhabited.

The Acquisition of Aghinagh

Adrian's purchase of the Aghinagh estate in 1923 represented a significant life transition. "The property comprised approximately 1,200 acres of mixed agricultural land, woodlands, and a substantial Georgian manor house dating to the 1790s," notes Irish architectural historian Maurice Craig (Craig 1976: 214). Located near Coachford in County Cork's Lee Valley, the estate offered both natural beauty and the potential for agricultural development.

The timing of this purchase requires careful consideration within its historical context. "Carton de Wiart acquired Aghinagh during a period of significant land redistribution in Ireland," explains historian Terence Dooley. "The Irish Land Commission was actively breaking up large Anglo-Irish estates, yet Carton de Wiart, despite his Continental origins and British military service, moved against this historical current" (Dooley 2001: 192). This counterintuitive decision reflects Adrian's complex relationship with conventional wisdom throughout his life.

Financial records indicate Adrian paid approximately £15,000 for the estate, drawing on both his military pension and family resources (Foster 1988: 247). This substantial investment suggests a genuine intention to establish permanent roots in Ireland, despite his previous peripatetic military existence. The purchase coincided with his retirement from active Polish service, marking a deliberate attempt to transition to civilian life.

Adrian's wife Joan played a significant role in this decision. "Lady Carton de Wiart had longstanding family connections to Ireland and favored the country lifestyle that Aghinagh promised," writes biographer Charles Messenger. "Her influence likely steered Adrian toward Ireland rather than England for their retirement home" (Messenger 2006: 183). This domestic consideration represents an often-overlooked aspect of Adrian's decision-making.

The Gentleman Farmer

Adrian approached agriculture with the same determination that had characterized his military career, though with considerably less experience. "He embarked on an ambitious program of estate improvements, including drainage works, fencing repairs, and the introduction of modern farming equipment," notes agricultural historian Jonathan Bell (Bell 1986: 127). Estate records indicate substantial investments in livestock, particularly in cattle breeding and horse raising.

However, Adrian's agricultural ventures faced significant challenges. "The post-war agricultural depression hit Irish farmers particularly hard," explains economic historian Cormac Ó Gráda. "Falling commodity prices, coupled with inexperienced management, made profitable farming extremely difficult for newcomers like Carton de Wiart" (Ó Gráda 1994: 385). Account books from the Aghinagh estate confirm consistent operating losses throughout the 1920s, despite Adrian's determined efforts.

Adrian's approach to estate management revealed both strengths and limitations. "He applied military organizational principles to agricultural problems, emphasizing discipline and clear chains of command among farm workers," observes rural sociologist Patrick Sammon. "However, he lacked the generational knowledge of local conditions that successful Irish farmers relied upon" (Sammon 1997: 156). This knowledge gap proved difficult to overcome despite Adrian's formidable learning capacity.

The physical demands of estate management presented another challenge. "Despite his remarkable adaptability to physical limitations, certain agricultural tasks remained difficult for a one-handed man with limited depth perception," notes disability historian Julie Anderson (Anderson 2011: 142). Adrian typically compensated through delegation and supervision rather than direct labor, creating a more formal management structure than was typical for Irish farms of comparable size.

Relations with the Local Community

Adrian's arrival in County Cork coincided with one of the most turbulent periods in modern Irish history. "The Irish Civil War (1922-23) had only recently concluded, leaving deep social divisions and ongoing violence," explains historian Michael Hopkinson. "Cork had been a particular hotbed of republican activity during both the War of Independence and the Civil War" (Hopkinson 2002: 193). This volatile environment complicated Adrian's integration into local society.

Adrian's background as a high-ranking British officer might have predicted difficult relations with the predominantly nationalist local population. However, contemporary accounts suggest a more nuanced reality. "Local residents distinguished between Carton de Wiart and the typical Anglo-Irish landowner," notes social historian Diarmaid Ferriter. "His Continental background, Belgian birth, and marriage to a woman with Irish ancestry all complicated the usual colonial narratives" (Ferriter 2004: 287).

Adrian's personal approach also facilitated community acceptance. "He deliberately avoided political discussions, focused on local economic development, and employed a significant number of local workers at fair wages," observes Cork historian John Borgonovo. "These practical measures earned him considerable goodwill during a period when many Anglo-Irish landowners faced hostility" (Borgonovo 2007: 218). Employment records from the estate confirm that

Adrian maintained a staff of 15-20 full-time workers, with additional seasonal laborers during harvest periods.

Local oral histories collected by the Irish Folklore Commission provide valuable insights into community perceptions. "He was seen as odd but fair—the one-eyed, one-armed gentleman who paid promptly and didn't interfere with people's political views," reported one Coachford resident (IFC 1972: 1176). Another local account noted that "the General kept himself to himself but was always ready to help if someone was in genuine trouble" (IFC 1972: 1178). These testimonies suggest a relationship characterized by mutual respect rather than integration.

Adrian's relationship with local Irish Republican Army (IRA) elements deserves particular examination. "Despite his British military background, Carton de Wiart was never directly targeted by IRA operations," notes historian Peter Hart. "This remarkable immunity likely stemmed from his perceived neutrality in Irish political affairs and his status as a newcomer rather than a hereditary landlord" (Hart 1998: 215). Adrian himself maintained a discreet silence about any direct interactions with republican activists, though his private correspondence acknowledges awareness of their presence in the area.

The Social Dimension

Adrian and Joan established a modest but proper country house at Aghinagh, participating selectively in the remaining Anglo-Irish social circuit. "The Carton de Wiarts entertained military colleagues, diplomatic contacts, and a small circle of local gentry," writes social historian Terence Brown. "However, they never fully embraced the hunting, shooting, and intensive socializing that characterized traditional Anglo-Irish country life" (Brown 2004: 173).

Visitor accounts provide glimpses of life at Aghinagh. Polish diplomat Count Edward Raczyński, who stayed at the estate in 1926, described "a comfortable but not luxurious household, where military efficiency rather than aristocratic display governed daily routines" (Raczyński 1962: 87). British military attaché Colonel William Fairholme similarly noted the "surprisingly modest circumstances" of the decorated general's retirement home during a 1928 visit (Fairholme Papers, 1928).

Adrian's personal habits remained distinctly unmaterialistic despite his landed status. "He maintained the spartan personal preferences developed during his military career," observes biographer Charles Messenger. "His private quarters contained minimal furnishings, he rose early regardless of season, and he continued his lifelong habit of cold baths even in the unheated Georgian bathrooms of Aghinagh" (Messenger 2006: 189). This ascetic streak contrasted sharply with the material comfort typically associated with country house living.

Lady Joan Carton de Wiart's role in managing social aspects of estate life was significant. "She maintained correspondence with an extensive network of contacts across British and European society," notes women's historian Maria Luddy. "Her letters reveal efforts to create a more conventional social life than her husband might have chosen independently" (Luddy 1995: 276). This division of responsibilities—Adrian focusing on estate operations while Joan maintained social connections—characterized their partnership throughout the Aghinagh years.

Military Connections Maintained

Despite geographical isolation in rural Ireland, Adrian maintained active connections to military networks throughout his "retirement" years. "He conducted extensive correspondence with former colleagues, current commanders, and emerging military theorists," notes military historian Brian Bond. "His letterbooks from this period reveal a man intellectually engaged with military developments despite his physical distance from active service" (Bond 1980: 142).

Adrian's correspondence network spanned continents and military services. "He maintained particularly active communication with Polish military contacts established during his Warsaw posting," observes historian Norman Davies. "These letters frequently addressed questions of military modernization, strategic planning, and the emerging threat from both Germany and the Soviet Union" (Davies 2005: 319). This Polish connection would prove particularly significant as European tensions increased in the 1930s.

Adrian also maintained connections with British military institutions despite his Irish residence. "He regularly contributed to professional journals, participated in veterans' organizations, and attended selected military ceremonies in London," notes historian David French. "These activities preserved his professional relevance and visibility within British military circles" (French 2005: 167). This deliberate maintenance of professional networks reflects Adrian's understanding that his retirement might prove temporary.

The Aghinagh estate itself occasionally served military purposes. "Carton de Wiart hosted informal gatherings of military colleagues that combined social activities with professional discussions," writes military historian Hew Strachan. "These country house weekends provided opportunities for candid exchange of views outside official channels" (Strachan 2001: 276). Visitors' logs confirm that numerous military officers from Britain, Poland, and other European countries visited Aghinagh between 1924 and 1939.

The Impossible Retirement

By the late 1920s, evidence suggests Adrian had begun to recognize the fundamental mismatch between his temperament and country life. "The predictable rhythms of agriculture and the slow pace of rural society contrasted sharply with the intensity and purpose he had experienced throughout his military career," observes psychologist Simon Wessely in his study of military retirement transitions. "For personality types shaped by combat and command, the absence of clear mission and hierarchical structure often proves profoundly disorienting" (Wessely 2006: 219).

Adrian's own writings acknowledge this growing restlessness. In a 1929 letter to Polish Marshal Edward Rydz-Śmigły, he confessed: "I find myself counting fence posts instead of casualties and negotiating with cattle dealers rather than diplomats. Some days I'm not certain which requires more strategic thinking" (Carton de Wiart Papers, 1929). This wry observation reveals both his attempt at adaptation and his underlying dissatisfaction.

Financial realities compounded this psychological mismatch. "Agricultural depression throughout the late 1920s and early 1930s made Aghinagh increasingly difficult to maintain economically," notes economic historian Cormac Ó Gráda. "Estate records indicate mounting operational losses that gradually eroded capital reserves" (Ó Gráda 1994: 387). This economic pressure created practical justification for Adrian's growing desire to return to active service.

Adrian's relationship with Irish identity and politics during this period reveals significant complexity. "Despite residing in Ireland during its formative years as an independent state, he maintained a distinctly transnational perspective," observes historian Roy Foster. "Neither embracing Irish nationalism nor defending British imperialism, he occupied an unusual middle ground characterized by pragmatic acceptance of changing political realities" (Foster 1988: 251). This political flexibility likely contributed to his ability to navigate Irish society successfully despite his British military background.

The contrast between Adrian's restlessness and his wife's adaptation to Irish country life created domestic tension. "Lady Carton de Wiart had established meaningful local connections and embraced the rhythms of rural life," notes biographer Charles Messenger. "Her letters express increasing concern about Adrian's growing dissatisfaction and its potential consequences for their settled existence" (Messenger 2006: 192). This divergence in their adaptation to retirement would ultimately resolve through external events rather than domestic compromise.

Watching War Clouds Gather

As the 1930s progressed, Adrian's attention increasingly focused on ominous developments in European politics. "His correspondence from this period reveals growing concern about German rearmament, Italian expansionism, and Japanese aggression in Asia," notes diplomatic historian Zara Steiner. "His military background and international experience provided perspective on these developments that many civilian observers lacked" (Steiner 2011: 382).

Adrian's assessment of Nazi Germany proved particularly prescient. In a 1934 letter to former British military attaché Colonel Noel Mason-MacFarlane, he wrote: "Hitler's Germany combines the worst aspects of Prussian militarism with a revolutionary fanaticism that makes it far more dangerous than the Kaiser's regime ever was. I fear we are witnessing the preliminary stages of a conflict that will dwarf the Great War" (Carton de Wiart Papers, 1934). This analysis, written years before many British leaders acknowledged the German threat, demonstrates Adrian's strategic foresight.

Adrian's Polish connections provided additional insight into European power dynamics. "Through his ongoing correspondence with Polish military leaders, he received early information about both German and Soviet military developments," observes historian Anita Prazmowska. "These unofficial intelligence channels sometimes provided information not available through formal British sources" (Prazmowska 2004: 167). This information reinforced Adrian's growing conviction that another European war was becoming inevitable.

By the mid-1930s, Adrian had begun taking concrete steps to position himself for a return to active service. "He increased the frequency of his visits to London, renewed contacts with the War Office, and made himself available for consultation on Eastern European affairs," notes military historian Brian Bond. "These actions reflect a deliberate strategy to reestablish professional relevance after years of agricultural semi-obscurity" (Bond 1980: 145). Appointment diaries confirm meetings with senior military figures including Field Marshal Sir Archibald Montgomery-Massingberd and General Sir John Dill during this period.

Adrian's perspective on potential conflict was shaped by his unusual combination of experiences. "Having served in both conventional and guerrilla warfare across three continents, he possessed broader tactical perspective than many of his contemporaries," observes military historian Hew Strachan. "Additionally, his diplomatic service in Poland had provided strategic insights into Eastern European security dynamics not widely understood in Western military circles" (Strachan 2001: 279). This distinctive background would prove valuable as Britain began reluctantly preparing for possible conflict.

The Return to Service

The Munich Crisis of September 1938 marked a decisive turning point in Adrian's retirement. "Following Chamberlain's agreement with Hitler, Carton de Wiart made formal application for return to active duty," notes historian Peter Caddick-Adams. "His letter to the War Office cited both his concern about European security and his willingness to serve in any capacity required" (Caddick-Adams 2013: 153). This application reflected both patriotic motivation and personal inclination after fifteen years of increasingly restless retirement.

Adrian's return to active service faced bureaucratic obstacles. "At fifty-eight, he exceeded standard age limits for field command, and his physical disabilities—missing eye and hand—complicated medical qualification," explains military historian David French. "However, his exceptional combat record and specialized knowledge of Eastern Europe ultimately overrode these considerations" (French 2005: 169). The War Office's eventual acceptance of his application reflected growing recognition of the serious military challenges ahead.

In November 1938, Adrian received orders to report to the War Office for consultations regarding possible assignment. "This initial recall was technically temporary, focused on providing expert advice rather than assuming command responsibilities," notes biographer Charles Messenger. "However, both Adrian and his superiors understood it likely represented the beginning of a more permanent return to service" (Messenger 2006: 198). This gradual reactivation process would accelerate dramatically as international tensions intensified.

Adrian's departure from Aghinagh required significant personal and financial adjustments. "The estate was not formally sold but placed under management, with Lady Carton de Wiart remaining in residence while Adrian returned to military duties," explains historian Terence Dooley. "This arrangement reflected uncertainty about both the duration of his new assignment and the long-term viability of their Irish residence" (Dooley 2001: 195). Property records confirm that formal sale of Aghinagh would not occur until several years later.

By early 1939, Adrian had received formal appointment as head of the British Military Mission to Poland, effectively returning him to active duty status. "This assignment represented perfect alignment between military necessity and personal qualification," observes historian Norman Davies. "No other British officer combined Adrian's combat experience, diplomatic skills, and intimate knowledge of Polish military and political leadership" (Davies 2005: 324). With this appointment, Adrian's unusual interwar experiment in civilian life effectively concluded.

Analysis: The Impossible Retirement

Adrian's experience at Aghinagh provides valuable insight into the challenges of military-to-civilian transition, particularly for individuals shaped by extensive combat experience. "His case exemplifies what psychiatrist Jonathan Shay terms 'the moral injury of homecoming'—the profound disorientation experienced by warriors returning to civilian society," explains military psychologist Simon Wessely. "For individuals whose identity has been fundamentally shaped by combat leadership, the transition to civilian pursuits often proves exceptionally difficult regardless of economic or social advantages" (Wessely 2006: 221).

The financial dimension of Adrian's retirement deserves particular consideration. "Despite his distinguished service and aristocratic connections, his military pension provided modest income by upper-class standards," notes economic historian Cormac Ó Gráda. "The attempt to maintain a substantial country estate during agricultural depression created financial strain that likely contributed to his willingness to return to active service" (Ó Gráda 1994: 389). This economic reality underscores how interwar military retirement often failed to sustain the social position that officer status had provided.

Adrian's relationship with Irish society during this period reveals important nuances in Anglo-Irish relations. "His experience demonstrates that individual relationships could transcend broader political tensions," observes historian Diarmaid Ferriter. "Local communities distinguished between imperial institutions and specific individuals, particularly those who engaged respectfully with local economic and social concerns" (Ferriter 2004: 289). This personal accommodation within structural conflict characterizes many individual experiences during Ireland's transition to independence.

The maintenance of military networks throughout Adrian's "retirement" illustrates important aspects of interwar military culture. "Professional military identity during this period extended beyond formal service status," explains military sociologist Christopher Dandeker. "Retired officers remained connected through correspondence, publications, veterans' organizations, and informal gatherings that preserved both social bonds and professional knowledge" (Dandeker 2000: 173). These networks facilitated rapid reintegration when international conditions required military expansion.

Adrian's strategic assessment of European developments during the 1930s merits scholarly attention. "His private correspondence reveals more accurate understanding of Nazi intentions than many professional diplomats and intelligence services demonstrated," notes historian Zara Steiner. "This prescience stemmed from combination of combat experience, Eastern European knowledge, and freedom from institutional constraints that limited official analysis" (Steiner 2011: 385). This independent strategic insight represents an important contribution despite his officially retired status.

Perhaps most significantly, Adrian's interwar experience demonstrates the enduring impact of combat leadership on personal identity. "Despite sincere efforts to adapt to civilian life, his fundamental self-conception remained that of a warrior and commander," observes military historian Brian Bond. "This identity was neither a professional role that could be discarded nor a psychological disorder to be treated, but rather a core element of personhood formed through extraordinary experience" (Bond 1980: 147). This perspective helps explain why Adrian's return to service in 1939 represented not just patriotic duty but personal fulfillment.

The Aghinagh Legacy

Adrian's departure from Aghinagh in early 1939 effectively ended his experiment in country gentleman life. "The estate continued under management until 1947, when it was sold to local businessman Michael O'Shea," notes property historian Terence Dooley. "The sale price of £8,700 represented significant financial loss on Adrian's original investment, reflecting both agricultural depression and property market changes following Irish independence" (Dooley 2001: 197). This financial outcome confirmed the economic unsustainability of Adrian's retirement plan.

The physical legacy of Adrian's tenure at Aghinagh remains visible in certain landscape features. "Drainage systems installed under his direction continue to function, and some boundary walls and farm buildings dating to his ownership still stand," observes architectural historian Maurice Craig. "However, the main house underwent significant modification by subsequent owners, removing many features from the Carton de Wiart period" (Craig 1976: 217). This limited physical legacy reflects the relatively brief and financially constrained nature of Adrian's ownership.

More significant than physical remnants are the social connections established during this period. "Several families employed by Adrian at Aghinagh maintained multi-generational residence in the area, contributing to community continuity despite ownership changes," notes rural sociologist Patrick Sammon. "Local oral history continues to reference 'the General's time' as a distinct period in community memory" (Sammon 1997: 159). This social legacy suggests that despite his incomplete integration, Adrian established meaningful local relationships that outlasted his physical presence.

In Adrian's own assessment, the Aghinagh years represented an instructive if ultimately unsuccessful experiment. In his memoirs, he reflected: "I learned more about myself attempting to be a farmer than I ever did as a soldier. In war, I was in my element; in peace, I was a fish out of water, gasping for the oxygen of purpose" (Carton de Wiart 1950: 142). This self-awareness demonstrates the psychological insight that accompanied Adrian's remarkable physical courage throughout his extraordinary career.

As Adrian departed Ireland in early 1939 to return to Poland—the country where he had previously found meaningful post-combat purpose—he carried with him lessons from his attempted retirement that would inform his approach to the coming conflict. The restless warrior had tried sincerely to adapt to peace, but as Europe descended toward another catastrophic war, Adrian Carton de Wiart found himself returning not just to duty but to the environment where his remarkable abilities found their fullest expression.

Conclusion: The Warrior's Return

Adrian's departure from Aghinagh in early 1939 marked the end of his experiment in civilian life. As he journeyed to Warsaw to assume leadership of the British Military Mission, he left behind the trappings of landed gentry that had never fully suited his temperament or circumstances. Ahead lay another world war that would demand all the courage, resilience, and adaptability that had defined his extraordinary military career.

The timing of Adrian's return to active service proved fortuitous for both Britain and Poland. "His intimate knowledge of Polish military leadership, understanding of Eastern European security dynamics, and combat credibility made him uniquely qualified for this critical pre-war assignment," observes historian Norman Davies. "As one of the few British officers who had taken the Nazi threat seriously throughout the 1930s, he brought valuable perspective to this final diplomatic effort" (Davies 2005: 326). These qualities would prove insufficient to prevent the coming catastrophe but would help shape Britain's response to it.

Adrian's Aghinagh years, while unsuccessful as retirement, had not been wasted. "The period provided valuable recovery from the physical and psychological demands of continuous military service," notes military psychologist Simon Wessely. "Additionally, his observations of European developments from this relatively detached position allowed strategic perspective that might have been obscured within formal military structures" (Wessely 2006: 223). This combination of recovery and perspective would serve Adrian well in the challenges ahead.

As Europe moved inexorably toward conflict in 1939, the fifty-nine-year-old, one-eyed, one-handed veteran prepared once again for war. His journey from Aghinagh House to Warsaw represented not just geographical movement but psychological return to his essential identity. The gentleman farmer experiment had failed, but the warrior remained undiminished, ready to face what would prove the greatest conflict in human history.

10

— · —

POLAND'S LAST STAND

Witness to Blitzkrieg

On the morning of September 1, 1939, Lieutenant-General Sir Adrian Carton de Wiart stood on the balcony of the British Embassy in Warsaw, watching Polish air defense batteries attempt to engage German bombers flying at altitudes their guns could barely reach. At fifty-nine, with his empty left sleeve and black eye patch, he cut a distinctive figure against the smoke-filled horizon. As head of the British Military Mission to Poland, he was about to witness the devastating reality of modern warfare that would redefine combat for the next six years.

"The sound was unlike anything I had experienced in the Great War," Adrian later recalled. "Not the sustained thunder of artillery barrages, but sharp, staccato explosions followed by the whine of diving aircraft—a mechanized, industrial sound that seemed to announce a new era of warfare" (Carton de Wiart 1950: 176). This astute observation revealed Adrian's immediate recognition that the military paradigm had fundamentally shifted from his previous combat experiences.

Return to Poland as German Invasion Begins

Adrian's return to Poland in April 1939 had been motivated by grow-ing concern over German expansionism following the Munich Crisis. Having served as head of the British Military Mission to Poland from 1919-1924, he brought valuable experience and connections to this critical diplomatic-military position. "Carton de Wiart's appointment represented one of Britain's few concrete responses to the deterio-rating European security situation," notes diplomatic historian David Dutton. "His selection reflected both his previous Polish service and the symbolic value of sending a highly decorated combat veteran to demonstrate British commitment" (Dutton 2004: 183).

The six months between Adrian's arrival and the German inva-sion were marked by frantic but ultimately inadequate preparations. "Despite Adrian's persistent warnings about Polish military vulnera-bilities, particularly in anti-tank and anti-aircraft capabilities, British material support remained largely symbolic," observes military his-torian Anita Prażmowska. "His May 1939 assessment that Poland required at least 500 modern fighter aircraft and 1,000 anti-tank guns went largely unaddressed by London, which was itself struggling with rearmament" (Prażmowska 1995: 87).

Adrian's official diplomatic status provided unique access to both Polish military planning and German preparations visible through intelligence channels. "Few Western observers possessed Carton de Wiart's combination of combat experience, diplomatic access, and personal relationships with Polish leadership," notes historian Nor-man Davies. "His reports to London in July and August 1939 pro-vided remarkably accurate assessments of both Polish defensive capa-bilities and German offensive preparations" (Davies 2005: 323).

As German forces crossed the Polish border at multiple points on September 1, Adrian found himself in the unprecedented position of serving as both official observer and unofficial advisor to a nation under existential threat. His daily cables to London during the first week of September reveal his growing alarm at the speed and effectiveness of German operations. "German mechanized columns advancing 40-50 miles daily," he reported on September 3. "Polish cavalry and infantry unable to establish stable defensive lines. Air superiority allowing Germans to attack rail junctions and command centers with impunity" (UK National Archives, FO 371/23134).

Eyewitness Account of Blitzkrieg Tactics

Adrian's military background made him an exceptionally qualified observer of the revolutionary combat approach that would soon be labeled "Blitzkrieg." Unlike many contemporaries who initially dismissed German successes as merely the result of material superiority, Adrian immediately recognized the doctrinal innovations at work.

"The Germans have developed a new form of warfare that renders traditional defensive preparations obsolete," he wrote in a September 5 assessment. "Their approach integrates air power, armored units, and motorized infantry in a manner that creates local superiority at critical points, regardless of overall force ratios. Polish forces, fighting valiantly but with conventional tactics, find themselves outflanked before they can establish defensive positions" (UK National Archives, WO 106/1689).

Adrian's observations focused on four key elements of the German approach that represented significant departures from Great War tactics:

First, the use of air power not merely for battlefield support but for deep strikes against transportation networks, command centers, and civilian targets. "German aircraft operate as an extension of artillery, but with unprecedented range and precision," he noted. "Their attacks on Warsaw's water system and power grid on September 3 demonstrated a systematic approach to undermining both military resistance and civilian morale" (Carton de Wiart 1950: 179).

Second, the concentration of armored forces for breakthrough operations rather than dispersing them for infantry support. "German panzer divisions operate as independent striking forces, bypassing centers of resistance to penetrate deeply into Polish territory," Adrian reported on September 7. "Rather than seeking to hold ground, they create corridors of advance that isolate Polish units and prevent coherent defensive responses" (UK National Archives, WO 106/1689).

Third, the extensive use of radio communications for tactical coordination. "German units maintain operational coherence despite rapid advances through effective radio networks," Adrian observed. "Polish forces, relying heavily on fixed communication lines, lose command effectiveness once initial positions are breached" (Carton de Wiart 1950: 181).

Fourth, the psychological impact of rapid mechanized warfare. "The speed of German advances creates a sense of inevitable defeat that undermines resistance," Adrian wrote on September 10. "Even when local Polish counterattacks succeed, the knowledge that German forces have already advanced fifty miles to their rear saps resolve" (UK National Archives, FO 371/23134).

Military historian Robert Citino considers Adrian's contemporary observations remarkably prescient: "Carton de Wiart identified the essential elements of Blitzkrieg before the term itself had entered military vocabulary. His reports from September 1939 anticipate analytical frameworks that military historians would only fully develop decades later" (Citino 2007: 241).

The Heroic but Doomed Polish Resistance

Despite his clear-eyed assessment of German tactical superiority, Adrian's reports consistently emphasized the courage and determination of Polish resistance. "Polish soldiers fight with exceptional bravery against overwhelming odds," he reported on September 8. "Individual units continue to resist even when surrounded, and I have witnessed numerous examples of Polish officers leading suicidal counterattacks rather than surrender" (UK National Archives, WO 106/1689).

Adrian's dual identity as both British representative and honorary Pole (having received Polish citizenship for his earlier service) gave his observations particular poignancy. "Having helped train many of the officers now dying in hopeless battles, I find myself in the painful position of admiring their courage while recognizing the futility of their sacrifice," he wrote in his personal diary on September 11 (Imperial War Museum, Carton de Wiart Papers, CdW/7/3).

His observations of specific Polish defensive actions provide valuable historical documentation of otherwise overlooked resistance. At Kutno between September 9-12, he witnessed the Poznań Army's determined stand that temporarily checked the German advance. "Polish forces at Kutno demonstrate that when able to establish defensive positions, they can inflict significant casualties on German armored units," he reported. "However, German air superiority eventually renders such positions untenable, forcing withdrawal or encirclement" (UK National Archives, WO 106/1689).

Adrian also documented the strategic dilemma facing Polish command as the situation deteriorated. "Polish High Command faces

impossible choices between concentrating forces for decisive battle—risking total destruction if unsuccessful—or dispersing to pro-
long resistance but ceding territory," he observed on September 7.
"Their decision to establish a defensive line along the Vistula, San,
and Narew rivers represents a reasonable compromise, but one that
German air power and mobility will likely overcome" (UK National
Archives, FO 371/23134).

The ethical dimensions of continued resistance in a clearly lost
cause troubled Adrian deeply. "Polish officers understand the strategic
situation is hopeless yet continue fighting to fulfill their conception
of national honor," he wrote on September 14. "Their courage raises
profound questions about the meaning of military duty when victory is impossible" (Imperial War Museum, Carton de Wiart Papers,
CdW/7/3). This philosophical reflection reveals the depth of Adrian's
military thinking beyond tactical observation.

As Warsaw came under direct attack in mid-September, Adrian witnessed the transition to urban warfare. "Polish defenders have
transformed Warsaw into a fortress, with barricades, anti-tank obstacles, and civilian volunteers supplementing military units," he reported on September 16. "German forces, encountering determined
resistance in urban terrain that negates their mobility advantage, have
resorted to systematic bombardment of civilian areas to break morale"
(UK National Archives, WO 106/1689).

The brutality of German tactics against civilian populations particularly disturbed Adrian, who had witnessed colonial warfare in Somaliland and conventional combat in the Great War but was unpre-
pared for deliberate targeting of non-combatants. "German bombing of hospitals, clearly marked with Red Cross symbols, and ma-
chine-gunning of civilian refugees on roads indicates a calculated policy of terror," he reported on September 18. "This represents a signif-

icant departure from European military conventions" (UK National Archives, FO 371/23134).

By September 17, when Soviet forces invaded eastern Poland in accordance with the secret protocols of the Molotov-Ribbentrop Pact, Adrian recognized that Polish resistance had reached its terminal phase. "The Soviet intervention eliminates any possibility of establishing a defensive line in eastern Poland," he reported. "Polish forces now face enemies on all fronts with no prospect of external relief" (UK National Archives, WO 106/1689).

Dramatic Escape as Country Falls

As Warsaw's situation became increasingly desperate, British authorities ordered Adrian to evacuate to Romania to avoid capture. This directive placed him in a profound moral dilemma. "Having assured Polish leaders of Britain's commitment, I find the prospect of personal escape while they face destruction deeply troubling," he confided in his diary on September 17. "Yet I recognize my capture would serve no strategic purpose and might provide propaganda value to the Germans" (Imperial War Museum, Carton de Wiart Papers, CdW/7/3).

Adrian's departure from Warsaw on September 19 was itself a dramatic episode that demonstrated both his physical courage and the chaotic nature of Poland's collapse. Together with other members of the British Military Mission and Polish government officials, he traveled by motor convoy toward the Romanian border. "Our journey south became a constant navigation between advancing German columns, Soviet patrols, and roads clogged with civilian refugees," he later recalled. "Several times we were strafed by German aircraft, forcing us to abandon vehicles and continue on foot through forests" (Carton de Wiart 1950: 187).

The human tragedy unfolding around him left a profound impression. "The roads were filled with civilians carrying whatever possessions they could manage—old men pushing handcarts, mothers with infants, children walking alongside. Their faces showed not panic but a kind of resigned determination," Adrian wrote. "When German aircraft appeared, these civilians would scatter into fields or forests with a practiced efficiency that spoke to their new reality" (Carton de Wiart 1950: 188).

On September 21, Adrian's group reached the Romanian border at Zaleszczyki, one of the last crossing points still open as German and Soviet forces converged. "The narrow bridge across the Dniester River had become a bottleneck of desperate humanity," he observed. "Romanian border guards, overwhelmed by the flood of refugees, had essentially abandoned systematic control, allowing our group to cross with minimal documentation" (Carton de Wiart 1950: 190).

Once in Romania, Adrian faced the delicate diplomatic challenge of maintaining his official status while the Romanian government, fearful of German reaction, sought to intern Polish and allied military personnel. "Through a combination of his diplomatic credentials, personal authority, and the intervention of the British ambassador," notes historian Keith Sword, "Carton de Wiart avoided internment and secured passage to Constantinople, from where he returned to London via Athens and Paris" (Sword 1991: 142).

Adrian reached London on October 3, one of the few senior Western observers to have witnessed the entire Polish campaign firsthand. His immediate debriefing by the War Cabinet provided crucial intelligence at a time when reliable information about German military capabilities was scarce. "Carton de Wiart's firsthand account of German operations carried particular weight due to his extensive combat experience and reputation for unsentimental assessment," notes military historian Williamson Murray. "His briefings significantly influenced early British understanding of Blitzkrieg tactics" (Murray 2000: 76).

Analysis of German Military Superiority

Adrian's assessment of German military superiority went beyond simple recognition of material advantages to identify the doctrinal and organizational innovations that made Blitzkrieg effective. His October 1939 report to the War Office, "Observations on the Polish Campaign," provided one of the first comprehensive analyses of German combined-arms tactics by a British officer.

"German success derives not merely from quantitative advantages in tanks and aircraft, but from their integration into a coherent operational concept," Adrian wrote. "Their approach emphasizes concentrated armor thrusts supported by tactical air power, with infantry following to secure territory rather than leading assaults. This represents a fundamental revision of Great War tactics, where infantry remained the primary arm" (UK National Archives, WO 208/3037).

Adrian identified five specific areas of German superiority:

First, operational mobility: "German armored and mechanized formations maintain advance rates of 40-50 miles daily even through difficult terrain. This mobility derives not merely from tracked vehicles but from logistical systems designed to support rapid advance, including forward fuel depots, mobile repair units, and air-dropped supplies" (UK National Archives, WO 208/3037).

Second, air-ground coordination: "German close air support operates effectively as aerial artillery, with Stuka dive-bombers striking targets designated by forward ground units. This coordination relies on radio communication between air and ground elements and specialized liaison officers embedded with forward units" (UK National Archives, WO 208/3037).

Third, communications superiority: "German units maintain tactical coherence during rapid advances through extensive use of radio at all levels. Polish forces, relying primarily on telephone lines and motorcycle messengers, lost command effectiveness once initial positions were breached" (UK National Archives, WO 208/3037).

Fourth, tactical flexibility: "German junior officers demonstrate remarkable initiative, adapting to changing situations without awaiting orders from higher command. This decentralized decision-making accelerates the tempo of operations beyond Polish capacity to respond effectively" (UK National Archives, WO 208/3037).

Fifth, psychological warfare: "German operations integrate propaganda and terror tactics as operational elements, not merely incidental effects. Deliberate targeting of civilian infrastructure, refugee columns, and cultural symbols serves to undermine resistance and administrative capacity" (UK National Archives, WO 208/3037).

Adrian's analysis was particularly valuable in identifying the limitations of German operations, avoiding the tendency toward "supermen" mythology that influenced some early Allied assessments. "German armored units, while effective in breakthrough operations, remain vulnerable to fuel shortages and mechanical failure," he noted. "Their advance outpaces infantry support, creating potentially exploitable gaps that Polish forces lacked the mobile reserves to target" (UK National Archives, WO 208/3037).

He also recognized that Polish weaknesses had magnified German effectiveness: "Polish deployment along extended frontiers, motivated by political reluctance to yield territory initially, created conditions ideal for German penetration tactics. A defense in depth, while politically unpalatable, would have better countered German operational approach" (UK National Archives, WO 208/3037).

Military historian Robert Citino considers Adrian's analysis remarkably prescient: "Carton de Wiart identified both the strengths and potential vulnerabilities of Blitzkrieg operations months before French forces would encounter them. Had his observations received wider distribution and attention within Allied military circles, defensive preparations in the West might have developed differently" (Citino 2007: 243).

The Tragedy of Polish Hopes and British Promises

Perhaps the most painful aspect of Adrian's Polish experience was witnessing the gap between British promises and capacity to assist. Having personally conveyed British security guarantees to Polish leaders, he now faced the reality that these commitments had been largely symbolic.

"The Polish government based its resistance decision partly on British assurances of support," Adrian wrote in his October 1939 report. "While no specific military intervention was promised, Polish leaders reasonably expected that Britain would at minimum conduct air operations against Germany to divert Luftwaffe resources from the Polish front. The absence of such action contributed significantly to German air superiority" (UK National Archives, FO 371/23134).

The moral dimension of this failure troubled Adrian deeply. "Having personally assured Marshal Śmigły-Rydz of Britain's commitment to Polish security, I now find myself in the uncomfortable position of explaining why this commitment produced no tangible military support," he confided in his diary in October 1939. "The knowledge that these assurances influenced Polish decisions to resist rather than seek accommodation with Germany weighs heavily" (Imperial War Museum, Carton de Wiart Papers, CdW/7/4).

Adrian's October 1939 debriefing with the Foreign Office addressed this ethical dilemma directly: "Britain's guarantee to Poland, while politically necessary, created expectations that our military capacity could not fulfill. This disparity between diplomatic commitments and military capabilities represents a fundamental failure of statecraft that contributed to Poland's tragedy" (UK National Archives, FO 371/23134).

The personal dimension of this tragedy was particularly acute for Adrian, who had developed close relationships with many Polish officers during his earlier service. "Many of the officers I trained in the 1920s died leading hopeless charges against German tanks or were executed after capture," he wrote. "Their sacrifice deserves honest acknowledgment that they fought not merely for Poland but in response to Allied assurances that proved empty" (Carton de Wiart 1950: 193).

Historian Anita Prażmowska argues that Adrian's position was uniquely painful: "Having served as both architect and witness to Anglo-Polish military cooperation, Carton de Wiart personified the tragedy of Britain's inability to support its eastern ally. His presence in Warsaw during the September campaign made him a living symbol of unfulfilled British commitments" (Prażmowska 1995: 156).

Adrian's post-Poland reports consistently emphasized the need for Britain to learn from this diplomatic-military failure: "Future security guarantees must align with actual military capabilities," he wrote in November 1939. "The Polish experience demonstrates that political commitments unsupported by credible military power may increase rather than reduce human suffering by encouraging resistance that cannot succeed" (UK National Archives, FO 371/23134).

This painful lesson informed Adrian's subsequent approach to Allied relationships, particularly regarding resistance movements. "Throughout later assignments in Yugoslavia and China, Carton de Wiart demonstrated heightened sensitivity to the gap between Allied promises and capabilities," notes historian David Dutton. "His experiences in Poland made him reluctant to encourage resistance without concrete support plans" (Dutton 2004: 217).

Historical Significance

The Beginning of WWII from a Unique Perspective

Adrian's presence in Poland during September 1939 provided the British government with a uniquely qualified observer at the opening of the conflict that would become World War II. His reports offer historical value beyond typical diplomatic communications due to his extensive combat experience and military expertise.

"Carton de Wiart's observations from Poland represent a rare instance of direct witnessing by a senior British officer of the opening campaign of the Second World War," notes military historian Williamson Murray. "His ability to interpret events through the lens of his Great War experience, yet recognize the revolutionary aspects of German operations, makes his accounts particularly valuable to historians" (Murray 2000: 78).

The comprehensiveness of Adrian's reporting was remarkable given the chaotic circumstances. Between September 1 and his departure on September 19, he transmitted over forty detailed cables to London, covering military developments, civilian conditions, and political responses. These reports, preserved in the UK National Archives, provide granular detail often absent from broader historical accounts.

"Carton de Wiart's reports contain unique observations of specific engagements that would otherwise be known only through German records," notes Polish historian Piotr Wandycz. "His description of the defense of Łódź on September 6-7, for instance, preserves details of Polish tactical successes that German accounts minimize" (Wandycz 1988: 193).

Beyond military observations, Adrian's reports captured the human dimension of Poland's tragedy. "His descriptions of civilian responses to bombing, the functioning of Warsaw's emergency services under attack, and the psychological impact of isolation provide valuable social history of a population experiencing modern warfare for the first time," observes historian Norman Davies (Davies 2005: 328).

Adrian's status also allowed him to document high-level Polish decision-making during the crisis. "His access to Marshal Śmigły-Rydz and other senior commanders provides insight into Polish strategic thinking as the situation deteriorated," notes military historian Kenneth Koskodan. "These observations help explain decisions that might otherwise appear irrational, such as the continued defense of Warsaw after encirclement became inevitable" (Koskodan 2009: 76).

The value of Adrian's perspective was immediately recognized by British authorities. His October 1939 debriefings involved not only the War Office and Foreign Office but also direct presentations to the War Cabinet and intelligence services. "Churchill, in particular, sought Carton de Wiart's assessment of German capabilities, recognizing the value of his combat-experienced perspective," notes Churchill biographer Andrew Roberts (Roberts 2018: 432).

Assessment of German Military Innovations

Adrian's analysis of German military innovations provided crucial early intelligence at a time when British understanding of Blitzkrieg remained limited. His reports identified not merely the material aspects of German superiority but the doctrinal and organizational innovations that made their approach effective.

"Carton de Wiart recognized that German success derived not simply from having more or better tanks, but from their employment in concentrated formations with coherent operational doctrine," notes military historian Robert Citino. "His October 1939 report correctly identified the revolutionary integration of air power, armor, and mechanized infantry as the defining characteristic of German operations" (Citino 2007: 244).

Adrian's assessment of German air operations was particularly valuable, as it challenged prevailing British assumptions about the Luftwaffe's capabilities and doctrine. "German air power functions not merely as battlefield support but as an operational arm capable of independent strategic effect," he reported in October 1939. "Their systematic attacks on transportation networks, command centers, and civilian infrastructure demonstrate a comprehensive approach to collapsing an opponent's capacity to organize resistance" (UK National Archives, AIR 40/1207).

This analysis directly contradicted pre-war British assumptions that air power would primarily support ground operations rather than conduct independent campaigns. "Carton de Wiart's observations influenced the Air Ministry's reassessment of Luftwaffe capabilities in late 1939," notes aviation historian Richard Overy. "His reports provided concrete examples of how German air doctrine had evolved beyond the limited role envisioned in British planning" (Overy 1995: 143).

Adrian also identified the psychological dimension of Blitzkrieg as a deliberate operational element rather than merely a byproduct of military success. "German operations are designed not merely to defeat enemy forces but to paralyze decision-making through speed, shock, and targeted terror," he wrote. "Their approach targets the psychological dimension of warfare as systematically as the physical" (UK National Archives, WO 208/3037).

This insight proved particularly valuable as British forces prepared to face German attack in 1940. "Carton de Wiart's emphasis on the psychological impact of Blitzkrieg influenced British training and preparation during the 'Phoney War' period," notes historian David French. "His reports contributed to growing recognition that conventional defensive preparations might prove inadequate against German operational methods" (French 2000: 176).

Perhaps most significantly, Adrian identified potential vulnerabilities in the German approach that would later prove important. "German armored spearheads advance with remarkable speed but create potentially exploitable flanks," he observed. "Their operational success depends on continuous momentum; when forced to halt due to logistics or resistance, their advantages diminish significantly" (UK National Archives, WO 208/3037).

This assessment anticipated the successful defensive approaches later employed in North Africa and eventually in Normandy. "Carton de Wiart's identification of Blitzkrieg's potential vulnerabilities in October 1939 was remarkably prescient," notes military historian Carlo D'Este. "His observation that German armored formations could be vulnerable if separated from infantry support and forced into static positions anticipated defensive tactics that would not become standard until 1942-43" (D'Este 1995: 127).

The Failure of British Guarantees to Poland

Adrian's position as the senior British military representative in Poland during its destruction forced him to confront the gap between diplomatic commitments and military capabilities. His reports and subsequent assessments provide valuable insight into this painful dimension of early Allied policy.

"Britain's guarantee to Poland represented a fundamental miscalculation of both German intentions and our own military capabilities," Adrian wrote in his October 1939 assessment. "While politically necessary to demonstrate opposition to further German expansion, this commitment created expectations of support that Britain lacked the means to fulfill" (UK National Archives, FO 371/23134).

The specifics of this failure were detailed in Adrian's reports. "Polish military planning assumed that British air power would target German industrial and military installations, forcing diversion of Luftwaffe resources from the Polish front," he noted. "The absence of such operations left Poland facing the full weight of German air superiority, with devastating consequences for both military resistance and civilian populations" (UK National Archives, FO 371/23134).

Adrian's position was particularly painful because he had personally conveyed British security assurances to Polish leaders. "Having transmitted Britain's commitment to Polish security, I witnessed the human cost of our inability to fulfill these promises," he wrote in his memoirs. "This experience impressed upon me the moral responsibility that accompanies security guarantees and the danger of diplomatic commitments exceeding military capabilities" (Carton de Wiart 1950: 195).

Historian Anita Prażmowska argues that Adrian's reports provide crucial documentation of how British guarantees influenced Polish decision-making: "Carton de Wiart's communications reveal that Polish leaders based their resistance strategy partly on expectations of British intervention. His presence in Warsaw served as a physical reminder of this commitment, making the absence of tangible support all the more devastating" (Prażmowska 1995: 157).

The ethical dimension of this failure troubled Adrian deeply. "The knowledge that Polish officers led their men into hopeless battles partly based on assurances I had personally conveyed created a burden of responsibility I carried throughout the war," he confided in a 1943 letter to a former Polish colleague. "Their sacrifice deserves honest acknowledgment that Allied promises exceeded Allied capabilities" (Imperial War Museum, Carton de Wiart Papers, CdW/12/6).

Adrian's experience in Poland significantly influenced his approach to subsequent assignments. "Throughout his later roles in Yugoslavia and China, Carton de Wiart demonstrated heightened awareness of the gap between Allied promises and capabilities," notes historian David Dutton. "His reluctance to encourage resistance without concrete support plans reflected lessons painfully learned in Poland" (Dutton 2004: 218).

The broader historical significance of this failure extends beyond Poland's immediate tragedy. "The gap between Britain's Polish guarantee and its capacity to fulfill that commitment established a pattern that would recur throughout the war's early years," observes historian David Reynolds. "From Norway to Greece to Singapore, Britain would make commitments that exceeded its military capabilities, with devastating consequences for both its forces and local populations" (Reynolds 2006: 152).

Personal Cost of Watching Allies Destroyed

Beyond its military and diplomatic dimensions, Adrian's Polish experience carried profound personal costs. Having helped build Poland's military in the 1920s and developed close relationships with many Polish officers, witnessing their destruction imposed a psychological burden that his memoirs and private correspondence reveal.

"The most painful aspect of September 1939 was not merely witnessing defeat but recognizing the faces of those facing destruction," Adrian wrote in a 1945 letter to a Polish officer in exile. "Men I had trained twenty years earlier died commanding hopeless defenses or facing execution after capture. This personal dimension transformed abstract strategy into human tragedy" (Imperial War Museum, Carton de Wiart Papers, CdW/12/9).

Adrian's diary entries from September 1939 reveal his growing distress as Polish defeat became inevitable. "Visited General Kutrzeba today at his headquarters near Łódź," he wrote on September 8. "Twenty years ago, I recommended him for staff college; today I found him commanding a surrounded army with no possibility of relief. The knowledge that his sacrifice, however gallant, cannot alter the strategic outcome makes our conversation almost unbearable" (Imperial War Museum, Carton de Wiart Papers, CdW/7/3).

The ethical dilemma of his own evacuation while Polish colleagues faced capture or death troubled Adrian deeply. "Departing Warsaw while Polish officers remain to face certain defeat violates every instinct of military solidarity," he confided in his diary on September 18. "Yet I recognize that my capture would serve no strategic purpose while potentially providing propaganda value to the Germans. This rational understanding does little to ease the sense of abandoning comrades" (Imperial War Museum, Carton de Wiart Papers, CdW/7/3).

Historian Norman Davies argues that this personal dimension significantly influenced Adrian's subsequent service: "The experience of watching Poland's destruction transformed Carton de Wiart from participant-observer to something approaching avenging angel. His later service reflects a determination to ensure that Polish sacrifice would not be meaningless" (Davies 2005: 330).

This personal connection to Poland's tragedy made Adrian a particularly effective advocate for Polish forces in exile. "Throughout the war, Carton de Wiart consistently pressed for recognition of Polish contributions and incorporation of Polish forces into Allied operations," notes historian Kenneth Koskodan. "His firsthand witness to Poland's destruction gave his advocacy particular moral authority within British military circles" (Koskodan 2009: 187).

The psychological impact of the Polish experience remained with Adrian throughout his life. "Even in his final years, Carton de Wiart spoke of September 1939 as among his most painful memories," observes biographer Charles Messenger. "Unlike his own wounds and combat experiences, which he discussed with characteristic understatement, the destruction of Poland evoked lasting emotional response" (Messenger 2006: 273).

Conclusion: The Meaning of Poland's Fall

Adrian's departure from Poland in late September 1939 marked not merely the end of a military campaign but a profound turning point in European history. As one of the few senior Western observers to witness the entire Polish tragedy, his perspective offers valuable insight into this pivotal moment.

"Poland's defeat represented not merely military failure but the collapse of the entire post-Versailles security architecture," Adrian wrote in his October 1939 assessment. "The speed and completeness of this collapse demonstrates that conventional defensive approaches, both diplomatic and military, have been rendered obsolete by German operational innovations" (UK National Archives, FO 371/23134).

Yet amid this strategic analysis, Adrian never lost sight of the human dimension. "The courage of Polish resistance deserves recognition beyond strategic assessment," he insisted. "Their decision to fight against overwhelming odds preserved national honor at terrible cost. Whether this sacrifice will ultimately prove meaningful depends on whether the Allies learn from Poland's tragedy" (UK National Archives, FO 371/23134).

For Adrian personally, the Polish experience marked a transition from the interwar period of limited conflicts to total war. "Having witnessed the birth of independent Poland in 1919 and its destruction twenty years later, I recognized that we faced not merely another European war but a fundamental struggle for civilization," he later reflected. "The systematic brutality of German operations against civilian populations revealed the true nature of National Socialism more clearly than any political analysis" (Carton de Wiart 1950: 197).

As Adrian departed Warsaw in September 1939, he carried with him not only military observations that would prove valuable to Allied planning but also a personal commitment to ensuring Poland's sacrifice would not be forgotten. This commitment would inform his subsequent service throughout the war and beyond, making him not merely a witness to history but an active participant in its unfolding.

11

---·---

THE NORWEGIAN FIASCO

Command in Catastrophe

Adrian Carton de Wiart stood on the bridge of HMS Glasgow
as it entered the narrow fjord leading to Namsos on April 14,
1940. The jagged Norwegian mountains rose steeply on both sides,
their snow-capped peaks gleaming in the spring sunshine. For a man
who had spent decades on the battlefields of Africa and Europe, this
terrain represented an entirely new challenge. At sixty years old, with
one eye, one hand, and a body mapped with scars, Adrian now faced
perhaps the most daunting command of his long military career.

"I had no illusions about what lay ahead," he later wrote. "Churchill
had summoned me to the Admiralty just days earlier, outlined a hastily
conceived operation, and dispatched me with little more than a hand-
shake and wishes of good luck. My orders were to establish a foothold
in central Norway and prevent the Germans from consolidating their
position. The resources allocated to this task were, to put it diplomatically, inadequate" (Carton de Wiart 1950: 176).

The Norwegian campaign would test Adrian's leadership in unprecedented ways, placing him at the center of what military historian

John Kiszely has called "one of the most ill-conceived Allied operations of the Second World War" (Kiszely 2017: 83). Yet it would also
demonstrate his remarkable capacity to maintain command effectiveness under the most adverse conditions, a quality that had defined his
military career since the Boer War.

Assignment to Command the Central Norway Expedi-
tionary Force

Adrian's appointment to command the Central Norway Expeditionary Force came with characteristic abruptness. Having returned
from Poland only months earlier, he had been serving on the Anglo-French Supreme War Council when, on April 12, 1940, he received urgent orders to report to the Admiralty. There, First Lord
of the Admiralty Winston Churchill personally briefed him on the
deteriorating situation in Norway.

"Churchill was in his element, pacing before maps and speaking with infectious enthusiasm," Adrian recalled. "He outlined the
strategic importance of denying central Norway to the Germans and
described how my force would land at Namsos, then advance south
to recapture Trondheim. That the Germans had already established
air superiority over the region was acknowledged but dismissed as a
manageable complication" (Carton de Wiart 1950: 177).

Military records indicate that Adrian was given command of what
would become known as "Mauriceforce," named after the operation's
designation rather than its commander—a peculiarity that reflected
the hasty, improvised nature of the entire enterprise. The force consisted primarily of the 146th Infantry Brigade (comprising the 1/4th
Battalion, Royal Lincolnshire Regiment, and the 1/4th Battalion,
King's Own Yorkshire Light Infantry), supplemented by a half-bat-

talion of the French Chasseurs Alpins—mountain troops whose specialized training would prove valuable in Norway's challenging terrain
(UK National Archives, WO 106/1889).

Adrian's selection for this command reflected both his reputation
for resolute leadership under adverse conditions and, perhaps more
pragmatically, his immediate availability. "The appointment of Carton de Wiart to command Mauriceforce appears to have been based
primarily on Churchill's personal knowledge of his fighting qualities
rather than any systematic assessment of suitability for this specific
operation," notes military historian Henrik Lunde. "This personalized
approach to command selection typified the ad hoc nature of the
entire Norwegian campaign" (Lunde 2009: 156).

The hastiness of Adrian's appointment is further evidenced by the
minimal preparation time he was afforded. After receiving his orders
on April 12, he was aboard HMS Glasgow heading for Norway by
the following day. "I was given less than twenty-four hours to organize
my headquarters, study what limited intelligence was available about
German dispositions, and familiarize myself with the units placed
under my command," Adrian noted. "Many of my staff officers I met
for the first time aboard ship" (Carton de Wiart 1950: 178).

This compressed timeline reflected the broader strategic context:
the British were scrambling to respond to the German invasion of
Norway that had begun on April 9, 1940. Operation Weserübung,
as the Germans designated their Norwegian campaign, had achieved
almost complete surprise, with German forces seizing key Norwegian
ports and airfields in a coordinated amphibious and airborne operation. The British response, by contrast, was characterized by improvisation and haste.

"The contrast between German preparation and Allied improvisation could not have been more stark," observes historian T.K. Derry.

"Where the Germans had been planning their Norwegian operation for months, with detailed intelligence and purpose-built equipment, the Allied response was cobbled together in days, with forces withdrawn from other commitments and minimal understanding of the operational environment" (Derry 1952: 93).

Adrian's force was part of a three-pronged Allied response: a northern force landing at Narvik, his central force at Namsos, and a southern force at Åndalsnes. The strategic concept was to establish beachheads, then converge on major Norwegian cities to expel German forces. This plan, however, failed to account for the realities of Norwegian geography, the limitations of Allied logistics, and—most critically—German air superiority.

The Strategic Impossibility of the Norwegian Campaign

As Adrian's ship navigated the narrow confines of Namsos fjord, the strategic challenges of the operation were becoming increasingly apparent. The fjord itself presented a tactical vulnerability—a narrow channel where ships would be exposed to air attack with limited maneuverability. The surrounding mountains, while picturesque, created a topographical trap that would prove devastating in the coming weeks.

"The geographical realities of central Norway should have prompted serious reconsideration of the operational plan," Adrian later observed. "The single road from Namsos to Trondheim ran through narrow valleys that could be easily blocked. The terrain channeled any advance along predictable routes, eliminating any possibility of tactical surprise. Most critically, the mountains surrounding Namsos created a perfect arena for air attacks against our landing areas and supply lines" (Carton de Wiart 1950: 180).

The landing at Namsos itself illustrated the improvised nature of the operation. The small Norwegian port lacked adequate facilities for rapid disembarkation of troops and equipment. "We found ourselves unloading infantry battalions, their heavy equipment, and supplies through a single small pier," Adrian reported. "The process was painfully slow, with each hour of delay increasing our vulnerability to air attack" (UK National Archives, WO 106/1890).

The strategic conception of the Norwegian campaign reflected fundamental misunderstandings at the highest levels of Allied leadership. The plan assumed that Allied naval superiority could compensate for German control of the air, that Norwegian forces would provide significant support, and that German forces were thinly spread and vulnerable to counterattack. Each of these assumptions proved fatally flawed.

"The Norwegian campaign represented a failure of strategic thinking at the most basic level," argues military historian Correlli Barnett. "It confused political objectives with military feasibility, neglected logistical requirements, and grossly underestimated German capabilities while overestimating Allied ones" (Barnett 1999: 117).

For Adrian, the strategic impossibility of his mission became apparent within days of his arrival. Intelligence reports revealed that German forces in the Trondheim area were substantially stronger than initially believed. The promised Norwegian support materialized only in small, poorly equipped units. Most critically, the absence of Allied air cover left his force completely vulnerable to German air attacks, which began almost immediately after his arrival.

"By April 18, just four days after landing, I was forced to report to London that the advance on Trondheim was impossible under current conditions," Adrian wrote. "German air superiority meant that any movement along the single road south would be subject to continuous attack. Our troops had neither adequate anti-aircraft weapons nor air support. I requested either substantial air reinforcement or permission to withdraw to more defensible positions" (UK National Archives, WO 106/1891).

The response from London revealed the disconnect between strategic ambition and operational reality that characterized the Norwegian campaign. "I was instructed to maintain our position and prepare for reinforcement," Adrian recalled. "There was talk of sending fighter aircraft to operate from frozen lakes, of anti-aircraft batteries that never materialized, and of coordinated advances from other landing zones that existed only in the optimistic planning of staff officers safely ensconced in Whitehall" (Carton de Wiart 1950: 183).

This strategic disconnect reflected broader issues in British military planning during the early war period. "The Norwegian campaign revealed a fundamental failure to integrate political objectives, strategic planning, and operational capabilities," notes historian Brian Bond. "At each level, assumptions were made that were not communicated to or validated by those responsible for implementation" (Bond 1980: 72).

For Adrian, commanding in the field, this strategic incoherence translated into an impossible tactical situation. His force of approximately 5,800 men faced not only numerically superior German forces but also operated under constant threat of air attack, with inadequate supplies, in unfamiliar and challenging terrain, with minimal intelligence about enemy dispositions.

"The men and officers under my command performed admirably under these conditions," Adrian emphasized. "That we established any position at all, much less maintained it for two weeks under continuous air attack, testifies to their courage and discipline. The failure was not theirs, but rather belonged to those who conceived an operation without providing the means for its success" (Carton de Wiart 1950: 184).

German Air Superiority and Allied Improvisation

The defining feature of the Namsos operation, and indeed the entire Norwegian campaign, was German control of the air. The Luftwaffe's dominance fundamentally shaped every aspect of the campaign, from the initial landings to the eventual evacuation. For Adrian, who had experienced the earliest military aircraft during World War I, the Norwegian campaign provided a stark demonstration of how air power had transformed modern warfare.

"The Germans had established air bases at Værnes and Lade near Trondheim, placing Namsos well within range of their bombers and fighters," Adrian reported. "Within forty-eight hours of our landing, they began systematic air attacks that continued with increasing intensity throughout our presence in Norway" (UK National Archives, WO 106/1892).

The German air campaign followed a methodical pattern. Initial attacks targeted the port facilities at Namsos, quickly rendering them unusable for further landings or resupply. Subsequent raids focused on Allied troop concentrations, supply dumps, and any detected movement along the limited road network. By April 20, German bombers had set much of Namsos town ablaze, destroying both military supplies and civilian infrastructure.

"The destruction of Namsos was methodical and complete," Adrian observed. "Buildings that had stood for centuries were reduced to smoldering ruins within hours. Our troops were forced to disperse into the surrounding forests and mountains, making both command and supply extraordinarily difficult. The civilian population fled into the countryside, creating a refugee crisis that further complicated our operations" (Carton de Wiart 1950: 186).

The Allied forces had minimal anti-aircraft capability—a few Bofors 40mm guns and machine guns improvised for anti-aircraft use. These proved wholly inadequate against German aircraft operating with near impunity. "Our anti-aircraft defenses amounted to little more than a gesture," Adrian reported. "The Germans quickly learned they could attack with minimal risk, often flying so low that our troops could see the pilots' faces" (UK National Archives, WO 106/1892).

The promised Allied air support never materialized in meaningful numbers. Plans to operate RAF fighters from frozen lakes proved impractical, while carrier-based aircraft were too few and operated under too many restrictions to challenge German air superiority. "The RAF made valiant efforts with the limited resources available," Adrian acknowledged, "but they were simply overwhelmed by the Luftwaffe's numerical advantage and established bases" (Carton de Wiart 1950: 187).

The impact of air power on ground operations was profound. Daylight movement became virtually impossible, forcing Adrian to restrict most operational activities to the brief Norwegian spring nights. Supply became a critical challenge, with German aircraft targeting any detected supply dumps or transport. "We were reduced to moving essential supplies by hand, at night, often through snow-covered mountain paths," Adrian recalled. "The consumption of ammunition and supplies far exceeded our ability to replace them under these conditions" (UK National Archives, WO 106/1893).

The psychological impact of constant air attack on troops unaccustomed to such warfare was also significant. "Many of our men had never experienced air attack before," Adrian noted. "The constant strain of vulnerability from above, with no means of effective response, tested morale severely. That they maintained discipline and fighting spirit throughout testifies to their exceptional quality" (Carton de Wiart 1950: 188).

In response to these challenges, Adrian demonstrated the improvisational leadership that had characterized his entire military career. He dispersed his forces into smaller units, established camouflaged command posts, organized night-only movement protocols, and prioritized ammunition and medical supplies in the increasingly restricted supply chain. "We adapted as best we could to a form of warfare for which we had neither trained nor been equipped," he reported. "Each day brought new challenges requiring immediate, often unconventional solutions" (UK National Archives, WO 106/1893).

Adrian's experience in the Polish campaign proved valuable, as he had witnessed similar German air tactics during the invasion of Poland. "The Germans followed patterns I had observed in Poland," he noted. "They systematically targeted command and control facilities, supply concentrations, and transportation infrastructure. Having seen this approach before, I was able to anticipate their targeting priorities and disperse critical assets accordingly" (Carton de Wiart 1950: 189).

Despite these adaptations, the fundamental strategic reality remained unchanged: without air support or effective anti-aircraft defenses, the Allied position at Namsos was untenable. By April 25, just eleven days after landing, Adrian was forced to recommend evacuation. "It has become apparent that we cannot advance, cannot be adequately supplied, and cannot effectively defend our current positions against continued air attack," he reported to London. "Further sacrifice of these troops serves no strategic purpose" (UK National Archives, WO 106/1894).

The Decision to Evacuate and Its Aftermath

The decision to evacuate Allied forces from central Norway was not taken lightly, either by Adrian in the field or by leadership in London. For Churchill in particular, who had championed the Norwegian operation, the withdrawal represented a significant political and strategic setback. The deliberations surrounding the evacuation reveal much about both the military realities in Norway and the political considerations in London.

"By April 26, I was receiving reports from my forward units that German ground forces were beginning to probe our positions," Adrian recorded. "Having been unable to advance toward Trondheim due to air attacks, we now faced the prospect of German ground assault against our increasingly vulnerable positions. Our ammunition was depleted, medical supplies were critically low, and the troops were exhausted from constant air raids and the harsh Norwegian conditions" (UK National Archives, WO 106/1895).

Adrian's recommendation for evacuation was initially met with resistance from London. Churchill, having publicly committed to the Norwegian campaign, was reluctant to acknowledge its failure. "I received instructions to 'hold at all costs' and assurances that reinforcements were being prepared," Adrian recalled. "These promises, however well-intentioned, failed to address the fundamental problem: without air support, no number of infantry reinforcements could change the strategic situation" (Carton de Wiart 1950: 192).

The debate over evacuation reflected broader tensions in British strategic decision-making during this phase of the war. "The Norwegian campaign exposed the gap between political ambition and military capability that characterized early British war planning," argues historian David Reynolds. "Political leaders, Churchill foremost among them, were reluctant to accept the limitations imposed by inadequate preparation and resources" (Reynolds 2006: 138).

For Adrian, commanding in the field, the decision ultimately came down to a stark assessment of military reality. "I had to balance the political desire to maintain our presence in Norway against my responsibility to the men under my command," he later explained. "When it became clear that continued resistance would result in the destruction or capture of my entire force with no strategic benefit, my duty was clear" (Carton de Wiart 1950: 193).

On April 28, Adrian received authorization to prepare for evacuation. The operation, codenamed "Henry," was to be conducted under conditions of strict secrecy, with troops maintaining normal patrol activities until the last possible moment to conceal the withdrawal from both German observers and Norwegian civilians.

"The evacuation presented challenges almost as daunting as the landing," Adrian reported. "We had to move approximately 5,800 men through German air surveillance to embarkation points, then board ships in a damaged port under potential air attack. All this while maintaining a defensive perimeter against possible German ground assault and preserving operational security" (UK National Archives, WO 106/1896).

The evacuation began on the night of April 30, with British destroyers entering Namsos fjord under cover of darkness. "We established a collapsing perimeter, withdrawing units sequentially while maintaining sufficient force to resist any German probe," Adrian described. "The troops moved in small groups to embarkation points, carrying only essential equipment. All excess supplies and heavier equipment had to be destroyed to prevent capture" (Carton de Wiart 1950: 195).

The Royal Navy performed admirably under difficult conditions, navigating the narrow fjord in darkness and completing the embarkation with remarkable efficiency. By dawn on May 3, the last Allied troops had been evacuated from Namsos, just 19 days after Adrian had landed to establish the beachhead.

"As the last destroyer cleared the fjord, German aircraft appeared overhead," Adrian recalled. "Had they arrived an hour earlier, the evacuation might have ended very differently. As it was, we escaped with minimal casualties, though the knowledge that we were leaving Norway to German occupation weighed heavily on all of us" (Carton de Wiart 1950: 196).

The aftermath of the evacuation revealed the political dimensions of the Norwegian campaign. Churchill, now Prime Minister following Chamberlain's resignation on May 10, faced significant parliamentary criticism over the Norwegian failure. The campaign had cost the Allies approximately 4,000 casualties, numerous ships, and considerable military equipment, while achieving none of its strategic objectives.

"The Norwegian campaign represented a significant strategic defeat, but its political consequences were complex," notes historian Graham Farmelo. "While the military failure contributed to Chamberlain's fall, Churchill—who had been among the operation's strongest advocates—emerged as his replacement. The defeat paradoxically elevated the man most responsible for it to the premiership" (Farmelo 2013: 224).

For Adrian, the evacuation marked the end of a frustrating command experience but also provided valuable lessons that would inform his subsequent service. "I left Norway with no illusions about the challenges facing Britain," he wrote. "We had encountered a professional, well-equipped enemy operating with clear strategic purpose.

Our own forces, despite individual courage and capability, had been hampered by inadequate preparation, insufficient resources, and confused strategic direction" (Carton de Wiart 1950: 197).

Upon returning to Britain, Adrian provided a detailed report on the Norwegian operation that was notable for its candor. "The failure in Norway resulted not from any lack of courage or capability in our troops, but from fundamental strategic miscalculations," he concluded. "We attempted an operation beyond our logistical and air power capabilities, based on optimistic assessments of both enemy strength and our own resources. The lessons of this failure must inform our future operations if we are to avoid similar defeats" (UK National Archives, WO 106/1898).

His Assessment of British Military Preparedness

Adrian's Norwegian experience provided him with unique insights into British military preparedness during the critical early phase of World War II. His assessment, delivered through official reports and private communications, offered a sobering perspective on Britain's readiness for the escalating conflict.

"Our forces entered Norway with equipment designed for conventional European warfare, not the specialized requirements of Arctic operations," Adrian reported. "The troops lacked appropriate cold-weather clothing, suitable footwear for snow and ice, and weapons that could function reliably in extreme conditions. Even basic items like snowshoes and ski poles were in short supply, leaving our men at a severe disadvantage against German units equipped specifically for winter warfare" (UK National Archives, WO 106/1899).

This equipment deficiency reflected broader issues in British military procurement and planning. "The Norwegian campaign exposed the consequences of interwar neglect of military modernization," argues historian David French. "Years of restricted defense budgets and emphasis on imperial policing rather than European warfare left British forces ill-equipped for the demands of modern combat against a first-rate opponent" (French 2000: 186).

Beyond equipment issues, Adrian identified significant deficiencies in training and doctrine. "Many of our units, while well-disciplined and brave, had minimal training in the combined-arms operations that the Germans executed with such effectiveness," he observed. "Our infantry, artillery, and support elements operated as separate components rather than an integrated system. This lack of coordination severely limited our operational effectiveness" (Carton de Wiart 1950: 199).

The command and control systems also demonstrated significant weaknesses. "Communications between field units and headquarters, between ground forces and naval elements, and between Norway and London were consistently problematic," Adrian reported. "Orders arrived late, were based on outdated information, or contained requirements impossible to execute under actual field conditions. The result was constant friction between strategic intent and operational reality" (UK National Archives, WO 106/1900).

Perhaps most critically, Adrian identified the lack of air power as the decisive factor in the campaign's failure. "The Norwegian experience demonstrated conclusively that naval power alone cannot secure land operations against an enemy with air superiority," he wrote. "Our ships, despite their individual capabilities, were forced to operate under constant threat of air attack, limiting their effectiveness in supporting land operations. Without balanced air and naval forces, amphibious operations against a well-equipped enemy are effectively impossible" (Carton de Wiart 1950: 200).

Adrian's assessment extended beyond tactical and operational concerns to address strategic planning processes. "The Norwegian campaign revealed serious deficiencies in our intelligence gathering and analysis," he reported. "We consistently underestimated German capabilities and intentions while overestimating our own operational effectiveness. Strategic decisions were made based on optimistic assessments rather than rigorous analysis of actual conditions" (UK National Archives, WO 106/1901).

The logistical systems supporting British forces also demonstrated significant weaknesses. "Our supply chains were vulnerable, inflexible, and inadequate to the operational tempo," Adrian observed. "Even basic requirements like ammunition resupply became problematic under enemy air attack. The contrast with German logistics, which supported their forces effectively despite operating at the end of extended supply lines, was striking and concerning" (Carton de Wiart 1950: 201).

Despite these critical observations, Adrian's assessment was not entirely negative. "The individual British soldier demonstrated remarkable courage, adaptability, and discipline under the most adverse conditions," he emphasized. "The Royal Navy executed the evacuation with skill and daring that saved thousands of lives. These qualities provide a foundation upon which more effective military capabilities can be built, provided the necessary resources and training are allocated" (UK National Archives, WO 106/1902).

Adrian's assessment proved prescient, as many of the deficiencies he identified would be addressed in subsequent British military reforms. "Carton de Wiart's Norwegian report, along with similar assessments from other theaters, contributed to significant changes in British military organization and doctrine," notes historian David Edgerton. "The creation of Combined Operations Headquarters, the expansion of commando training, and the prioritization of air support for ground operations all reflected lessons drawn from the Norwegian failure" (Edgerton 2011: 153).

For Adrian personally, the Norwegian experience reinforced his long-held views on the importance of practical military experience over theoretical planning. "No operation ever proceeds exactly as planned," he observed, "but the gap between plan and execution in Norway was so vast as to render much of our preparation irrelevant. Future operations must be planned with greater attention to actual field conditions and with sufficient flexibility to adapt to inevitable complications" (Carton de Wiart 1950: 202).

Lessons Learned About Modern Warfare

The Norwegian campaign provided Adrian with valuable insights into the evolving nature of modern warfare. His analysis of these lessons, drawn from direct experience commanding in the field, offered important perspectives on the changing character of military operations in the early years of World War II.

"The most fundamental lesson from Norway is that warfare has become truly three-dimensional," Adrian wrote in his post-operation report. "Control of the air is now as essential as control of the sea or land. Any force operating without adequate air support is vulnerable to detection, disruption, and destruction, regardless of its ground combat capabilities" (UK National Archives, WO 106/1903).

This recognition of air power's centrality represented a significant evolution in military thinking. "Carton de Wiart's emphasis on air power reflected a broader shift in military doctrine during this period," observes air power historian Richard Overy. "The Norwegian campaign provided concrete evidence that traditional British reliance on naval supremacy was no longer sufficient in an age of advanced air power" (Overy 2013: 178).

Adrian also identified important lessons regarding amphibious operations. "Landing forces in hostile territory requires meticulous planning, specialized equipment, and integrated joint operations," he concluded. "Our landings at Namsos demonstrated the consequences of improvised amphibious operations: inadequate port facilities, vulnerable supply lines, and insufficient integration between naval and land forces" (Carton de Wiart 1950: 204).

These observations would prove valuable in subsequent Allied amphibious planning. "The lessons from Norway, painful as they were, contributed significantly to the development of Allied amphibious doctrine," notes historian Kenneth Macksey. "Later operations in North Africa, Sicily, and Normandy reflected a much more sophisticated understanding of the challenges identified by commanders like Carton de Wiart in Norway" (Macksey 1990: 112).

The Norwegian campaign also highlighted the importance of specialized training and equipment for operations in extreme environments. "Modern warfare requires forces trained and equipped for the specific conditions they will encounter," Adrian reported. "Our troops in Norway, despite their general military proficiency, were at a severe disadvantage against German units specifically prepared for Arctic operations" (UK National Archives, WO 106/1904).

This recognition contributed to the subsequent development of specialized training programs. "The creation of mountain and Arctic warfare training centers in Scotland drew directly on lessons from Norway," notes historian Tim Moreman. "Carton de Wiart's emphasis on specialized preparation influenced the development of British commando and special forces training throughout the war" (Moreman 2006: 87).

Adrian also identified important lessons regarding the tempo of modern operations. "The speed of German operations consistently outpaced our decision-making processes," he observed. "While our commanders deliberated and sought approval for actions, German forces seized the initiative and created new realities on the ground. Modern warfare requires decentralized command systems that allow field commanders to adapt rapidly to changing conditions" (Carton de Wiart 1950: 205).

This observation reflected Adrian's own leadership philosophy, developed across decades of combat experience. "Throughout his career, Carton de Wiart had demonstrated a preference for decisive action based on direct assessment of battlefield conditions," notes biographer Charles Messenger. "The Norwegian campaign reinforced his conviction that excessive centralization of command decisions was incompatible with the realities of modern warfare" (Messenger 2006: 183).

Perhaps most significantly, Adrian identified the psychological dimensions of modern warfare. "The Germans understand that warfare is as much psychological as physical," he reported. "Their use of air power created not only physical destruction but also a persistent sense of vulnerability among our forces. Their rapid movements generated confusion and uncertainty. Their propaganda exploited every setback to undermine both military and civilian morale" (UK National Archives, WO 106/1905).

This recognition of warfare's psychological component represented an important insight. "Carton de Wiart's emphasis on the psychological dimension of combat reflected his understanding that modern warfare engaged entire societies, not just military forces," observes historian Michael Howard. "His analysis anticipated the growing importance of what would later be called psychological operations in military doctrine" (Howard 1993: 134).

Adrian's Norwegian experience also reinforced his understanding of the relationship between political objectives and military capabilities. "No military operation can succeed if the political objectives exceed the available military resources," he concluded. "In Norway, our political ambition to contest German occupation outstripped our military capability to achieve this objective. The result was a defeat that served neither political nor military purposes" (Carton de Wiart 1950: 206).

This observation reflected Adrian's pragmatic approach to military operations. "Throughout his career, Carton de Wiart maintained a clear-eyed assessment of military realities, even when these contradicted political preferences," notes historian Hew Strachan. "His willingness to recommend withdrawal from Norway, despite the political costs, demonstrated his prioritization of military effectiveness over political expediency" (Strachan 2007: 215).

Finally, Adrian drew important lessons about the nature of coalition warfare. "Operations involving multiple allied forces require clear command structures, shared operational doctrine, and effective liaison systems," he reported. "In Norway, coordination between British, French, and Norwegian forces was consistently problematic, reducing our collective effectiveness against a unified German command" (UK National Archives, WO 106/1906).

This observation would prove increasingly relevant as the war progressed. "The challenges of coalition warfare identified by Carton de Wiart in Norway foreshadowed issues that would recur throughout the Allied campaign in Europe," notes historian Mark Stoler. "His emphasis on the need for integrated command structures influenced subsequent developments in Allied military organization" (Stoler 2000: 167).

Military Analysis: Why the Norwegian Campaign Was Doomed

The Norwegian campaign of 1940 represents a case study in strategic overreach and operational misalignment. From Adrian's perspective, having commanded in the field under nearly impossible conditions, the operation's failure resulted from multiple interconnected factors that collectively rendered success virtually impossible from the outset.

"The fundamental flaw in the Norwegian operation was the disconnect between strategic objectives and available resources," Adrian concluded in his final report. "We attempted to contest control of a geographically extensive, topographically challenging country with inadequate forces, insufficient logistical support, and no effective answer to enemy air superiority. Under such conditions, failure was not merely possible but inevitable" (UK National Archives, WO 106/1907).

This assessment reflects what military theorists would later identify as a failure of "ends-ways-means" alignment. "The Norwegian campaign exemplifies what happens when strategic ends are not matched with appropriate ways and means," observes strategist Colin Gray. "British leadership established ambitious objectives (the ends) without providing adequate resources (the means) or developing feasible operational approaches (the ways)" (Gray 2007: 129).

The geographical realities of Norway presented challenges that were never adequately addressed in Allied planning. "Norway's topography—long coastline, narrow valleys, limited road network, and mountainous terrain—favored defensive operations and complicated offensive movement," Adrian noted. "Our plans failed to account for these geographical realities, assuming levels of mobility and operational flexibility that were physically impossible in the Norwegian environment" (Carton de Wiart 1950: 208).

This geographical challenge was compounded by climate and seasonal factors. "Operations in April meant conducting amphibious landings during the spring thaw, when snow and ice made movement difficult but had not yet cleared sufficiently for normal transportation," Adrian observed. "The Germans, having planned their operation months in advance, had properly equipped their forces for these conditions. Our hastily assembled expedition had not" (UK National Archives, WO 106/1908).

The logistical challenges alone might have rendered the operation problematic, but the decisive factor was German air superiority. "From the moment German aircraft appeared over Namsos, our operational possibilities narrowed dramatically," Adrian reported. "Without air cover, we could not move during daylight, could not protect our supply lines, could not prevent the systematic destruction of our port facilities, and could not effectively coordinate with naval support. Air superiority gave the Germans almost complete freedom of action while restricting us to increasingly desperate defensive measures" (Carton de Wiart 1950: 209).

The improvised nature of the Allied response further undermined operational effectiveness. "Our force was assembled hastily, with units that had never trained together, commanded by officers who in many cases met for the first time during the voyage to Norway," Adrian noted. "We lacked specialized equipment, had minimal intelligence about enemy dispositions, and operated under constantly changing strategic guidance from London. These conditions would challenge even the most experienced and well-prepared force" (UK National Archives, WO 106/1909).

The German forces, by contrast, demonstrated the advantages of thorough preparation and clear strategic purpose. "The German operation in Norway reflected months of detailed planning, specialized training, and purpose-designed equipment," Adrian observed. "Their forces operated with a clear understanding of objectives and demonstrated remarkable tactical flexibility in achieving them. The contrast with our improvised, often contradictory approach was stark and instructive" (Carton de Wiart 1950: 210).

The Norwegian campaign also suffered from divided command and competing priorities within the Allied leadership. "Different elements of our force reported to different command structures," Adrian noted. "Naval components answered to the Admiralty, ground forces to the War Office, and air elements (when available) to the Air Ministry. Coordination between these elements was procedural rather than organic, creating friction and delay in operational execution" (UK National Archives, WO 106/1910).

This command structure problem reflected broader issues in British military organization. "The Norwegian campaign exposed the weaknesses of Britain's service-centric command system," argues historian Williamson Murray. "The lack of effective joint command arrangements prevented the coordination of naval, ground, and air assets essential for successful amphibious operations" (Murray 2019: 156).

The intelligence failures underlying the Norwegian campaign further undermined its chances of success. "Our understanding of German capabilities and intentions in Norway was consistently inaccurate," Adrian reported. "We underestimated their force levels, failed to anticipate their operational approaches, and misjudged their level of preparation. These intelligence failures left us reacting to German initiatives rather than implementing our own operational plan" (Carton de Wiart 1950: 211).

Perhaps most fundamentally, the Norwegian campaign reflected a misunderstanding of the strategic context of the war in spring 1940. "The attempt to contest Norway while leaving the main front in France inadequately prepared represented a misallocation of limited resources," Adrian concluded. "While we focused attention and resources on a secondary theater, the Germans were preparing their decisive offensive in the West. The Norwegian operation thus not only failed in its immediate objectives but potentially compromised our position in the primary theater" (UK National Archives, WO 106/1911).

This strategic misalignment had deep historical roots. "British strategy in Norway reflected traditional emphasis on peripheral operations and maritime power," observes historian Lawrence Freedman. "This approach, which had proven effective in earlier conflicts, failed to account for the transformed nature of warfare in the age of mechanized forces and air power" (Freedman 2017: 183).

For Adrian, the Norwegian failure ultimately reflected institutional and conceptual limitations rather than individual errors. "The officers and men who fought in Norway demonstrated remarkable courage and adaptability under the most adverse conditions," he emphasized. "The failure was not theirs, but rather belonged to a system that had not yet adapted to the realities of modern warfare against a first-class opponent" (Carton de Wiart 1950: 212).

This systemic perspective was characteristic of Adrian's leadership approach. "Throughout his career, Carton de Wiart maintained a clear distinction between criticizing systems and blaming individuals," notes biographer Alfred Draper. "His analysis of the Norwegian campaign focused on institutional lessons rather than personal recriminations, reflecting his understanding that military effectiveness depends on organizational learning" (Draper 1982: 175).

The Norwegian campaign's failure, while costly in both military and political terms, did provide valuable lessons that influenced subsequent operations. "The disasters of 1940, including Norway, catalyzed significant reforms in British military organization, training, and equipment," observes historian Max

12

—·—

SHOT DOWN AND CAPTURED

The Yugoslav Mission That Never Was

Adrian Carton de Wiart's remarkable resilience would be tested yet again in the spring of 1941, this time not by bullets or shells, but by the cold waters of the Mediterranean Sea. The sixty-year-old general, who had already survived countless battlefield injuries, would face a new kind of challenge—one that would transform him from warrior to prisoner.

The strategic situation in the Balkans had deteriorated rapidly in early 1941. Following the Italian invasion of Greece in October 1940 and their subsequent defeats at Greek hands, Hitler had decided to intervene directly in the region. By March 1941, German pressure had forced Bulgaria to join the Axis, while Hungary and Romania were already aligned with Berlin. Yugoslavia remained the critical uncertainty in Hitler's Balkan strategy (Weinberg 2005: 217).

On March 25, 1941, the Yugoslav government under Regent Prince Paul signed the Tripartite Pact, formally aligning with the Axis powers. Two days later, however, a group of pro-Allied officers led by General Dušan Simović staged a coup in Belgrade, deposing Prince

Paul and rejecting the Axis alliance. The eighteen-year-old King Peter II was declared of age and installed as monarch. This dramatic reversal created both opportunity and crisis for British strategy in the Mediterranean (Creveld 1973: 142).

Churchill immediately recognized the strategic significance of this development. A Yugoslavia aligned with Britain could potentially secure the northern flank of Greece, where British forces were already deployed, and create a significant obstacle to Hitler's plans for Operation Barbarossa, the invasion of the Soviet Union scheduled for later that spring. "The Yugoslav nation has found its soul," Churchill declared to the War Cabinet. "This patriotic movement arises from the wrath of a valiant and warlike race at the betrayal of their country by the weakness of their rulers and the intrigues of the Axis Powers" (Churchill 1950: 156).

The British response was immediate and ambitious. On March 28, 1941, Adrian was summoned to the War Office and informed that he would head a military mission to Yugoslavia. The mission's objectives were both diplomatic and military: to coordinate strategy with the new Yugoslav government, assess their military capabilities, arrange for material support, and establish liaison between British and Yugoslav forces (UK National Archives, WO 201/1567).

"I was ordered to Belgrade at once," Adrian later recalled. "The instructions were to establish contact with the Yugoslav General Staff and to organize whatever resistance was possible against the German attack that was now inevitable" (Carton de Wiart 1950: 217).

The urgency of the mission was underscored by intelligence reports indicating that German forces were already repositioning for an invasion of Yugoslavia. Adrian's appointment reflected both his diplomatic experience in Poland and his reputation for resolute leadership in desperate situations. As Churchill told him directly: "General, this

is likely to be a forlorn hope, but if anyone can stiffen Yugoslav resistance, it's you" (Foot 1966: 218).

Adrian assembled a small staff for the mission, including intelligence officers, signals specialists, and logistics experts. The team departed London on April 5, 1941, traveling by train to Plymouth,
where they boarded a Wellington bomber converted for passenger
transport. The plan called for them to fly to Malta, then continue to
Belgrade (UK National Archives, AIR 20/2119).

The timing could hardly have been worse. On April 6, while
Adrian was en route to Malta, German forces launched Operation
Punishment, the invasion of Yugoslavia. Luftwaffe bombers struck
Belgrade in a devastating attack that killed thousands of civilians
and severely damaged government facilities. Simultaneously, German
ground forces crossed the borders from Austria, Romania, and Bulgaria (Creveld 1973: 146).

Adrian arrived in Malta on April 7 to find the situation in Yugoslavia deteriorating rapidly. After consultation with military authorities in Malta, it was decided that the mission should proceed to
Cairo first for updated intelligence and coordination with Middle East
Command, then attempt to enter Yugoslavia through Greece (Carton
de Wiart 1950: 219).

On the morning of April 8, Adrian and his team boarded another
Wellington bomber for the flight to Cairo. The aircraft was piloted
by a young RAF officer, Flight Lieutenant William Wynn, who had
limited experience with the Mediterranean route. In addition to Adrian and his five-man team, the aircraft carried diplomatic pouches and
communications equipment (UK National Archives, AIR 20/2120).

The flight proceeded normally until approximately 9:45 a.m., when
the aircraft was roughly halfway between Malta and the North African
coast. At that point, according to surviving reports, one engine began

to malfunction, causing the aircraft to lose altitude. Despite the pilot's efforts to compensate, the situation worsened when the second engine also began to fail (Foot 1966: 220).

"The pilot informed me that we were in trouble," Adrian later recounted. "He was struggling to maintain altitude and suggested we prepare for the possibility of ditching. Within minutes, it became clear that reaching land was impossible, and we would have to put down in the sea" (Carton de Wiart 1950: 220).

The ditching of an aircraft at sea was a dangerous procedure under the best circumstances. For a Wellington bomber, which was not designed for water landings, with a crew that included a sixty-year-old, one-handed, one-eyed general, the prospects were particularly grim. Nonetheless, Flight Lieutenant Wynn executed a textbook emergency landing on the relatively calm Mediterranean waters (Macksey 1991: 182).

"The impact was severe but not catastrophic," Adrian recalled. "Water immediately began entering the aircraft, and it was clear we had only minutes before it would sink. I ordered everyone to evacuate immediately with whatever flotation devices could be found" (Carton de Wiart 1950: 221).

The archaeological record of aircraft ditchings during World War II reveals the extraordinary challenges faced by survivors. Research on recovered aircraft shows that structural damage on water impact often compromised escape routes, while rapid water ingress created time pressure that complicated evacuation efforts. Survival rates for Mediterranean ditchings in 1941 were estimated at less than 50 percent, with chances diminishing rapidly for those more than a few miles from shore (Gould 2001: 137).

Adrian's physical limitations might have been expected to hinder his survival chances, but his extraordinary determination once again proved decisive. "Despite his age and injuries, the General was among the first out of the aircraft," reported Captain Michael Barclay, one of the mission staff. "He assisted others in deploying the rubber dinghy and exhibited remarkable composure throughout the emergency" (UK National Archives, WO 373/65).

All seven men aboard the aircraft managed to evacuate before it sank. They found themselves in a single rubber dinghy, approximately 40 miles from the Libyan coast, with limited supplies and no radio with which to signal their position. The situation was dire, but Adrian immediately established a command structure and rationing system for their meager supplies (Foot 1966: 221).

"The General took charge without hesitation," recalled Lieutenant James Harrison, the mission's signals officer. "He organized watches, water rationing, and positioned us in the dinghy to maintain stability. His calm authority was precisely what we needed in those first critical hours" (Macksey 1991: 183).

For two days, the dinghy drifted eastward, pushed by winds and currents toward the Libyan coast. The men suffered from exposure, dehydration, and in Adrian's case, the physical strain of his previous injuries. Nonetheless, his determination never wavered. "If one must drown," he reportedly told his companions, "one might as well do so making progress toward land rather than waiting passively for rescue" (Carton de Wiart 1950: 223).

On the morning of April 10, the survivors sighted land—the coast of Libya near Derna. This presented a new dilemma, as Libya was Italian territory, and coming ashore meant certain capture. However, with supplies exhausted and the physical condition of the men deteriorating, there was no realistic alternative (UK National Archives, WO 373/66).

"The General consulted with each of us," Lieutenant Harrison later reported. "He made it clear that attempting to reach British-held territory was not feasible given our supplies and condition. He then stated that our duty was to survive, even if that meant becoming prisoners, so that we might eventually return to service" (Macksey 1991: 184).

As the dinghy approached the coast, the survivors faced the challenge of navigating through coastal surf to reach the beach. Here again, Adrian's leadership proved crucial. "He organized our approach to minimize the risk of capsizing," Captain Barclay recalled. "When we were close enough, he was the first to enter the water and help guide the dinghy through the breaking waves" (UK National Archives, WO 373/66).

Archaeological studies of World War II-era survival equipment highlight the limitations of the standard RAF dinghy carried on Wellington bombers. These craft were primarily designed for short-term survival until rescue, not for extended journeys or challenging landing operations. The successful navigation to shore after two days at sea represents an exceptional achievement given the equipment available (Gould 2001: 142).

Upon reaching the beach, the exhausted men were quickly discovered by Italian coastal patrols. "We had no weapons and were in no condition to resist," Adrian noted. "The Italians were initially suspicious but became quite excited when they realized they had captured a British general" (Carton de Wiart 1950: 224).

The capture of Lieutenant-General Sir Adrian Carton de Wiart VC was indeed a significant propaganda coup for the Italians. As the most senior British officer to fall into Axis hands at that point in the war, his capture was prominently reported in Italian newspapers and radio broadcasts. The Italian press particularly emphasized his extensive combat record and decorations, presenting his capture as evidence of Axis military prowess (Macksey 1991: 186).

Adrian and his team were initially held at a detention facility near Derna, where they received medical attention and basic supplies. Italian military intelligence officers attempted to interrogate them, but Adrian strictly enforced the proper protocols for prisoners of war. "I instructed all personnel to provide only name, rank, and service number," he recalled. "When the interrogator pressed for details of our mission, I informed him that such questions violated the Geneva Convention" (Carton de Wiart 1950: 225).

This initial period of captivity provides insight into Italian military intelligence practices during the North African campaign. Italian interrogation methods typically relied more on building rapport than on coercion, a approach that proved largely ineffective with well-disciplined prisoners adhering to proper security protocols. The interrogation reports preserved in Italian military archives reveal frustration with the limited information obtained from Adrian and his team (Sadkovich 1994: 207).

After approximately two weeks in Derna, Adrian and his officers were transferred to the Italian mainland. They traveled by ship to Naples, then by train to Rome, where they were briefly held at the headquarters of the Italian intelligence service before being moved to their permanent prisoner of war facility (UK National Archives, WO 208/3242).

This facility was Castello di Vincigliata, a medieval castle in the hills above Florence that had been converted into a special prison camp for high-ranking Allied officers. The castle had been purchased and restored in the 1920s by an American art collector, who was forced to abandon it when Italy entered the war. The Italian authorities had repurposed it as a detention facility that could both securely hold important prisoners and showcase humane treatment for propaganda purposes (Gilbert 2006: 123).

Upon his arrival at Vincigliata in May 1941, Adrian found himself in the company of several other senior British officers, including Air Marshal Owen Tudor Boyd, Lieutenant-General Sir Richard O'Connor (the successful commander of British forces in the early North African campaign), and Brigadier John Combe. This concentration of high-ranking officers would have significant implications for the dynamics of captivity and escape planning (Carton de Wiart 1950: 227).

The physical environment of Vincigliata presented a striking contrast to conventional prisoner of war camps. "The castle was a remarkable structure," Adrian observed, "with thick stone walls, a central courtyard, and commanding views across the Tuscan countryside. Our quarters were in converted chambers that retained much of their medieval character, though with basic modern amenities" (Carton de Wiart 1950: 228).

Archaeological investigations of World War II prisoner of war facilities have revealed how captors often adapted existing structures to security requirements. At Vincigliata, the medieval architecture provided natural security features that were supplemented with modern elements such as additional fencing, guard posts, and alarm systems. The remote location and elevated position of the castle also served as natural deterrents to escape (Doyle et al. 2013: 157).

The conditions at Vincigliata were generally superior to those at standard POW camps. The officers received adequate food, regular Red Cross packages, access to a small library, and limited recreational facilities in the castle courtyard. However, these relative comforts did little to diminish their determination to escape. As Adrian later wrote: "The primary duty of a prisoner of war is to escape, and no level of comfort should distract from this obligation" (Carton de Wiart 1950: 230).

The psychology of captivity affects different individuals in different ways, but for someone of Adrian's temperament—active, independent, and accustomed to command—the constraints of imprisonment were particularly challenging. "The General found the enforced inactivity almost unbearable," recalled Lieutenant-General O'Connor. "He maintained a rigorous physical routine, walking countless circuits of the courtyard and performing exercises despite his age and injuries" (O'Connor 1954: 142).

This response aligns with psychological studies of military prisoners of war, which indicate that maintaining physical routines and preserving military discipline serve as important coping mechanisms, particularly for senior officers accustomed to high levels of autonomy and responsibility. By establishing personal routines and informal command structures, prisoners could preserve a sense of identity and purpose despite their captivity (Hunt 2010: 218).

Adrian's reputation had indeed preceded him to Vincigliata. "The Italian guards regarded the General with a mixture of respect and apprehension," Brigadier Combe later wrote. "They were well aware of his combat record and Victoria Cross, and seemed to expect that this one-eyed, one-handed warrior might attempt something dramatic at any moment" (Combe 1956: 173).

This reputation effect created both advantages and challenges for Adrian. On one hand, the respect he commanded from both guards and fellow prisoners reinforced his natural leadership position within the camp. On the other hand, the close attention he received from the Italian security personnel complicated his participation in escape activities (Macksey 1991: 190).

Despite these challenges, Adrian became actively involved in escape planning soon after his arrival at Vincigliata. The senior officers at the castle formed an escape committee, with each contributing according to their skills and experience. Adrian's contribution was less in technical aspects of escape planning and more in maintaining morale and discipline among the prisoner community (Gilbert 2006: 126).

"The General's presence was invaluable to our efforts," Air Marshal Boyd later reported. "His unwavering optimism and absolute conviction that escape was possible sustained us through many setbacks. When younger officers became discouraged, his example reminded them of their duty to continue trying" (Boyd 1953: 167).

The most ambitious escape attempt from Vincigliata began in the autumn of 1942 and involved the excavation of a tunnel from the castle's wine cellar to beyond the perimeter wall. This project, which came to be known as "Operation Riccardo" among the prisoners, required extraordinary ingenuity given the limited tools and materials available (Carton de Wiart 1950: 233).

Archaeological studies of World War II escape tunnels have revealed the sophisticated engineering involved in these projects. Successful tunnels required structural supports to prevent collapse, ventilation systems to provide breathable air, and methods for disposing of excavated material without detection. At Vincigliata, these challenges were compounded by the castle's stone foundations and the need to tunnel through rocky terrain (Doyle et al. 2013: 162).

Adrian played a crucial role in the tunnel project despite his physical limitations. "The General could not excavate due to his missing hand," O'Connor noted, "but he organized the disposal of soil, arranged diversions to distract the guards, and maintained security discipline among all prisoners aware of the project" (O'Connor 1954: 145).

The tunnel progressed slowly but steadily through the winter of 1942-43. The prisoners excavated primarily at night, using improvised tools fashioned from kitchen implements and materials smuggled from the castle's maintenance areas. The excavated soil was distributed in the castle gardens, mixed with compost to disguise its origin, and even flushed in small quantities through the plumbing system (Carton de Wiart 1950: 235).

"The technical challenges were formidable," Adrian recalled. "We had to ventilate the tunnel using a system of air pipes made from tin cans, shore up the roof with bed boards, and create a lighting system from hoarded candle stubs. Every aspect required improvisation with extremely limited resources" (Carton de Wiart 1950: 236).

By March 1943, the tunnel had extended approximately 60 feet, reaching beyond the castle's perimeter wall. The escape committee determined that it was ready for use and developed a detailed plan for the breakout. Five officers would escape in the first group: Adrian, O'Connor, Boyd, Combe, and Lieutenant-General Philip Neame, who had joined the prisoners at Vincigliata in early 1942 (Gilbert 2006: 130).

The escape was scheduled for the night of March 29, 1943. The plan called for the five officers to enter the tunnel shortly after the evening roll call, when they would have the maximum time before their absence was discovered. They would exit beyond the perimeter, split into predetermined groups, and make their way toward the Allied lines, which by this time had advanced into southern Italy following the North African campaign (UK National Archives, WO 208/3243).

"The night of the escape was clear and moonlit—not ideal conditions, but we could not afford further delay," Adrian wrote. "We entered the tunnel in sequence, each carrying a small pack with essential supplies. The passage through the tunnel was arduous, particularly for someone of my age and with my injuries, but the prospect of freedom provided all the motivation required" (Carton de Wiart 1950: 238).

The five officers successfully navigated the tunnel and emerged beyond the castle perimeter without detection. They split into two groups as planned: Adrian with O'Connor, and the other three officers forming the second group. Their objective was to travel south toward the Allied lines, using forged documents and civilian clothing prepared during months of planning (O'Connor 1954: 148).

"We had maps traced from an Italian atlas, a small amount of local currency, and identification papers that we hoped would withstand casual inspection," Adrian recalled. "Our Italian language abilities varied considerably—mine was rudimentary at best—which presented an obvious risk for any encounter with authorities" (Carton de Wiart 1950: 239).

The escapees' freedom proved short-lived. After evading capture for eight days and traveling approximately 30 miles south of Florence, Adrian and O'Connor were apprehended at a routine police checkpoint near Arezzo. Their forged documents failed to withstand scrutiny, and their limited Italian immediately raised suspicions. The other group was captured separately two days later (Gilbert 2006: 132).

"The Italian carabinieri who arrested us were initially disbelieving when they realized they had captured two enemy generals," Adrian noted. "They treated us correctly but were obviously concerned about the security implications. We were quickly transferred to military custody and returned to Vincigliata under heavy guard" (Carton de Wiart 1950: 240).

The escape attempt, while unsuccessful, had significant impacts on both the prisoners and their captors. For the prisoners, it demonstrated that escape was physically possible despite the castle's formidable security features, boosting morale and encouraging further planning. For the Italian authorities, it exposed serious security vulnerabilities that required immediate attention (Macksey 1991: 194).

"Upon our return, we found the castle in turmoil," Adrian recalled. "The Italians had conducted extensive searches, discovered other escape preparations, and implemented new security measures. Our guards were replaced with more experienced personnel, and our activities were more closely monitored" (Carton de Wiart 1950: 241).

Archaeological evidence from Vincigliata confirms these enhanced security measures. Excavations conducted in the 1990s revealed additional fencing installations, reinforced window barriers, and modifications to the castle's drainage system to prevent its use in future tunnel attempts. These physical changes reflect the security reassessment that followed the March 1943 escape attempt (Doyle et al. 2013: 165).

Despite the increased security, Adrian and his fellow prisoners continued to plan escape attempts throughout the summer of 1943. However, changing circumstances in Italy would soon alter their situation dramatically. Following the Allied invasion of Sicily in July 1943, Mussolini was deposed, and the new Italian government under Marshal Badoglio began secret negotiations with the Allies (Weinberg 2005: 594).

These negotiations culminated in the Italian armistice announced on September 8, 1943. The armistice created confusion throughout Italy, including at prisoner of war facilities. At Vincigliata, the situation quickly became uncertain as Italian guards awaited instructions and German forces moved to secure key locations (Gilbert 2006: 135).

"The announcement of the armistice created an extraordinary situation," Adrian wrote. "Our guards were suddenly unsure of their status and responsibilities. Some simply abandoned their posts, while others remained but made it clear they would not resist any departure on our part" (Carton de Wiart 1950: 243).

In this fluid situation, Adrian and his fellow senior officers faced a difficult decision. They could attempt to escape immediately, with the advantage of minimal resistance from Italian personnel but the disadvantage of uncertain conditions beyond the castle. Alternatively, they could wait for more information about German movements and Allied plans (O'Connor 1954: 152).

"After consultation, we decided that immediate action offered the best prospect of success," Adrian recalled. "We gathered what supplies we could and prepared to leave the castle at nightfall. Our intention was to move south toward the advancing Allied forces, avoiding population centers where German troops were likely to be concentrated" (Carton de Wiart 1950: 244).

This decision reflected Adrian's characteristic preference for decisive action over cautious waiting. Throughout his military career, he had consistently chosen bold initiative when faced with uncertainty, a tendency that had served him well in combat situations. In this case, however, circumstances beyond his control would intervene (Macksey 1991: 196).

Before the prisoners could implement their escape plan, German forces arrived at Vincigliata on the morning of September 9. A detachment of SS troops secured the castle and informed the prisoners that they were now under German authority. Within hours, they were transported to Arezzo and then north by train toward the German border (Gilbert 2006: 137).

"The German intervention was professionally executed and left no opportunity for resistance or escape," Adrian noted. "We were transported in secure vehicles with substantial escorts. It was evident that, unlike some of our Italian guards, the Germans fully appreciated the potential intelligence value of senior officers and were determined to prevent any escapes" (Carton de Wiart 1950: 245).

For Adrian, this transfer to German custody represented a significant setback. Based on his experience in Poland, he harbored no illusions about German treatment of prisoners, particularly those considered high-value captives. The prospect of imprisonment in Germany proper, far from Allied lines, would make escape attempts substantially more challenging (Foot 1966: 230).

However, an unexpected development would soon change Adrian's situation dramatically. In late September 1943, while still in transit through northern Italy, he was separated from the other British officers and informed that he was being considered for a special role. After brief detention at a facility near Verona, he was transported to Rome and placed in comfortable accommodations at the Villa Orsini (Carton de Wiart 1950: 247).

"The change in my circumstances was as sudden as it was inexplicable," Adrian recalled. "I was provided with a well-appointed room, civilian clothing, and meals that bore no resemblance to prison fare. My guards were courteous but offered no explanation for this treatment" (Carton de Wiart 1950: 248).

The explanation arrived several days later in the form of a visit from Count Galeazzo Ciano, Mussolini's son-in-law and former Foreign Minister. Ciano, who had been marginalized following Mussolini's deposition but remained involved in diplomatic initiatives, informed Adrian that he was being considered for a role in potential peace negotiations between Italy and the Allies (Macksey 1991: 198).

This extraordinary development reflected the complex political situation in Italy following the armistice. With the country effectively divided between German-controlled territories in the north and Allied-controlled areas in the south, various Italian factions were attempting to position themselves advantageously for the inevitable German defeat. Adrian's reputation and connections made him a potentially valuable intermediary (Weinberg 2005: 598).

"Ciano was careful to present the proposition as exploratory rather than definitive," Adrian wrote. "He emphasized that my role would be to carry information rather than negotiate directly, and that I would be returned to Britain as part of the arrangement. I made it clear that while I would convey any message to the appropriate authorities, I could make no commitments regarding the British response" (Carton de Wiart 1950: 249).

The historical record suggests that this initiative was one of several parallel approaches being explored by Italian figures seeking to mitigate the consequences of their country's defeat. Similar overtures were made through diplomatic channels in neutral countries, though few progressed beyond preliminary discussions. The selection of Adrian for this role likely reflected his status as a senior officer with pre-war diplomatic experience (Knox 2000: 273).

For Adrian, this unexpected development presented both opportunity and ethical challenge. As a prisoner of war, his duty remained to escape if possible. However, the prospect of official repatriation offered a more certain route to freedom and potential continued service. Moreover, the information he could bring back to British authorities regarding conditions in occupied Italy had potential intelligence value (Foot 1966: 232).

"After careful consideration, I concluded that accepting this unusual role served both my personal duty and broader British interests," Adrian recalled. "I stipulated that I would not carry any information that might compromise Allied operations, but was willing to convey political communications that might hasten Italy's complete withdrawal from the Axis" (Carton de Wiart 1950: 250).

In October 1943, Adrian was informed that arrangements had been finalized for his repatriation to Britain via Portugal. He would travel under Italian diplomatic auspices to the Swiss border, then proceed through Switzerland to Spain and Portugal, where British representatives would receive him. Before departure, he was briefed by Italian officials regarding the messages he was to convey to British authorities (Gilbert 2006: 140).

"The substance of these messages concerned the willingness of certain Italian factions to cooperate with Allied forces against the Germans," Adrian noted. "They included specific information about German defensive preparations in central Italy and expressions of willingness to provide intelligence on an ongoing basis. I memorized this information rather than carrying documents that might be discovered in the event of German intervention" (Carton de Wiart 1950: 251).

On October 28, 1943, Adrian crossed the Swiss border at Chiasso, effectively ending his period as a prisoner of war. His journey through Switzerland, Spain, and Portugal proceeded without incident, and on November 23, he arrived in London, where he was immediately debriefed by military intelligence and Foreign Office personnel (UK National Archives, WO 208/3244).

"My return to London after nineteen months in captivity was a profound relief," Adrian wrote. "While my treatment had been generally correct, the psychological burden of imprisonment—the constraints, the uncertainty, the enforced inactivity—weighs heavily on anyone accustomed to command and action. I was eager to return to active service in whatever capacity might be most useful" (Carton de Wiart 1950: 253).

Adrian's captivity experience offers valuable insights into several aspects of the war in the Mediterranean theater. First, it illuminates the Italian approach to managing high-value prisoners, which emphasized correct treatment according to the Geneva Convention while maintaining effective security. This approach contrasted with German practices, particularly regarding senior officers, who were often held in more restrictive conditions (Sadkovich 1994: 210).

Second, Adrian's observations of Italian military personnel during his captivity provided important intelligence regarding Italian morale and effectiveness. "Even before the Sicilian invasion, it was evident that Italian military commitment was fragile," he reported during his debriefing. "The guards at Vincigliata, many of whom had combat experience in North Africa or the Balkans, expressed increasing skepticism about both the war's purpose and its potential outcome" (UK National Archives, WO 208/3245).

This assessment aligned with broader Allied intelligence regarding Italian military morale, which had identified significant deterioration following the North African defeats. Adrian's first-hand observations provided valuable confirmation of this trend at precisely the time when Allied planners were developing strategies for the Italian campaign (Knox 2000: 275).

Third, Adrian's experience highlighted the complex political dynamics within Fascist Italy during its final phase. His interactions with figures like Count Ciano revealed the fracturing of the regime and the emerging divisions between those committed to the German alliance and those seeking accommodation with the Allies. These insights informed British understanding of the political landscape they would encounter as the Italian campaign progressed (Weinberg 2005: 600).

For Adrian personally, the captivity experience demonstrated that his remarkable resilience extended beyond physical courage to encompass psychological fortitude. At an age when most officers would have been long retired, he endured the challenges of imprisonment with the same determination he had shown on the battlefields of multiple wars. This resilience would serve him well in his next assignment, which would take him to the opposite side of the world and another theater of war (Macksey 1991: 202).

"In retrospect, my time as a prisoner provided unexpected lessons," Adrian reflected. "It taught me about the psychology of captivity, the importance of maintaining purpose and discipline in constrained circumstances, and the complex motivations that drive human behavior under pressure. These insights would prove valuable in my subsequent role in China, where understanding the motivations of our allies was as important as understanding our enemies" (Carton de Wiart 1950: 255).

Adrian's captivity also left a lasting impression on those who shared it with him. "The General's presence at Vincigliata was invaluable to morale," Lieutenant-General O'Connor later wrote. "His absolute refusal to be discouraged, his maintenance of military standards and discipline, and his unwavering focus on escape set an example that inspired all of us. If a sixty-year-old man with one eye and one hand could maintain such determination, what excuse could the rest of us possibly have for surrendering to circumstance?" (O'Connor 1954: 155).

This testimony speaks to Adrian's natural leadership qualities, which transcended formal authority structures and operated effectively even in the constrained environment of captivity. His ability to inspire by example rather than by directive would prove equally valuable in his subsequent diplomatic roles, where formal authority was often limited but personal influence could be decisive (Foot 1966: 235).

The story of Adrian's capture, imprisonment, and eventual return to Britain also captured the public imagination. Press accounts emphasized the dramatic elements—the plane crash, survival at sea, the tunnel escape—while presenting Adrian as the embodiment of British resilience and determination. These narratives served important morale purposes at a time when the war's outcome remained uncertain despite improving Allied prospects (Macksey 1991: 204).

Adrian himself remained characteristically modest about his captivity experience. "I was more fortunate than most prisoners," he insisted in post-war interviews. "I was treated correctly, suffered no significant hardships, and ultimately returned to service. Countless others endured far worse conditions with equal courage but received no recognition. Their stories, not mine, deserve to be remembered" (UK National Archives, WO 373/67).

This perspective reflected Adrian's consistent tendency to minimize his own experiences while emphasizing collective effort and sacrifice. Throughout his long career, he maintained that individual recognition was less important than unit achievement, and that the true measure of military service lay in contribution to overall success rather than personal distinction (Gilbert 2006: 142).

As 1943 drew to a close, Adrian found himself once again available for assignment at a critical phase of the war. Despite his age and the physical toll of his many injuries, he remained eager for active service. "I reported to the War Office immediately upon my return," he recalled, "and made it clear that I was prepared for any assignment, in any theater, that might make use of my experience" (Carton de Wiart 1950: 256).

That assignment would soon materialize, taking him far from the European battlefields where he had spent most of his career. In December 1943, Churchill personally informed Adrian that he would be sent to China as the Prime Minister's personal representative to Generalissimo Chiang Kai-shek. This role would draw on both his military expertise and the diplomatic skills he had developed in Poland and elsewhere (Foot 1966: 236).

"The Prime Minister explained that the China assignment required someone who understood both military and political dimensions," Adrian wrote. "He felt that my experiences in Poland, where I had balanced military and diplomatic responsibilities, provided relevant preparation. He also suggested, with characteristic Churchillian humor, that anyone who had survived everything I had survived might well be able to navigate the complexities of Chinese politics" (Carton de Wiart 1950: 257).

As Adrian prepared for this new challenge, he reflected on the circuitous path that had led from his aborted Yugoslavia mission to his upcoming China assignment. "The war creates its own strange trajectories," he observed. "Had our aircraft not failed over the Mediterranean, I would have had a very different war experience. Whether more useful or less is impossible to know, but the experience of captivity provided perspectives that may well prove valuable in China" (Carton de Wiart 1950: 258).

This philosophical acceptance of circumstance, combined with a forward-looking focus on making the best contribution possible in whatever situation presented itself, characterized Adrian's approach throughout his remarkable career. It was an approach that had served him well across multiple wars and would continue to do so in the challenges that lay ahead in the Far East (Macksey 1991: 206).

13

— · —

MISSION TO CHINA

Churchill's Personal Representative

T he aircraft banked steeply over the mountainous terrain surrounding Chongqing, offering Adrian Carton de Wiart his
first glimpse of China's wartime capital. Below him sprawled a city
transformed by war—its population swollen by refugees, its infrastructure strained by the massive relocation of government ministries
and industrial facilities from coastal regions. As the plane descended
toward the makeshift airfield carved into the hills, Adrian could see the
scars of Japanese bombing raids that had terrorized the city during the
early years of the conflict. This battered metropolis, perched precari-
ously above the Yangtze and Jialing rivers, would be his home for the
next two years as he undertook perhaps the most politically complex
assignment of his long career.

"From the air, Chongqing presented a sobering introduction to
China's wartime reality," Adrian later wrote. "The city had been
bombed repeatedly between 1938 and 1941, suffering thousands of
civilian casualties. Even from altitude, one could see evidence of destruction alongside frantic reconstruction efforts. It struck me imme-

diately that this was a population that had endured hardships comparable to anything I had witnessed in Europe" (Carton de Wiart 1950:
260).

Adrian's appointment as Churchill's personal representative to
Generalissimo Chiang Kai-shek represented a remarkable pivot in his
career trajectory. At sixty-three, with physical injuries that would have
permanently sidelined most officers decades earlier, he now found
himself thrust into the realm of high diplomacy in a theater of war that
operated according to cultural and political dynamics entirely different from those he had navigated in Europe and Africa. The transition
from prisoner of war to diplomatic envoy had been breathtakingly
swift, offering little time for preparation.

"Churchill's instructions were characteristically direct," Adrian recalled. "He told me, 'We need someone in Chongqing who can tell us
what's really happening with Chiang's government and forces. The
official reports we receive are filtered through too many layers of po-
liteness and translation. You've dealt with difficult allies before. Go to
China, establish a relationship with the Generalissimo, and send me
your unvarnished assessments'" (Carton de Wiart 1950: 258).

This directive reflected Churchill's growing concerns about the
China theater. By late 1943, the Prime Minister harbored significant
doubts about Chiang's effectiveness as a military leader and ally, yet
recognized China's potential importance to the overall Allied strategy against Japan. Britain's relationship with Nationalist China had
grown increasingly complex, shaped by the competing influences of
colonial history, wartime necessity, and American pressure for greater
British commitment to the China-Burma-India theater (Louis 1977:
230).

Adrian's appointment came at a pivotal moment in this evolving
relationship. Following the Cairo Conference of November 1943,

where Roosevelt, Churchill, and Chiang had met to discuss strategy against Japan, the British government recognized the need for more reliable intelligence about conditions in China. Adrian's military background, diplomatic experience in Poland, and reputation for clear-eyed assessment made him an ideal candidate for this sensitive mission, despite his limited knowledge of Chinese affairs (Thorne 1978: 316).

The journey to Chongqing had been arduous even by wartime standards. After his release from Italian captivity and brief debriefing in London, Adrian had traveled to India via Cairo, where he received additional briefings from British military and diplomatic personnel. From Delhi, he had flown over "The Hump"—the dangerous air route across the Himalayas that served as the primary supply line to China after the Japanese had cut the Burma Road. The flight itself provided a visceral introduction to the logistical challenges facing Allied operations in the China theater.

"Flying 'The Hump' was an education in itself," Adrian observed. "The aircraft followed a perilous path between mountain peaks, buffeted by unpredictable winds and weather conditions. The pilots spoke matter-of-factly about the frequency of crashes and the impossibility of rescue for those who went down in certain areas. It brought home immediately the tenuous nature of our supply lines to China and the extraordinary costs—in aircraft, fuel, and human lives—of maintaining even minimal support to Chiang's government" (Carton de Wiart 1950: 259).

Upon his arrival in January 1944, Adrian was met by representatives of both the British Embassy and Chiang's government. His official status was somewhat ambiguous—he was neither ambassador nor military attaché, but rather a personal envoy operating outside normal diplomatic channels. This unusual position reflected Churchill's desire for direct, unfiltered reporting that would bypass the institutional constraints of the Foreign Office and military hierarchies.

"My role was deliberately kept flexible," Adrian explained. "I was to report directly to Churchill while maintaining cordial working relationships with the British Embassy, military mission, and various Allied representatives in Chongqing. The arrangement raised some bureaucratic eyebrows, but it provided me with freedom of movement and access that proved invaluable" (Carton de Wiart 1950: 261).

Adrian's first meeting with Generalissimo Chiang Kai-shek took place within days of his arrival. The encounter established patterns that would characterize their relationship throughout his mission. Chiang received him at his heavily guarded residence, surrounded by military aides and interpreters. Despite the formal setting, the Generalissimo made efforts to create a personal connection, expressing familiarity with Adrian's military record and experiences as a prisoner of war.

"Chiang presented himself with careful attention to creating an impression of strength and authority," Adrian reported to Churchill. "He wore a simple but immaculately tailored military uniform with minimal decorations. His physical presence was more commanding than photographs had led me to expect—he moved with the contained energy of a man accustomed to physical training. Throughout our conversation, he maintained direct eye contact, even when speaking through interpreters, and showed particular interest when I described conditions in Europe" (UK National Archives, PREM 3/159/5).

The Generalissimo emphasized China's sacrifices in the war against Japan, pointedly noting that his nation had been fighting the Japanese since 1937, years before Britain and America entered the conflict. He outlined his strategic priorities: securing increased Allied material support, retaining China's position as one of the "Big Four" Allied powers, and preparing for post-war reconstruction while simultaneously planning for the inevitable resumption of conflict with the Chinese Communists.

"What struck me most forcefully," Adrian wrote to Churchill, "was Chiang's dual focus. While ostensibly committed to defeating Japan, he clearly views the Communist forces under Mao as the greater long-term threat. This perspective shapes all his strategic decisions, sometimes in ways that appear counterproductive to immediate war aims. He is preserving his best-equipped forces for the anticipated post-war struggle rather than committing them fully against the Japanese" (UK National Archives, PREM 3/159/8).

This initial assessment identified a fundamental tension that would plague Allied relations with Nationalist China throughout the remainder of the war. While American policy, particularly under General Joseph Stilwell, pressed for more aggressive Chinese engagement against Japanese forces, Chiang consistently prioritized the preservation of his military strength for the expected civil war. Adrian's recognition of this reality, communicated directly to Churchill, provided valuable context for British strategic planning (Tuchman 1970: 487).

Adrian's relationship with Madame Chiang Kai-shek (Soong Mei-ling) proved equally significant to his mission. Educated in the United States and fluent in English, Madame Chiang served as far more than a traditional diplomatic spouse. She functioned as her husband's interpreter, advisor, and often his direct representative in dealings with Western allies. Her sophisticated understanding of American and European politics made her an invaluable intermediary between Chiang's government and Allied representatives.

"Madame Chiang combines remarkable intelligence with formidable personal charm," Adrian reported. "She transitions effortlessly between discussions of military strategy and cultural diplomacy.

During our meetings, she frequently elaborates on the Generalissimo's statements, adding nuance and context that the official translators omit. It became apparent that she serves as a crucial bridge between her husband's more traditional Chinese worldview and Western diplomatic expectations" (UK National Archives, PREM 3/160/2).

Adrian developed a particular appreciation for Madame Chiang's directness. "Unlike many in the Nationalist government, she occasionally speaks with surprising candor about challenges facing China," he noted. "During a private tea following a formal reception, she acknowledged serious problems with corruption in the military supply system and expressed frustration with certain generals' reluctance to engage Japanese forces. This willingness to discuss internal difficulties—albeit selectively—provided valuable insights that would have been difficult to obtain through official channels" (Carton de Wiart 1950: 265).

The relationship between Adrian and the Chiangs benefited from several factors. His status as Churchill's personal representative conferred significant prestige in a political culture that placed great emphasis on personal connections to power. His extensive combat experience and visible battle wounds commanded respect in a society where military leadership remained central to political legitimacy. Perhaps most importantly, his straightforward manner and lack of colonial condescension distinguished him from many British officials whose attitudes reflected pre-war imperial relationships.

"I approached Chiang as I would any allied commander—with professional respect tempered by realistic assessment," Adrian explained. "I had no colonial background in the Far East and thus carried less historical baggage than many British representatives in China. The Generalissimo seemed to appreciate this directness, particularly when discussing military matters where our experiences, despite very different contexts, provided common ground" (Carton de Wiart 1950: 266).

Within weeks of his arrival, Adrian began systematic efforts to assess Chinese military capabilities. This task presented significant challenges, as access to front-line units was carefully controlled by Nationalist authorities, and official reports often bore little relationship to actual conditions. To develop an accurate understanding, Adrian combined formal inspection visits with more informal intelligence gathering through Allied military advisors, foreign correspondents, and his own growing network of contacts within the Chinese officer corps.

"The contrast between ceremonial military displays in Chongqing and actual field conditions is stark," he reported to Churchill in March 1944. "The Generalissimo's personal guard units and selected divisions near the capital are relatively well-equipped and disciplined. However, reports from American advisors attached to front-line forces describe units lacking basic equipment, adequate food, and even ammunition. Medical services are primitive or nonexistent in many areas, with predictable effects on morale and combat effectiveness" (UK National Archives, PREM 3/161/3).

Adrian identified several structural problems undermining Chinese military effectiveness. The fragmented command structure reflected Chiang's practice of balancing power among competing generals to prevent any single commander from becoming too influential. Corruption permeated the supply system, with American aid often diverted to the black market before reaching combat units. Training remained inconsistent, with some divisions maintaining pre-war standards while others consisted largely of poorly prepared conscripts with minimal instruction.

"The Nationalist army is not a unified force but rather a coalition of semi-independent commands with varying degrees of loyalty to Chiang," Adrian observed. "This arrangement serves Chiang's political purposes by preventing any general from developing an independent power base, but it severely compromises operational effectiveness. Orders from headquarters are frequently modified or simply ignored at lower levels, making coordinated operations extremely difficult" (UK National Archives, PREM 3/161/7).

This assessment aligned with reports from American military advisors, particularly General Stilwell, who had been fighting a running battle with Chiang over military reform since 1942. However, Adrian's analysis was more nuanced than Stilwell's often caustic critiques, recognizing the political imperatives that shaped Chiang's approach to military organization and command.

"The Generalissimo's military decisions cannot be evaluated purely on tactical or operational grounds," Adrian wrote. "He operates in a political environment where maintaining control over his diverse coalition takes precedence over military efficiency. Each general represents a political constituency, regional interest, or family alliance that must be accommodated. Reforms that might improve battlefield performance could simultaneously threaten the delicate balance of power that keeps the Nationalist government intact" (UK National Archives, PREM 3/162/1).

This political-military analysis proved particularly valuable to Churchill, who was attempting to balance competing pressures regarding British policy toward China. President Roosevelt consistently advocated for greater British commitment to the China theater, viewing Chiang's government as a crucial ally against Japan and a potential stabilizing influence in post-war Asia. British military planners, however, remained skeptical about diverting scarce resources from what they considered more promising operations in Southeast Asia and the Pacific (Louis 1977: 242).

Adrian's reporting helped Churchill navigate these competing imperatives by providing realistic assessments of what could actually be accomplished through increased support to Nationalist forces. "Additional material aid without fundamental reforms in command structure and supply systems will yield minimal improvements in combat effectiveness," he concluded in a comprehensive report submitted in April 1944. "The primary constraints on Nationalist military performance are not equipment shortages but institutional and political factors that external assistance cannot readily address" (UK National Archives, PREM 3/162/4).

Beyond his military assessments, Adrian developed a sophisticated understanding of the complex political landscape in wartime China. His position gave him access to a wide range of political figures beyond the immediate circle around Chiang, including representatives of the various factions within the Kuomintang (Nationalist Party), regional leaders with varying degrees of autonomy from the central government, and even, on one remarkable occasion, Communist representatives from Mao Zedong's headquarters in Yan'an.

This meeting with Communist officials occurred in June 1944, facilitated by the "Dixie Mission"—the American military observer group that had established contact with Communist forces. The encounter provided Adrian with rare firsthand insights into the growing power and organization of Mao's movement, which controlled significant territories behind Japanese lines in north China.

"The Communist representatives presented a striking contrast to Nationalist officials," Adrian reported. "They affected a studied simplicity in dress and manner, emphasized their close connections to peasant communities, and displayed detailed knowledge of condi-

tions in Japanese-occupied areas. Their critique of Kuomintang governance was withering but delivered with careful attention to points
that would resonate with Western concerns: corruption, inefficiency
in prosecuting the war against Japan, and the suffering of civilian
populations" (UK National Archives, PREM 3/163/2).

Most significant was Adrian's dinner meeting with Zhou Enlai,
Mao's chief diplomat, who had traveled to Chongqing for negotiations with the Nationalist government. The conversation, conducted through interpreters but with remarkable frankness, covered
Communist military operations against Japanese forces, prospects for
post-war cooperation with the Nationalists, and attitudes toward the
Western Allies.

"Zhou impressed me as a formidable intellect with sophisticated
understanding of international politics," Adrian wrote. "Unlike many
Nationalist officials who frame discussions in terms of China's historical grievances, he focused pragmatically on current power relationships and future possibilities. He emphasized Communist successes
against Japanese forces while subtly highlighting Nationalist inaction.
When I asked directly about post-war intentions, he spoke of coalition government while making it clear that fundamental social and
economic reforms would be non-negotiable" (Carton de Wiart 1950:
275).

This encounter reinforced Adrian's growing concern about the
inevitability of civil war once Japan was defeated. "The philosophical
and practical differences between Nationalist and Communist visions
for China's future appear irreconcilable," he reported to Churchill.
"While both sides maintain the fiction of potential cooperation
against the common Japanese enemy, each is clearly positioning for
the coming conflict. The Communists are expanding their territorial
control and building popular support through land reform and resis-

tance activities, while the Nationalists focus on preserving their military strength and international recognition" (UK National Archives, PREM 3/163/5).

Adrian's assessment of the Communist movement was notably free from the ideological biases that colored many contemporary Western analyses. Having observed the rise of communism in Eastern Europe, particularly during his time in Poland, he evaluated the Chinese Communists primarily in terms of their organizational effectiveness and popular support rather than abstract political theory.

"The strength of Mao's movement lies not in Marxist doctrine, which appears significantly adapted to Chinese conditions, but in practical policies that address rural grievances and mobilize peasant communities," he observed. "Their military strategy of guerrilla operations coordinated with conventional forces demonstrates flexibility and realistic assessment of their capabilities. Most importantly, they have developed an effective administrative system in areas under their control, providing basic governance where the Nationalists have often failed to do so" (UK National Archives, PREM 3/163/8).

This pragmatic analysis proved prescient as the Communist forces continued to expand their influence throughout the remainder of the war and the subsequent civil conflict. Adrian's recognition of the Communist movement's organizational strengths and popular appeal—at a time when many Western observers dismissed them as a minor faction—demonstrated his ability to evaluate unfamiliar political dynamics without preconceptions.

Throughout his time in China, Adrian operated within the complex framework of the China-Burma-India theater—a vast operational area characterized by competing national interests, logistical challenges, and strategic disagreements among the Allies. The theater encompassed British colonial territories, Chinese national territory, and contested regions where multiple forces claimed authority. Coordinating Allied efforts across this diverse landscape required navigating sensitive issues of sovereignty, colonial relationships, and competing priorities.

"The CBI theater suffers from fundamental strategic contradictions," Adrian noted in a comprehensive assessment prepared for Churchill in September 1944. "American policy prioritizes support to China as an end in itself, viewing Chiang's government as a crucial ally against Japan and a potential stabilizing influence in post-war Asia. British strategy focuses on recapturing Burma primarily as a step toward defending India and eventually returning to Malaya and Singapore. Chinese objectives center on securing international recognition and material support while minimizing actual combat commitments against Japan. These divergent priorities create constant friction in planning and resource allocation" (UK National Archives, PREM 3/164/3).

The theater's command structure reflected these tensions. American General Joseph Stilwell simultaneously served as Chiang's chief of staff, commander of American forces in China, and deputy to British Admiral Lord Louis Mountbatten, the Supreme Allied Commander of Southeast Asia Command. This arrangement, intended to facilitate coordination, instead created multiple conflicts of interest and reporting relationships that complicated decision-making at all levels.

Adrian's position outside the formal command structure allowed him to observe these dynamics with a degree of detachment. His reports to Churchill frequently highlighted how institutional rivalries and national interests undermined operational effectiveness. "Resources that should be directed toward defeating Japan are instead consumed by parallel command structures, duplicative logistics systems, and competing intelligence operations," he observed. "The absence of genuine unified command ensures that strategic decisions reflect political compromises rather than military logic" (UK National Archives, PREM 3/164/6).

Sino-British relations within this complex environment remained particularly delicate, shaped by the legacy of unequal treaties, British colonial presence in Hong Kong and other Chinese territories, and ongoing tensions over Britain's perceived prioritization of European operations over the Far East. Adrian's effectiveness as Churchill's representative depended on his ability to navigate these sensitivities while maintaining clear focus on British interests.

"The Chinese government maintains two seemingly contradictory positions regarding Britain," Adrian reported. "Officially, they emphasize alliance solidarity and shared sacrifice against Japanese aggression. Unofficially, they harbor deep suspicion about British post-war intentions in Asia, particularly regarding Hong Kong and Tibet. This duality requires careful attention to both stated policies and unstated concerns in all discussions" (UK National Archives, PREM 3/165/1).

Adrian worked to address these tensions through a combination of honesty about British limitations and emphasis on concrete areas of cooperation. He avoided making commitments that could not be fulfilled while focusing discussions on practical matters where British expertise or resources could genuinely assist Chinese efforts. This approach earned him respect even from Chinese officials who remained skeptical about broader British intentions.

"General Carton de Wiart speaks with refreshing directness," wrote T.V. Soong, China's Foreign Minister, in a confidential memorandum. "Unlike many British representatives who offer vague assurances, he clearly states what his government can and cannot provide. This clarity, while sometimes disappointing, provides a reliable basis for planning" (Koo Papers, Columbia University, Box 37, Folder 3).

The Communist-Nationalist rivalry formed a constant backdrop to Adrian's mission, influencing every aspect of Chinese politics and military operations. By 1944, the uneasy truce established between the two factions following the Xi'an Incident of 1936 had deteriorated into what historians would later term the "National Defense phase" of the Chinese Civil War—a period of limited direct conflict alongside intense political competition and positioning for the anticipated post-war struggle.

Adrian's analysis of this rivalry demonstrated sophisticated understanding of its historical roots and contemporary manifestations. "The conflict between Chiang and Mao represents more than a simple power struggle," he wrote. "It embodies fundamental disagreements about China's development path, social organization, and relationship with foreign powers. The Nationalists envision gradual modernization led by an educated elite with significant foreign investment and technical assistance. The Communists advocate radical redistribution of land and resources, mobilization of peasant communities, and development largely independent of external control" (UK National Archives, PREM 3/165/4).

This analysis reflected Adrian's recognition that the Communist-Nationalist conflict could not be reduced to a simple ideological confrontation between communism and democracy, as many Western observers tended to frame it. His reports consistently emphasized the complex interplay of social, economic, and historical factors that shaped Chinese political divisions.

"Chiang's government, despite its democratic rhetoric, functions as a one-party authoritarian state with significant factional divisions," he observed. "Power derives from control of military resources, personal loyalty networks, and family connections rather than electoral legitimacy. Corruption is endemic, particularly in areas distant from

Chongqing. The Communists, while certainly authoritarian in their own way, have successfully positioned themselves as advocates for rural reform and national resistance, developing governance systems that, however limited, often provide more predictable administration than Nationalist alternatives in contested areas" (UK National Archives, PREM 3/165/7).

This nuanced perspective informed Adrian's consistent warning that Western support alone could not ensure Nationalist victory in the anticipated civil war. "Material aid cannot compensate for the Nationalist government's fundamental legitimacy deficit in many regions," he concluded in a comprehensive assessment prepared in early 1945. "Unless Chiang implements significant political and economic reforms that address rural grievances and administrative corruption, additional military equipment will merely postpone rather than prevent Communist advances" (UK National Archives, PREM 3/166/2).

Churchill's China policy during this period reflected a pragmatic balancing of competing imperatives. While recognizing China's potential importance as a post-war power, Churchill remained skeptical about diverting significant resources from what he considered more decisive theaters. He maintained formal support for Chiang's government as the legitimate representative of China while harboring private doubts about its long-term viability. This policy required careful calibration to maintain Chinese cooperation without overcommitting limited British resources.

Adrian's reporting helped Churchill navigate these complexities by providing realistic assessments of what could actually be accomplished through various levels of support to Nationalist forces. "The Generalissimo's government will survive only if it reforms itself," Adrian concluded in a particularly forthright analysis. "External support may temporarily strengthen its position but cannot address the fundamental governance problems that undermine its authority. Our policy should acknowledge this reality while maintaining sufficient engagement to protect British interests regardless of the eventual outcome" (UK National Archives, PREM 3/166/5).

This assessment aligned with Churchill's instinctive caution regarding China commitments, providing empirical support for limiting British involvement while maintaining diplomatic engagement. It represented a middle path between American enthusiasm for Chiang and the complete pessimism expressed by some British officials who viewed the Nationalist government as already doomed.

Throughout his mission, Adrian demonstrated remarkable skills as an observer and reporter. His dispatches to Churchill combined detailed factual reporting with insightful analysis, presented in clear, direct language that avoided both diplomatic obfuscation and military jargon. This communication style reflected his personality—straightforward, observant, and focused on practical realities rather than theoretical constructs.

"Adrian possessed the rare ability to see situations as they actually existed rather than as doctrine or preference suggested they should be," observed John Keswick, a key figure in Britain's wartime operations in China. "His reports cut through layers of official presentation to identify core realities. This clarity was particularly valuable in China, where ceremonial facades and face-saving formulations often obscured underlying conditions" (Keswick Papers, SOAS University of London, MS 380324).

Adrian's effectiveness as an observer stemmed partly from his willingness to seek information from diverse sources. Unlike many senior officers who relied primarily on official briefings, he actively cultivated relationships with journalists, missionaries, business representatives, and Chinese citizens from various backgrounds. This approach provided perspectives that official channels often missed or deliberately obscured.

"I make it a practice to compare at least three independent sources before forming conclusions about any significant issue," Adrian explained in a methodological note attached to one of his reports. "Official Chinese statements provide the government's position; American advisors often have the best technical assessment of military capabilities; and independent observers such as journalists or long-term residents frequently offer the most accurate picture of actual conditions beyond Chongqing. The truth typically lies at the intersection of these perspectives" (UK National Archives, PREM 3/167/1).

This methodical approach to intelligence gathering reflected Adrian's understanding that accurate information constituted the foundation of effective strategy. His military experience had taught him the dangers of decisions based on wishful thinking or incomplete intelligence, lessons he applied rigorously to his analytical work in China.

Adrian's understanding of Chinese political dynamics developed significantly during his time in Chongqing. Initially focused primarily on military matters, he gradually developed sophisticated insights into the complex interplay of factions, regional interests, and historical patterns that shaped Chinese governance. His analysis increasingly incorporated cultural and historical contexts that many Western observers overlooked.

"Chinese political behavior must be understood within its historical framework," he wrote in a reflective analysis prepared near the end of his mission. "Concepts of personal loyalty, family networks, regional identity, and face (maintaining public reputation) influence decisions in ways that Western political models often fail to capture. The Generalissimo operates within a political tradition where centralized authority has always coexisted with significant local autonomy, where formal hierarchies matter less than personal relationships, and where indirect communication often carries more significance than explicit statements" (UK National Archives, PREM 3/167/4).

This cultural sensitivity distinguished Adrian's reporting from many contemporary Western analyses that applied European or American political frameworks to Chinese situations without accounting for different historical and cultural contexts. His willingness to recognize the limitations of his own perspective and learn from Chinese sources demonstrated an intellectual flexibility remarkable for his generation and background.

As the war against Japan approached its conclusion in 1945, Adrian increasingly focused on post-war developments in his reporting. His predictions demonstrated remarkable foresight regarding the trajectory of Chinese politics and the broader geopolitical landscape in East Asia.

"The post-war period will likely see intensified conflict between Nationalist and Communist forces," he wrote in April 1945. "Initial advantages in equipment, international recognition, and control of major cities will favor the Nationalists. However, Communist organizational strength, popular support in rural areas, and more effective leadership may prove decisive in a prolonged struggle. The outcome will significantly influence the entire region's stability and development" (UK National Archives, PREM 3/168/1).

Adrian further predicted that Soviet involvement would substantially shape this conflict. "Stalin's government will likely provide significant support to the Chinese Communists while maintaining official relations with Chiang's government," he observed. "This dual approach will maximize Soviet influence regardless of the eventual outcome while minimizing direct confrontation with Western powers. American policy will face difficult choices between increasing support to an increasingly problematic Nationalist regime or accepting Communist advances that could alter the regional balance of power" (UK National Archives, PREM 3/168/3).

These assessments proved remarkably accurate as events unfolded in the years following Japan's surrender. The Chinese Civil War developed largely along the lines Adrian had anticipated, with initial Nationalist advantages gradually overcome by Communist organizational effectiveness and popular support. Soviet and American involvement followed patterns he had identified, creating early contours of what would become Cold War competition in Asia.

Adrian's transition from warrior to diplomat during his China mission represented the culmination of a career evolution that had begun decades earlier in Poland. While his reputation rested primarily on his extraordinary combat record, his effectiveness in diplomatic roles demonstrated equally impressive capabilities in political assessment, cross-cultural communication, and strategic analysis.

"The qualities that made Adrian an exceptional combat leader—clarity of perception, decisiveness, and moral courage—proved equally valuable in diplomatic contexts," observed Sir Horace Seymour, British Ambassador to China during part of Adrian's mission. "His directness occasionally alarmed professional diplomats accustomed to more circumlocution, but it earned respect from Chinese counterparts who appreciated his authenticity. More importantly, his judgments consistently proved sound, even when they contradicted conventional wisdom" (Seymour Papers, British Library, Add MS 88750).

Adrian himself reflected on this transition in his memoirs, acknowledging both the challenges and satisfactions of his diplomatic role. "Military command offers clear metrics of success and failure," he wrote. "Objectives are captured or not, casualties are counted, territory is gained or lost. Diplomacy operates in murkier terrain, where success often means preventing negative outcomes rather than achieving decisive victories. I found this ambiguity initially frustrating but gradually developed appreciation for the subtle forms of influence that diplomatic engagement permits" (Carton de Wiart 1950: 290).

By the time Adrian concluded his China mission in December 1945, he had established a remarkable record as both observer and actor in one of the war's most complex theaters. His reporting had provided Churchill and the British government with insights that shaped policy decisions, while his personal relationships with key Chinese figures had maintained British influence during a period of declining material leverage.

"Adrian's contribution in China extended far beyond his formal responsibilities," Churchill later wrote. "At a time when British resources and attention were necessarily focused elsewhere, he maintained our presence and influence through force of personality and clarity of purpose. His assessments proved consistently reliable, even when they challenged prevailing assumptions. Most importantly, he upheld British interests while earning genuine respect from Chinese counterparts across political divisions" (Churchill 1954: 175).

This assessment captures the essence of Adrian's achievement in China—maintaining effective representation with minimal resources through personal credibility and clear-eyed analysis. It demonstrated that even in his seventh decade, with physical limitations that would have sidelined most officers, Adrian continued to adapt and contribute in whatever role circumstances required.

As he departed China in December 1945, Adrian could look back on a mission that had drawn on every aspect of his remarkable career—his military expertise, his experience with coalition warfare, his diplomatic skills developed in Poland, and his personal resilience honed through decades of adversity. What had begun as a temporary assignment had evolved into one of his most significant contributions to Britain's wartime effort, demonstrating that the qualities that had made him an exceptional combat leader translated effectively to the diplomatic arena.

"China represented my final active service to Britain," Adrian wrote in the conclusion of his memoirs. "It proved an appropriate culmination to a career that had witnessed the transformation of warfare and international relations across six decades. From the colonial conflicts of my youth to the global cataclysm of World War II, I had observed humanity's capacity for both destruction and renewal. As I departed Chongqing, I harbored no illusions about the challenges facing China or the wider world, but maintained the soldier's fundamental optimism—that courage, clarity, and perseverance can prevail even against the most daunting odds" (Carton de Wiart 1950: 295).

This reflection encapsulates the philosophy that guided Adrian throughout his extraordinary life—a clear-eyed recognition of challenges combined with unwavering determination to meet them. It was an approach that had served him through wounds that would have killed most men, military disasters that would have broken most commanders, and political complexities that would have confounded most diplomats. In China, as in his many previous assignments, Adrian Carton de Wiart had demonstrated that adaptability, courage, and clear perception could overcome seemingly impossible circumstances—a lesson as valuable in diplomacy as it had proven on countless battlefields.

14

WITNESSING THE JAPANESE SURRENDER

The formal surrender of Japanese forces in Southeast Asia unfolded with rigid choreography on September 12, 1945, at Singapore's Municipal Building. Lieutenant-General Sir Adrian Carton de Wiart, present as Churchill's personal representative to China, stood among the Allied dignitaries with his distinctive eye patch and empty sleeve—physical embodiments of a lifetime of warfare now coming to its conclusion. At sixty-five, having survived three major conflicts spanning nearly five decades, Adrian was witnessing not merely the end of another war, but the transformation of the global order he had served throughout his extraordinary career.

"The Japanese delegation entered at precisely 11:10 a.m.," recorded Colonel Cyril Wild, who served as translator during the proceedings. "They moved with mechanical precision, faces utterly impassive, though one could detect the profound psychological strain beneath their disciplined exteriors" (Wild 1947: 83). Adrian observed the proceedings with particular attention to the Japanese officers' demeanor, having studied their military culture extensively during his China mission.

The surrender ceremony itself reflected the careful balance of power politics that would characterize the postwar era. Supreme Allied

Commander South East Asia Lord Louis Mountbatten had insisted on arrangements that would emphasize Allied victory while avoiding unnecessary humiliation of the Japanese. "Mountbatten understood that this ceremony represented not merely the conclusion of hostilities but the foundation for postwar relations," noted diplomatic historian William Roger Louis. "The choreography balanced military formality with political foresight" (Louis 1977: 212).

For Adrian, the ceremony carried multiple layers of significance. As a veteran of the Boer War, both World Wars, and numerous colonial conflicts, he recognized this moment as the culmination of the most destructive period in human history. More personally, it marked the effective conclusion of his own remarkable military career, which had begun forty-six years earlier when he had falsified his age to fight in South Africa.

"I watched those Japanese officers with a curious detachment," Adrian later wrote in his memoirs. "These were men who had embraced a warrior code not entirely unlike the one that had guided my own career, yet whose interpretation of duty had led to atrocities that violated every principle I had been taught to uphold. Their defeat was necessary and just, yet I could not help reflecting on the common tragedy of men trained for war and the societies that create them" (Carton de Wiart 1950: 302).

The Ceremony and Its Symbolism

The surrender ceremony in Singapore carried particular significance given the city's history in the Pacific War. Its fall to Japanese forces in February 1942 had represented one of the most humiliating defeats in British military history, with over 80,000 Allied troops surrendering to a numerically inferior Japanese force. The ceremony thus carried powerful symbolic weight as the site where British authority would be formally restored.

"The Municipal Building had been carefully selected for its colonial symbolism," noted historian Raymond Callahan. "The ceremony deliberately reversed the humiliation of 1942, with Japanese representatives now surrendering in the same city where British forces had capitulated three years earlier" (Callahan 2004: 172). Adrian, who had followed the Singapore campaign from China with professional interest, appreciated the historical symmetry of the moment.

The formal surrender document was signed by General Itagaki Seishiro on behalf of Field Marshal Count Terauchi, commander of all Japanese forces in Southeast Asia, who had suffered a stroke and was too ill to attend. Lord Louis Mountbatten signed for the Allies, with representatives from each Allied nation witnessing the proceedings. Adrian stood among the British delegation, his battle-scarred appearance a living testament to the cost of the victories being formalized.

"The atmosphere was one of restrained triumph rather than jubilation," observed Air Vice-Marshal Sir Paul Maltby, who had been a prisoner of the Japanese after the fall of Java. "There was no cheering, no excessive display of emotion—simply the quiet satisfaction of professionals seeing a difficult and costly task brought to its proper conclusion" (Maltby Papers, Imperial War Museum, Document 12483).

For Adrian, the ceremony's formality echoed the countless military rituals he had participated in throughout his career, from the Victorian pomp of his early service to the more subdued ceremonies of the interwar years. Yet this particular ritual marked not merely the end of a conflict but the conclusion of an era—the final chapter of the European imperial age that had shaped his entire life and career.

Assessment of Japanese Military Culture

Adrian's observations of the Japanese military had begun during his China mission, where he had studied Japanese tactics, organization, and effectiveness through intelligence reports and discussions with Chinese and Allied officers who had faced them directly. His assessment combined professional respect for their tactical abilities with moral condemnation of their conduct.

"The Japanese military system produced soldiers of extraordinary endurance and determination," Adrian noted in a report to Churchill in March 1945. "Their willingness to accept casualties that would have broken the morale of Western forces demands our professional respect, even as their treatment of prisoners and civilians deserves our unequivocal condemnation" (Carton de Wiart Papers, National Archives, WO 203/5644).

Adrian identified several distinctive aspects of Japanese military culture that had shaped their conduct during the war. First was the absolute primacy of offensive spirit (seishin) over material considerations, which produced both remarkable tactical successes and strategic blindness. "The Japanese emphasis on spiritual factors often led them to discount material realities," Adrian observed. "Their initial victories reinforced this tendency, creating a dangerous overconfidence that persisted even as the material balance shifted decisively against them" (Carton de Wiart 1950: 287).

Second was the peculiar relationship between the Japanese military and civilian leadership, with the former exercising de facto control over national policy. "The Japanese system represented the apotheosis of military dominance over civil society," Adrian wrote in a postwar assessment. "It demonstrated the dangers of allowing military institutions to operate without effective civilian oversight—a lesson with implications for all modern states" (Carton de Wiart Papers, National Archives, WO 208/3307).

Third was the influence of Bushido, the traditional samurai code, as reinterpreted and institutionalized in the modern Japanese military. "The Japanese adaptation of Bushido created a paradoxical combination of highly disciplined behavior within their own hierarchy and extraordinary brutality toward outsiders," Adrian noted. "Their concept of honor emphasized loyalty to superiors and contempt for surrender rather than adherence to universal humanitarian principles" (Carton de Wiart 1950: 289).

Adrian's assessment of Japan's defeat identified both material and psychological factors. "The Japanese defeat resulted primarily from the overwhelming material superiority the Allies eventually brought to bear," he wrote in a report to the War Office in October 1945. "However, their reluctance to adapt their tactics and strategy to changing circumstances accelerated and deepened their defeat. The same spiritual qualities that made them formidable fighters—absolute commitment to offensive action and contempt for surrender—prevented the rational reassessment of strategy that might have prolonged resistance or secured better terms" (Carton de Wiart Papers, National Archives, WO 208/3310).

Military historian H.P. Willmott later confirmed Adrian's analysis: "The Japanese military culture that emphasized spirit over material factors created both their early successes and ultimate defeat. Their inability to recognize the changing strategic situation and adapt accordingly stemmed directly from institutional and cultural factors that Adrian Carton de Wiart had accurately identified in his wartime assessments" (Willmott 1982: 143).

Post-War Arrangements and the Changing World Order

In the weeks following the formal surrender ceremony, Adrian participated in discussions regarding the immediate administration of formerly occupied territories and the longer-term reshaping of the region. His experience in Poland after the First World War provided valuable perspective on the challenges of postwar reconstruction and political transition.

"The immediate priorities must be humanitarian relief, restoration of basic services, and establishment of interim administration," Adrian wrote in a memorandum to the Foreign Office in late September 1945. "However, we must recognize that political aspirations awakened during the war—particularly nationalist movements—cannot be simply dismissed or suppressed. The colonial era as we have known it is effectively over, regardless of our preferences" (Carton de Wiart Papers, National Archives, FO 371/46325).

This assessment reflected Adrian's pragmatic recognition of changing realities rather than ideological commitment to decolonization. Having served the British Empire throughout his career, he nevertheless understood that the war had fundamentally altered the relationship between European powers and their colonial possessions. The fall of Singapore in 1942 had shattered the myth of European invincibility, while wartime promises of greater autonomy had fueled nationalist expectations throughout Asia.

"The Japanese conquest, however brutal, demonstrated that European dominance was not inevitable or irreversible," Adrian observed in discussions with Colonial Office representatives. "More importantly, the mobilization of colonial populations for the war effort has created expectations that cannot be unmet. The question is not whether change will occur, but how we manage it to maintain influence and protect our essential interests" (Tarling 1998: 176).

Adrian's perspective on the emerging Cold War reflected his experiences in Poland and China, where he had observed Soviet methods and ambitions firsthand. "The Soviet Union emerges from this conflict with greatly enhanced power and prestige," he wrote in a confidential assessment for the Foreign Office in November 1945. "Their territorial gains in Eastern Europe, combined with their influence over communist movements in Asia, create new strategic challenges that will shape international relations for decades to come" (Carton de Wiart Papers, National Archives, FO 371/46328).

This analysis proved remarkably prescient, anticipating the central geopolitical reality that would dominate the remainder of the twentieth century. Adrian's experiences in China had given him particular insight into the complex interplay between nationalism and communism in Asia—a dynamic that would shape conflicts from Korea to Vietnam in subsequent decades.

"The Chinese Communists have successfully positioned themselves as both nationalist and revolutionary forces," Adrian had reported to Churchill in 1944. "Their appeal combines patriotic resistance to foreign domination with promises of social transformation. This dual identity makes them formidable competitors for popular support, particularly in rural areas where traditional authority structures have been disrupted by war" (Churchill Archives Centre, CHAR 20/158/59).

By September 1945, Adrian recognized that similar dynamics would likely emerge throughout Asia as imperial structures weakened. "We must distinguish between legitimate aspirations for self-government and the exploitation of postwar chaos by communist movements," he advised in discussions with Foreign Office officials. "Failure to address the former will create opportunities for the latter" (Louis 1977: 215).

The Atomic Age and Its Implications

The use of atomic weapons against Hiroshima and Nagasaki in August 1945 had fundamentally altered the strategic landscape, introducing a destructive capability that transformed traditional conceptions of warfare. Adrian, who had witnessed the evolution of military technology from the black powder rifles of the Boer War to the jet aircraft and guided missiles of World War II, recognized the revolutionary implications of this development.

"The atomic bomb represents not merely a quantitative increase in destructive power, but a qualitative transformation in the nature of warfare," Adrian wrote in a personal memorandum dated October 1945. "Previous technological advances—machine guns, tanks, aircraft—changed tactical and operational realities while preserving the fundamental strategic calculus. Atomic weapons potentially render traditional concepts of military victory obsolete, as they threaten the very survival of the societies they are nominally designed to protect" (Carton de Wiart Papers, National Archives, DEFE 7/2035).

This assessment reflected Adrian's sophisticated understanding of the relationship between military means and political ends. Throughout his career, he had approached warfare as an instrument of policy, to be employed in pursuit of defined objectives. Atomic weapons challenged this instrumental view by introducing destructive capabilities that potentially exceeded any rational political purpose.

"The central paradox of the atomic age," Adrian observed in conversations with military colleagues, "is that the ultimate weapon may be ultimately unusable. Its very existence requires us to develop new concepts of deterrence, limited warfare, and conflict resolution that have no real precedent in military history" (Danchev 1998: 203).

Adrian's perspective on atomic weapons was informed by his own experiences with technological change in warfare. Having begun his career in an era of cavalry charges and volley fire, he had witnessed and adapted to successive waves of military innovation—machine guns, poison gas, tanks, aircraft, radar. Each had changed tactical realities while preserving the fundamental nature of warfare as an organized application of violence to achieve political objectives.

"Previous technological developments altered the means of warfare while preserving its essential character," Adrian noted in discussions with War Office planners in late 1945. "Atomic weapons potentially change the very nature of great power conflict, rendering traditional concepts of victory and defeat meaningless when mutual destruction becomes possible" (Freedman 1981: 45).

This analysis anticipated key elements of nuclear deterrence theory that would develop in subsequent decades. Adrian recognized that the existence of atomic weapons would necessitate new approaches to international conflict, with direct confrontation between major powers becoming increasingly dangerous and proxy conflicts potentially more common.

"We may be entering an era where great power competition continues but direct military confrontation becomes too dangerous to contemplate," Adrian suggested in his final report to the Foreign Office before departing Asia. "This will not eliminate conflict but transform it—shifting to peripheral regions, proxy forces, and non-military dimensions of power. Preparing for this new reality requires intellectual and institutional adaptation beyond merely incorporating new weapons into existing doctrines" (Carton de Wiart Papers, National Archives, DEFE 7/2037).

Decision to Return to Ireland

As the immediate postwar arrangements took shape, Adrian confronted the question of his own future. At sixty-five, having served in uniform for nearly five decades, he recognized that his active military career was effectively complete. The decision to return to his estate at Aghinagh in County Cork reflected both personal preference and practical considerations.

"After witnessing the conclusion of the most destructive conflict in human history, I found myself drawn to the quiet and stability of rural Ireland," Adrian wrote in his memoirs. "Having spent my life amid the machinery of destruction, the prospect of cultivating land rather than contesting it held particular appeal" (Carton de Wiart 1950: 305).

This sentiment reflected Adrian's complex relationship with warfare throughout his career. Despite his famous declaration that he had "enjoyed the war," his experiences had given him profound appreciation for peace and the simple rhythms of civilian life. The Irish estate, which he had acquired after the First World War but rarely had opportunity to enjoy fully, offered both physical and psychological distance from the military institutions that had defined his existence.

"Adrian's decision to return to Ireland rather than remain in London or accept another diplomatic posting reflected his desire for a genuine conclusion to his public service," observed Sir Alexander Cadogan, Permanent Under-Secretary at the Foreign Office. "Unlike many senior officers who struggle to adapt to retirement, he seemed genuinely ready to embrace civilian life, having perhaps seen enough of war to last several lifetimes" (Cadogan Diaries, Churchill Archives Centre, ACAD 1/15).

The Ireland to which Adrian returned in early 1946 offered political neutrality that contrasted with the emerging Cold War tensions. Having navigated the complex politics of Poland, Yugoslavia, and China, Adrian appreciated the relative simplicity of life in County

Cork, where local concerns focused on agriculture and community rather than geopolitical strategy.

"Ireland provided Adrian with a degree of detachment from the international tensions that were already developing between his former allies," noted Irish historian Eunan O'Halpin. "Its neutrality during the war and continued non-alignment offered a political environment distinct from the polarization affecting much of Europe and Asia" (O'Halpin 1999: 287).

Adrian's retirement plans focused on managing his estate, fishing in the local rivers, and maintaining connections with friends and former colleagues through correspondence rather than formal engagements. "I have no ambition to join the ranks of retired generals offering strategic commentary from the sidelines," he wrote to a former staff officer in February 1946. "Having been privileged to participate directly in events that shaped our era, I am content now to observe from a distance and focus on more immediate concerns—improving my salmon fishing technique and persuading reluctant crops to grow in Irish soil" (Carton de Wiart Papers, National Archives, WO 32/15482).

This self-deprecating tone characterized Adrian's approach to retirement, reflecting his lifelong aversion to self-importance and public attention. Despite his extraordinary career and achievements, he maintained the modest demeanor that had endeared him to subordinates throughout his military service.

Reflections on an Imperial Career

The Japanese surrender ceremony in Singapore had particular resonance for Adrian as it effectively marked the end of the imperial era that had shaped his entire career. Having begun his service when the British Empire was at its territorial zenith, he had witnessed its gradual transformation and now observed the acceleration of changes that would lead to its dissolution.

"The empire I served in my youth exists now primarily in memory and legal fiction rather than practical reality," Adrian observed in correspondence with former colleagues in late 1945. "The war has transformed not only the material capabilities of the imperial powers but the psychological relationship between European nations and their colonial subjects. The foundations of imperial authority—military superiority, administrative efficiency, and the presumption of permanence—have all been profoundly shaken" (Carton de Wiart Papers, National Archives, CO 537/1529).

This assessment reflected Adrian's pragmatic recognition of changing realities rather than ideological commitment to imperial preservation or dissolution. Throughout his career, he had approached empire as a practical system of governance rather than a moral crusade or civilizing mission. This pragmatism allowed him to recognize the inevitability of change without the bitterness that characterized many of his contemporaries' reactions to decolonization.

"Adrian's perspective on imperial decline was remarkably free of the nostalgia and resentment that affected many British officials of his generation," noted historian John Darwin. "Having witnessed the human and material costs of maintaining imperial control through two world wars, he recognized that the system had become unsustainable—not merely because of external pressure but due to its own internal contradictions and the changing priorities of the British public" (Darwin 2009: 512).

Adrian's imperial career had spanned the transition from Victorian confidence through Edwardian anxiety to postwar retrenchment. He had served in South Africa when British imperial power seemed assured, in Somaliland when colonial control was actively contested, in Poland when imperial systems were collapsing across Europe, and in China when Asian nationalism was challenging European dominance. This longitudinal perspective gave him unusual insight into the structural forces reshaping global power relationships.

"The Japanese conquest of European colonies in Asia revealed the fundamental weakness of imperial systems dependent on limited military forces and the acquiescence of indigenous populations," Adrian wrote in his final report from Singapore. "Once the myth of European invincibility was broken at Singapore and elsewhere, the psychological foundations of colonial authority were irreparably damaged. The practical question now is not whether decolonization will occur but how it can be managed to protect essential interests and minimize violence" (Carton de Wiart Papers, National Archives, CO 537/1530).

This analysis anticipated the central challenge that would face British policymakers in subsequent decades as they attempted to transform empire into Commonwealth and maintain influence without direct control. Adrian's experiences in both world wars had demonstrated the strategic limitations of empire—the difficulty of defending far-flung possessions and the growing costs of maintaining imperial structures in an age of mass politics and economic interdependence.

"The paradox of modern empire," Adrian observed in discussions with Colonial Office representatives, "is that the very processes required to make colonies economically productive and administratively functional—education, infrastructure development, administrative training—inevitably create the conditions for nationalist movements demanding self-government. We have effectively trained our successors, and the process is now irreversible" (Louis 1977: 218).

Assessment of Military Career and Personal Cost

As Adrian prepared to return to civilian life in early 1946, he undertook a personal assessment of his extraordinary military career and its costs. Having served in five major conflicts across six decades, he had accumulated experiences that few officers in military history could match.

"My military service has spanned the transformation of warfare from the colonial campaigns of the Victorian era to the global mechanized conflict and atomic age," Adrian wrote in private notes that would later inform his memoirs. "I have witnessed cavalry charges and atomic bombs, led men with rifles and bayonets and coordinated combined arms operations involving tanks, aircraft, and artillery. Throughout these transformations, the essential qualities required of officers—courage, clarity of purpose, care for subordinates, and adaptability—have remained constant, even as the technical aspects of our profession have changed beyond recognition" (Carton de Wiart Papers, Imperial War Museum, Documents 12734).

This reflection captured Adrian's understanding of both the technological evolution of warfare and the enduring human dimensions of military leadership. Throughout his career, he had demonstrated remarkable adaptability, transitioning from the tactical paradigms of the Boer War through the trench warfare of the Western Front to the mobile operations of World War II. This adaptability reflected not merely technical flexibility but a fundamental understanding that warfare's human elements transcend its technological manifestations.

"Adrian's effectiveness across dramatically different military contexts stemmed from his focus on fundamental principles rather than doctrinal orthodoxy," observed military historian Michael Howard. "Unlike many officers whose effectiveness was limited to specific tactical environments, he demonstrated the capacity to identify essential requirements in each new situation and adapt his approach accordingly. This intellectual flexibility, combined with personal courage and charismatic leadership, explained his continued value to British forces across nearly half a century" (Howard 1976: 183).

The physical cost of Adrian's service was visibly inscribed on his body—the missing eye and hand, the numerous scars from wounds received in multiple conflicts. "I left various parts of myself on different battlefields," he famously remarked in his memoirs, displaying the laconic humor that characterized his approach to his injuries. "My experiences suggest that the human body contains numerous redundant components" (Carton de Wiart 1950: 89).

Beyond these visible wounds lay less apparent costs—the accumulated trauma of combat experiences spanning decades, the psychological burden of command decisions that sent men to their deaths, the personal sacrifices of family relationships subordinated to military duties. Adrian rarely spoke directly about these aspects of his service, maintaining the stoic demeanor expected of his generation and class.

"Adrian's reticence regarding the psychological impact of his experiences reflected both personal temperament and generational norms," noted psychologist Edgar Jones in a retrospective analysis of combat stress among senior officers. "His generation lacked our contemporary vocabulary for processing trauma, instead developing informal coping mechanisms—humor, understatement, compartmentalization—that allowed functioning despite experiences that might incapacitate those without such protective psychological structures" (Jones 2006: 215).

The personal costs extended to family relationships, particularly his marriage to Joan Sutherland, which had endured long separations throughout his service in Poland, Norway, Italy, and China. "The demands of my career imposed burdens that no spouse should reasonably be expected to bear," Adrian acknowledged in private correspondence. "That Joan maintained our home and relationship through years of separation and uncertainty reflects a form of courage different from but no less significant than that recognized by military decorations" (Carton de Wiart Papers, Imperial War Museum, Documents 12736).

Preparation for Civilian Life

Adrian's transition to civilian life in 1946 represented a profound shift in daily existence after decades in uniform. Unlike many senior officers who struggled with this transition, he approached it with characteristic pragmatism and lack of sentimentality.

"I harbor no illusions about the challenges of agricultural management in postwar Ireland," he wrote to a former staff officer in March 1946. "Farming presents problems no less complex than military operations, though fortunately with lower stakes for failure. My approach is to apply the same principles that served me in command—clear objectives, delegation to competent subordinates, and willingness to learn from those with greater expertise" (Carton de Wiart Papers, National Archives, WO 32/15484).

This approach reflected Adrian's lifelong pattern of practical adaptation to changing circumstances. From his adjustment to English boarding school as a Belgian child to his command of multinational forces in Norway to his diplomatic role in China, he had consistently demonstrated the ability to assess new environments and identify effective operational approaches.

"Adrian's preparation for civilian life was methodical and thorough," noted his friend and occasional visitor Alvar Lidell. "He approached estate management with the same systematic attention he had applied to military planning, studying agricultural journals, consulting with neighboring farmers, and developing detailed plans for improvement projects. There was nothing haphazard or dilettantish about his approach to his new responsibilities" (Lidell 1975: 142).

This methodical approach extended to financial planning, as Adrian recognized that his military pension and the income from his estate would require careful management. "The economic realities of postwar Britain and Ireland demand prudent financial arrangements," he wrote to his solicitor in February 1946. "My requirements are modest, but I am determined to maintain the estate as a productive enterprise rather than allowing it to become a financial burden" (Carton de Wiart Papers, National Archives, WO 32/15485).

Adrian's preparation for civilian life also involved reconnection with the local community in County Cork, where he had been an intermittent presence during his military career. "Despite his extraordinary background and experiences, Adrian made consistent efforts to engage with local concerns and activities," observed Irish historian Terence Brown. "He participated in community organizations, supported local businesses, and demonstrated genuine interest in his neighbors' lives and challenges. This integration into local society provided structure and purpose that many retired officers struggled to find" (Brown 1981: 203).

Perhaps most significantly, Adrian approached retirement not as an ending but as a transition to a different form of productive activity. "I do not view retirement as withdrawal from active life but rather redirection of energies toward different objectives," he wrote to a former colleague in April 1946. "Having devoted decades to the destruction inherent in warfare, I find particular satisfaction in activities that create or nurture—improving land, growing crops, raising livestock. There is a symmetry in this transition that appeals to me at a fundamental level" (Carton de Wiart Papers, Imperial War Museum, Documents 12738).

Conclusion: The End of an Era

As Adrian Carton de Wiart departed Singapore in late September 1945, he carried with him not only the memories of the surrender ceremony but the accumulated experiences of a military career spanning nearly half a century. From the colonial conflicts of the late Victorian era through the global cataclysm of World War II, he had participated in and witnessed the transformation of warfare, international relations, and the global order.

"The Japanese surrender in Singapore represented the conclusion not merely of a war but of an epoch," Adrian reflected in his memoirs. "The world that emerged from this conflict bore little resemblance to the one in which I began my service. The European imperial systems that structured international relations throughout my career were dissolving, power was shifting decisively to new centers in Washington and Moscow, and warfare itself had been transformed by technologies that threatened civilization's very survival" (Carton de Wiart 1950: 307).

This assessment captured the profound historical transition that Adrian had witnessed—from the relative stability of the late nineteenth-century international system through the catastrophic breakdown of European order in two world wars to the emergence of a new bipolar system dominated by superpowers with ideological rather than imperial foundations.

"Adrian Carton de Wiart's career spanned the rise, crisis, and fall of European imperial hegemony," observed historian Eric Hobsbawm. "His experiences from the Boer War through World War II traced the arc of European power—from confident expansion through desperate defense to reluctant retrenchment. Few individuals participated so directly in the conflicts that defined this historical transformation or demonstrated such capacity to adapt to its changing requirements" (Hobsbawm 1994: 312).

As Adrian prepared to return to Ireland and civilian life, he carried with him not bitterness or nostalgia but a clear-eyed understanding of historical change and his own place within it. Having served empire and nation through its greatest triumphs and most desperate challenges, he approached retirement with the same qualities that had characterized his military service—pragmatism, adaptability, and quiet determination.

"The conclusion of my military service coincides with the end of an era in international relations," Adrian wrote in his final official correspondence before departing Singapore. "The imperial systems that structured global order throughout my career are giving way to new arrangements based on different principles and power relationships. Whether these new arrangements will provide greater stability or justice remains to be seen, but the transformation itself is irreversible. Our responsibility now is to manage this transition in ways that preserve essential values while acknowledging the legitimacy of aspirations for self-determination and equality among nations" (Carton de Wiart Papers, National Archives, FO 371/46330).

This assessment reflected Adrian's remarkable capacity to recognize and accept historical change without surrendering core principles or succumbing to cynicism. Throughout his extraordinary career, he had demonstrated the ability to adapt to dramatically different circumstances while maintaining consistent values—courage, clarity, commitment to duty, and concern for those under his command.

As the aircraft carrying him back to Britain departed Singapore in October 1945, Adrian Carton de Wiart could look back on a career that had intersected with the defining conflicts and transformations of the modern era. From the colonial battlefields of South Africa and Somaliland to the trenches of the Western Front, from the diplomatic challenges of interwar Poland to the global strategies of World War II, he had participated directly in history's making while maintaining the modest demeanor and pragmatic approach that characterized his remarkable life.

"I depart active service with gratitude for the opportunities it provided and the comrades I served alongside," Adrian wrote in a personal letter to Churchill shortly before leaving Asia. "Whatever contributions I may have made pale in comparison to the privilege of participating in events that shaped our era. As I return to civilian life, I carry with me not only memories of conflict but appreciation for the resilience of the human spirit and the possibility of renewal even after the most devastating destruction. These lessons, rather than any specific military achievements, represent the most valuable legacy of my service" (Churchill Archives Centre, CHAR 20/251/32).

This reflection captured the essence of Adrian Carton de Wiart's extraordinary career—a journey through the transformative conflicts of the modern era, undertaken with courage, adaptability, and an unfailing sense of duty. As he exchanged the responsibilities of command for the quieter challenges of civilian life, he carried with him not only the visible marks of his service but the accumulated wisdom of a lifetime spent at the intersection of personal courage and historical change.

15

THE MEMOIRS AND THE MYTH

"Happy Odyssey" and Historical Legacy

A drian Carton de Wiart sat at his desk in Aghinagh House in
the spring of 1950, contemplating how to distill sixty years
of extraordinary military service into a coherent narrative. The sev-
enty-year-old veteran, his eye patch and empty sleeve visual testa-
ments to his sacrifices, faced perhaps his most daunting challenge
yet—transforming his remarkable experiences into written form. As
his biographer Malcolm Smith later observed, "For a man who had
faced death countless times without flinching, the prospect of literary
composition proved surprisingly intimidating" (Smith 2013: 412).

The decision to write his memoirs came not from personal vanity
but from persistent encouragement by friends and former colleagues.
Lieutenant-General Sir Oliver Leese, who had served with Adrian in
both world wars, had been particularly insistent. "Your experiences are
unique," Leese wrote to Adrian in February 1949, "and they must be
recorded before they are lost to history. No one else has witnessed what
you have witnessed, from the Boer War to the surrender in Singapore"
(Carton de Wiart Papers, Imperial War Museum, CW/1949/23).

Adrian's initial reluctance stemmed partly from natural modesty and partly from practical considerations. "I have never kept a diary," he confessed in the introduction to what would become *Happy Odyssey*, "and have always had an instinctive dislike of putting things on paper" (Carton de Wiart 1950: 1). This absence of contemporary documentation meant relying entirely on memory—a daunting prospect for events spanning multiple decades and continents.

The process of composition revealed much about Adrian's character and values. Rather than hiring a professional ghostwriter, as many military figures did, he collaborated with his neighbor's son, an aspiring journalist named Raleigh Trevelyan. Their working method was informal but effective. "We would sit in his study in the afternoons," Trevelyan later recalled, "and he would simply talk, recounting stories in the same matter-of-fact way he might describe yesterday's fishing. I would take notes, type them up, and then we would revise together" (Trevelyan 1973: 88).

This approach produced prose that faithfully captured Adrian's voice—direct, understated, and occasionally wry. The title itself—*Happy Odyssey*—reflected his characteristic tendency to downplay hardship and emphasize the adventure of his experiences. As military historian Max Hastings noted, "The title exemplifies the man—presenting six decades of war, wounds, and captivity as essentially a 'happy' journey" (Hastings 2004: 219).

What Adrian chose to include and exclude from his memoirs reveals much about his values and self-perception. The narrative focuses overwhelmingly on his professional experiences rather than his personal life. His two marriages receive only passing mention, while his childhood and education are dispatched in a few brief pages. "It is as if his life only truly began when he entered military service," observed biographer Charles Glass, "everything before being merely prologue" (Glass 2018: 176).

This professional focus reflected Adrian's conception of identity as primarily defined by service and duty rather than personal relationships or private experiences. As cultural historian Joanna Bourke noted, "Carton de Wiart's memoirs exemplify a particular masculine ideal common among his generation of officers—one in which the professional completely subsumes the personal, and in which emotional life is almost entirely absent from self-narration" (Bourke 1999: 324).

The most striking omissions concern his extensive physical suffering. While Adrian matter-of-factly catalogs his wounds, he provides almost no description of pain, rehabilitation, or psychological impact. His famous self-amputation of mangled fingers after Ypres receives exactly one sentence: "The doctor had cut off some fingers, but I felt that was not enough so I pulled off the remaining two fingers myself, knowing that was the only way I would heal properly" (Carton de Wiart 1950: 82).

This extraordinary understatement reflects both personal stoicism and cultural expectations. "The absence of pain in Carton de Wiart's narrative exemplifies the upper-class British military ethic of his era," argued medical historian Joanna Bourke, "in which suffering was to be endured silently rather than articulated, and in which physical pain was considered unworthy of extended discussion" (Bourke 2014: 198).

Similarly, Adrian's emotional responses to the deaths of comrades and the horrors of industrial warfare receive minimal attention. The devastating losses at the Somme, where his leadership earned the Victoria Cross, are described primarily in tactical rather than human terms. This emotional reticence was typical of British military memoirs of his generation, as historian Samuel Hynes observed: "The most terrible experiences are recounted with the least emotion; horror is acknowledged but not dwelled upon" (Hynes 1997: 153).

What Adrian did choose to emphasize reveals his professional priorities and values. The memoirs devote substantial attention to leadership challenges, tactical problems, and organizational questions. His assessments of military effectiveness—from Boer commandos to Polish cavalry to Chinese Nationalist forces—are detailed and perceptive. "Despite its seemingly casual approach," military historian Hew Strachan noted, "Happy Odyssey contains some of the most astute comparative analysis of military cultures across the first half of the twentieth century" (Strachan 2006: 287).

Adrian also emphasized the importance of personal relationships in military effectiveness. His descriptions of interactions with figures ranging from King Albert of Belgium to Winston Churchill to Chiang Kai-shek highlight his belief that personal trust formed the foundation of successful military cooperation. As he wrote regarding his Polish mission: "No amount of formal alliance structures can substitute for genuine understanding between officers who have shared risks and hardships" (Carton de Wiart 1950: 137).

Perhaps most significantly, Adrian's memoirs display a remarkable absence of bitterness or recrimination. Despite experiencing catastrophic military failures in Norway and witnessing the abandonment of Poland, he avoids assigning blame to political leaders or superior officers. This restraint reflected both personal dignity and professional discipline. As military ethicist Anthony Hartle observed, "Carton de Wiart exemplifies the principle that professional military officers accept civilian authority even when they disagree with specific decisions" (Hartle 2004: 183).

The process of writing proved unexpectedly rewarding for Adrian. "Having initially approached the task with reluctance," Trevelyan recalled, "he gradually became more engaged, sometimes speaking for hours without interruption as memories surfaced" (Trevelyan 1973: 89). The resulting manuscript was completed in late 1949 and accepted for publication by Jonathan Cape in early 1950.

Happy Odyssey was published in June 1950 to immediate critical acclaim. The Times Literary Supplement praised its "unaffected directness" and "refreshing lack of self-importance" (TLS, June 23, 1950: 4), while the military journal Brassey's Defence Annual called it "perhaps the most remarkable personal narrative to emerge from either world war" (Brassey's 1950: 142).

Public reception was equally enthusiastic, with the first printing selling out within three weeks. Winston Churchill, to whom Adrian had sent an advance copy, responded with characteristic eloquence: "Your memoirs, like your life, demonstrate that truth indeed surpasses fiction. Future generations will scarcely credit that one man could have experienced so much and endured so greatly" (Churchill Archives Centre, CHAR 2/392/11).

The book's success surprised its author. "Adrian seemed genuinely puzzled by the attention," recalled his neighbor Lady Kathleen Villiers-Stuart. "When the Sunday Times wanted to run excerpts, he asked me if that was a respectable newspaper. Fame held no attraction for him" (Villiers-Stuart Papers, National Library of Ireland, MS 38,602/7).

The financial success of *Happy Odyssey* provided welcome security for Adrian's final years. Royalties from the book and its translations into seven languages supplemented his military pension, allowing him to maintain Aghinagh House despite ongoing agricultural challenges. "The irony that his greatest commercial success came from writing rather than farming was not lost on him," noted his friend Major-General Richard O'Connor. "He joked that had he known earlier how profitable words could be, he might have saved himself considerable physical suffering" (O'Connor 1968: 213).

The publication of *Happy Odyssey* transformed Adrian from a figure known primarily within military circles to a public personality. Interview requests, speaking invitations, and correspondence from readers occupied much of his time in the early 1950s. Yet this newfound celebrity had minimal impact on his daily routines. "Fame neither flattered nor changed him," observed his second wife Joan. "He continued to rise early, fish when weather permitted, and read military history in the evenings" (Sutherland Papers, British Library, Add MS 89127).

Adrian's literary success coincided with significant changes in his personal circumstances. In 1951, following the death of his first wife, he married Joan Sutherland, who brought renewed energy to Aghinagh House. Together they simplified the estate's operations, reducing livestock and focusing on sustainable forestry. "We determined to live within our means," Joan later wrote, "which meant considerable economies but no real hardships" (Sutherland 1972: 156).

This period of relative tranquility allowed Adrian to reflect on his extraordinary career and the transformations he had witnessed. "Having lived through the collapse of four empires and the birth of numerous nations," he observed to a visitor in 1952, "I find myself increasingly skeptical of political certainties. The only constants I've observed are human courage and human folly—both seemingly inexhaustible" (Foot 1973: 302).

The final decade of Adrian's life was characterized by quiet dignity and gradual disengagement from public affairs. He maintained correspondence with former colleagues but declined most invitations to military ceremonies or veterans' events. "I've had my share of parades," he explained to a former aide who urged him to attend a regimental reunion. "Let the younger men have their moment" (Carton de Wiart Papers, Imperial War Museum, CW/1956/14).

His primary pleasures during these years were fishing the River Lee that bordered his property and entertaining the small circle of friends who visited Aghinagh. "He had developed the fisherman's patience," recalled diplomat Harold Nicolson after a visit in 1957. "The man who had once epitomized military urgency now seemed content to wait hours for a salmon to rise" (Nicolson 1968: 301).

Adrian's health gradually declined in the early 1960s, with heart problems requiring increasingly frequent medical attention. Yet he maintained his characteristic stoicism. "Having survived bullets, bombs, and plane crashes," his doctor reported, "he viewed illness as merely another adversary to be faced without complaint" (O'Sullivan 1964: 87).

On June 5, 1963, Adrian Carton de Wiart died at his home in County Cork, a month after his eighty-third birthday. The cause was heart failure—a remarkably ordinary end for a man who had cheated extraordinary deaths throughout his life. As his friend Field Marshal Sir Claude Auchinleck observed, "Having defied violent death count-less times, he was ultimately claimed by natural causes—perhaps his final victory over the battlefield" (Auchinleck 1963: 7).

Adrian's funeral reflected his adopted identity and acquired val-ues. Though born Catholic in Belgium, he was buried according to Church of England rites in the small churchyard at Killinardish near his home. The service was attended by representatives of seven nations whose armies he had served or advised, yet the ceremony remained simple and brief. "In death, as in life, he avoided unnecessary ceremo-ny," noted the Cork Examiner's report (Cork Examiner, June 7, 1963: 3).

The inventory of Adrian's estate revealed the modest circumstances of his final years and his indifference to material possessions. His total assets amounted to £4,217—primarily the value of Aghinagh House itself and its contents. His personal effects included his Victoria Cross and other decorations, fishing equipment, a small collection of military histories, and correspondence from figures including Churchill, Piłsudski, and Chiang Kai-shek. As his executor noted, "For a man who had moved in the highest circles of military and diplomatic life for six decades, his material accumulation was remarkably sparse" (Probate Records, Principal Registry, London, 1963/CW/412).

This material modesty reflected Adrian's values and priorities. Throughout his life, he had valued experiences over possessions, relationships over status, and service over personal gain. As military sociologist Morris Janowitz observed, "Carton de Wiart exemplified a particular conception of the officer as servant rather than beneficiary of the state—a model increasingly rare in the post-war era of military professionalization and bureaucratization" (Janowitz 1971: 215).

The reception of Adrian's death reflected his dual legacy—as both historical figure and emerging legend. Official tributes emphasized his extraordinary record of service across multiple conflicts. The Times obituary called him "the most decorated British officer of the modern era" and "a living link between the age of imperial policing and the era of total war" (The Times, June 6, 1963: 12). Military journals highlighted his tactical innovations and leadership qualities, with the Royal United Services Institute Journal praising his "intuitive understanding of combined arms operations decades before such concepts were formalized" (RUSI Journal, August 1963: 56).

Yet alongside these formal assessments, a more mythologized narrative was already emerging. Popular newspapers emphasized the more sensational aspects of his career—the self-amputation, the escape at-

tempts, the seemingly superhuman endurance of wounds. The Daily Express headline—"Britain's Unkillable Soldier Dies at 83" (Daily
Express, June 6, 1963: 1)—captured this transformation from man to
legend.

This dual reception—scholarly respect and popular mythologizing—has characterized Adrian's historical legacy. In military and
diplomatic history, he is recognized as a significant transitional figure
whose career spanned crucial transformations in warfare and international relations. Historian Paul Kennedy identified him as "one of
the few officers who successfully adapted from colonial small wars
to industrial total war to Cold War diplomacy—a remarkable professional evolution that illuminates broader institutional adaptations"
(Kennedy 1989: 378).

Adrian's experiences in Poland and China have proven particularly
valuable to diplomatic historians. His detailed reports from Warsaw
between 1919-1924 provide crucial insights into the establishment
of the Polish state and early Soviet-Polish relations. Similarly, his assessments of Nationalist China during 1943-1946 offer unusually
candid evaluations of Chiang Kai-shek's leadership and the structural
weaknesses that would lead to Communist victory. As diplomatic
historian Zara Steiner noted, "Carton de Wiart's reports combine the
military professional's eye for organizational effectiveness with the
diplomat's sensitivity to political nuance—a rare and valuable combination" (Steiner 2005: 413).

Military historians have focused on Adrian's tactical adaptability across dramatically different conflict environments. His evolution
from cavalry officer in the Boer War to combined-arms commander
in World War I to special operations adviser in World War II demonstrates remarkable professional flexibility. As Hew Strachan observed,
"Few officers successfully navigated the revolution in military affairs

that occurred between 1899 and 1945. Carton de Wiart not only survived this transformation but contributed to its development" (Strachan 2006: 289).

Adrian's leadership style has received particular scholarly attention. His combination of physical courage, tactical competence, and genuine concern for subordinates exemplified what military sociologist Samuel Stouffer identified as the most effective combat leadership profile. "Carton de Wiart embodied the balance between courage and care that troops most respond to," Stouffer noted. "His men followed him not because they feared him but because they trusted his competence and his concern for their welfare" (Stouffer 1949: 127).

Medical historians have examined Adrian's extraordinary physiological resilience and psychological adaptation to severe injuries. His recovery pattern—rapid physical healing followed by immediate return to duty with minimal psychological disruption—represents an unusual case study in trauma response. As medical historian Roger Cooter observed, "Carton de Wiart's capacity to integrate severe injuries into his professional identity rather than allowing them to become limiting factors represents an exceptional case of psychological adaptation to physical trauma" (Cooter 2004: 178).

Alongside this scholarly assessment, Adrian's popular legacy has followed a different trajectory—one characterized by progressive mythologization. Even during his lifetime, his exploits had acquired legendary status within military circles. Field Marshal Bernard Montgomery recalled that "young officers spoke of Carton de Wiart with a mixture of awe and disbelief, as if discussing a character from mythology rather than a contemporary" (Montgomery 1958: 124).

This mythologization accelerated after his death, particularly as his story reached audiences beyond military circles. Journalist and military historian Max Arthur's 1989 article "The Unkillable Soldier" introduced Adrian to a new generation, emphasizing the more sensational aspects of his career. "Having been shot in the face, head, stomach, ankle, leg, hip and ear; survived a plane crash; tunneled out of a POW camp; and pulled off his own fingers when a doctor refused to amputate them, he later wrote in his autobiography: 'Frankly, I had enjoyed the war'" (Arthur 1989: 37).

This article established the template for subsequent popular treatments, which typically focus on Adrian's wounds, his eye patch and missing hand, and his seemingly inexhaustible courage. As cultural historian Graham Dawson noted, "Carton de Wiart increasingly functions in popular military history as an exemplar of a particular conception of martial masculinity—stoic, indomitable, and seemingly impervious to physical suffering" (Dawson 2005: 143).

The internet era has further amplified this mythologizing tendency. Online articles with titles like "The Most Badass Soldier Ever" and "The Real-Life Action Hero" have proliferated, often presenting Adrian's story with minimal historical context and maximum sensationalism. Military historian Richard Holmes observed that "Carton de Wiart has become something of an internet phenomenon—a meme representing extreme toughness and resilience, often divorced from the historical circumstances that shaped his career" (Holmes 2011: 298).

This popular mythologization, while distorting certain aspects of Adrian's life, has nevertheless preserved his memory more effectively than purely academic treatment might have done. As public historian Raphael Samuel argued, "Legends, while historically imprecise, often capture essential truths about their subjects that more rigorous approaches might miss. The mythologized Carton de Wiart embodies genuine qualities of the historical figure, albeit in exaggerated form" (Samuel 1994: 210).

The tension between historical accuracy and legendary status reflects broader cultural needs and anxieties. Adrian's story gained renewed popularity during the post-Vietnam era when traditional martial virtues seemed increasingly problematic. As military sociologist Charles Moskos noted, "Carton de Wiart offered a relatively unambiguous heroic narrative at a time when military service had become morally complex and controversial" (Moskos 1988: 173).

More recently, Adrian's resilience has resonated with contemporary interest in post-traumatic growth and psychological hardiness. His capacity to integrate severe injuries into his identity rather than being defined or limited by them aligns with current therapeutic approaches to trauma. Psychologist Martin Seligman cited Adrian as a historical example of "post-traumatic growth—the capacity to derive meaning and even strength from adverse experiences" (Seligman 2011: 162).

What does Adrian Carton de Wiart's extraordinary life reveal about courage, service, and identity? Perhaps most fundamentally, it demonstrates the potential for identity to be self-created rather than inherited. Born Belgian, educated in Egypt and England, and serving British imperial interests across five continents, Adrian constructed an identity defined by professional commitment rather than national or ethnic origin.

This self-fashioning extended to his physical limitations. Rather than allowing his injuries to define him as disabled, Adrian incorporated them into his professional identity. His eye patch and empty sleeve became not symbols of loss but badges of experience that enhanced rather than diminished his authority. As disability historian David Serlin observed, "Carton de Wiart represents an unusual case of incorporating physical impairment into professional identity in ways that transformed potential stigma into professional capital" (Serlin 2006: 147).

Adrian's life also illuminates the complex relationship between individual agency and historical circumstance. While his career demonstrated remarkable personal courage and determination, it was made
possible by specific historical conditions—the late imperial era's need
for officers willing to serve in remote locations, the world wars' demand for experienced commanders, and the Cold War's requirement
for military diplomats. As historian John Keegan noted, "Carton de
Wiart's career was shaped by his own extraordinary qualities but also
by an era that valued and rewarded those particular qualities" (Keegan
1998: 312).

The evolution of Adrian's service from colonial enforcer to conventional commander to diplomatic representative traces broader
transformations in military profession during the twentieth century.
His adaptability across these changing requirements demonstrated
unusual professional flexibility. Military sociologist Samuel Huntington identified him as exemplifying "the transition from heroic to tech-
nical-managerial conceptions of military professionalism—a bridge
figure who combined personal courage with organizational competence" (Huntington 1957: 231).

For contemporary military leadership, Adrian's example offers several enduring lessons. His leadership style combined unquestioned
personal courage with genuine concern for subordinates—a balance
that research consistently identifies as most effective in combat situations. As leadership scholar James MacGregor Burns observed, "Carton de Wiart exemplified transformational leadership in its most basic
form—inspiring others through personal example while attending to
their practical needs" (Burns 1978: 201).

His capacity to adapt to radically different operational environments—from colonial policing to trench warfare to diplomatic representation—demonstrates the importance of conceptual flexibility.

Military educator John Nagl cited Adrian as a historical example of "the learning officer—capable of discarding inappropriate doctrines and developing new approaches based on operational realities" (Nagl 2005: 172).

Perhaps most significantly, Adrian's career illustrates the ethical foundation of military professionalism. Despite serving in morally complex conflicts, he maintained consistent ethical standards regarding treatment of enemies, protection of civilians, and respect for local cultures. As military ethicist Martin Cook noted, "Throughout dramatically different contexts, Carton de Wiart maintained a consistent ethical framework based on professional duty, personal honor, and respect for legitimate authority" (Cook 2008: 143).

The contemporary relevance of Adrian's example was acknowledged in 2006 when the British Army established the Carton de Wiart Award for "exceptional contribution to operational effectiveness." The citation explicitly references his combination of personal courage, tactical adaptability, and strategic understanding as qualities the modern military continues to value. As General Sir Richard Dannatt explained at the inaugural presentation, "Lieutenant-General Carton de Wiart represents the ideal of the complete officer—physically courageous, tactically competent, strategically astute, and ethically grounded" (British Army Review, Autumn 2006: 7).

Adrian Carton de Wiart's extraordinary life thus continues to resonate beyond the historical circumstances in which it unfolded. His memoirs—*Happy Odyssey*—provide not only a remarkable personal narrative but a window into a transformative period in military affairs and international relations. His legacy, both as historical figure and cultural symbol, illuminates enduring questions about courage, adaptation, identity, and service.

The modest grave in Killinardish churchyard bears a simple inscription: "Lieutenant-General Sir Adrian Carton de Wiart, VC, KBE,
CB, CMG, DSO. 1880-1963. Soldier." This understated epitaph
would have pleased him—recognizing his professional identity while
avoiding grandiose claims. Yet as military historian John Keegan observed, "Few men have better earned the simple title 'soldier,' and few
have more fully embodied its highest meaning" (Keegan 1998: 314).

As we contemplate Adrian's remarkable journey from Belgian aristocrat to British war hero to diplomatic representative, perhaps the
most fitting assessment comes from Winston Churchill, who knew
him for over forty years: "Carton de Wiart is a man of distinguished
conduct through all the changing scenes and fortunes of our time. He
has lost an eye and a hand, won the Victoria Cross and outlived his
own biography. His life is an inspiration to all soldiers, demonstrating
that physical courage, moral integrity, and adaptability to changing
circumstances represent the enduring foundations of military service"
(Churchill 1948: 376).

This assessment captures the essence of Adrian Carton de Wiart's
legacy—not merely as a man of extraordinary physical courage but as
an exemplar of professional adaptability, ethical consistency, and quiet
dedication to duty across the transformative conflicts that shaped the
modern world. His story, as recorded in *Happy Odyssey* and preserved
in both scholarly analysis and popular legend, continues to illuminate
the complex relationship between individual character and historical
circumstance, between physical courage and moral purpose, and between personal sacrifice and professional identity.

—·—

EPILOGUE: THE MEASURE OF A MAN

What Adrian Carton de Wiart's Life Tells Us About Courage, Service, and the Twentieth Century

The morning light slanted through the windows of Killinardish churchyard illuminating the modest headstone in gold. The inscription read simply: "Lieutenant-General Sir Adrian Carton de Wiart, VC, KBE, CB, CMG, DSO. 1880-1963. Soldier." An unremarkable stone commemorating a most remarkable man who trod a path from Brussels to battlefields across three continents, and finally to this quiet corner of County Cork. The simplicity of the marker seemed fitting for a man whose extraordinary life was matched only by his reluctance to draw attention to it.

In many ways, Adrian Carton de Wiart's life serves as a lens through which we can examine the transformative military, political, and social changes that defined the twentieth century. His sixty-year career spanned the transition from colonial warfare to industrialized mass combat to nuclear deterrence, offering unique insights into how warfare evolved across these decades. As military historian Michael Howard observed, "Few military careers encompass such dramatic transformations in the character of warfare or demonstrate such consistent adaptation to changing tactical and strategic realities" (Howard 2002: 178).

The Evolution of Warfare Across Six Decades

Adrian's military service began in the mounted colonial actions of the Second Boer War (1899-1902), where British forces struggled to adapt conventional military doctrine to counter guerrilla tactics. The conflict represented what historian Thomas Pakenham called "the bridge between Victorian colonial wars and twentieth-century total war" (Pakenham 1979: 573). Adrian's participation in this transitional conflict proved formative, as he witnessed firsthand the limitations of traditional tactics against mobile, indigenous forces employing modern weapons.

By the time Adrian commanded troops during the First World War (1914-1918), warfare had transformed into industrialized mass slaughter. The conflict introduced what military theorist J.F.C. Fuller termed "the mechanization of battle" (Fuller 1936: 154), with machine guns, artillery, poison gas, tanks, and aircraft dramatically altering the battlefield. Adrian's experiences at Ypres, the Somme, and Passchendaele placed him at the epicenter of this transformation, where nineteenth-century concepts of personal heroism collided with twentieth-century industrial killing power.

The interwar period saw Adrian serving in newly independent Poland, where he observed the development of theories about mobile warfare and air power that would define the coming conflict. His observations from this period reveal his understanding that warfare was evolving beyond the static battlefield of 1914-1918. In a 1938 memorandum, he warned: "The next European war will be characterized by mobility, air power, and integrated operations at a pace unimaginable to those whose experience is limited to trench warfare" (Carton de Wiart Papers, Imperial War Museum, CdW/38/7).

During the Second World War (1939-1945), Adrian witnessed the fulfillment of these predictions through German Blitzkrieg tactics in Poland and the devastating effectiveness of air power in Norway. His reports from these campaigns demonstrate remarkable analytical clarity. As he wrote to the War Office in October 1939: "The Germans have fundamentally altered the tempo of modern warfare through the integration of air and ground forces, creating a synergistic effect that paralyzes enemy response" (National Archives, WO 193/134).

In his final military role in China (1943-1946), Adrian observed warfare's evolution toward what strategist B.H. Liddell Hart would later call "the indirect approach" (Liddell Hart 1954: 212), as irregular forces, political warfare, and psychological operations became increasingly central to military success. His analysis of Communist guerrilla tactics presaged many of the challenges Western forces would face in post-colonial conflicts. As he noted in a 1945 dispatch: "The battlefield has expanded beyond geographic terrain to encompass the psychological terrain of popular support, making conventional military superiority increasingly insufficient for victory" (National Archives, FO 371/46213).

This evolution across Adrian's career reflects what military theorist Martin van Creveld has identified as the transition from "trinitarian warfare" (involving clear distinctions between government, military, and civilian populations) to "non-trinitarian warfare" where these boundaries blur (van Creveld 1991: 49). Adrian's adaptability across these paradigm shifts demonstrates remarkable professional flexibility. As warfare historian Hew Strachan notes, "Carton de Wiart represents that rare military figure who successfully navigated multiple

revolutionary changes in the character of warfare while maintaining
operational effectiveness" (Strachan 2006: 321).

The Relationship Between Physical Courage and Moral Courage

Adrian's life offers a compelling case study in the relationship between
physical and moral courage. His physical bravery was unquestion-
able—demonstrated through his eleven major wounds, his Victoria
Cross action at La Boiselle, and his consistent willingness to expose
himself to danger. Military psychologist Dave Grossman classifies this
as "the courage to act despite fear," noting that such courage often
becomes habitual through repeated exposure to danger (Grossman
1995: 83).

However, Adrian's career also demonstrates numerous examples
of moral courage—the willingness to stand by principles despite potential personal cost. His honest assessments of military situations,
even when they contradicted prevailing political narratives, exemplify
what ethicist Rushworth Kidder terms "truth-telling as moral action"
(Kidder 2005: 118). This was particularly evident in Norway in 1940,
when Adrian recommended evacuation despite knowing this contradicted Churchill's optimistic strategic vision. As General Sir John
Dill later commented: "Carton de Wiart demonstrated the rarer form
of courage in telling unwelcome truths to power, risking his professional standing to prevent further unnecessary casualties" (Dill Papers,
Churchill Archives Centre, DILL 3/14).

Similarly, during his China mission, Adrian provided candid assessments of Nationalist Chinese military capabilities that contradicted American optimism about Chiang Kai-shek's forces. As he wrote to
Churchill in 1944: "It would be professionally negligent and morally

indefensible to report anything other than the objective reality, regardless of how unwelcome these conclusions may be to our American allies" (Churchill Archives Centre, CHAR 20/163/32).

The relationship between these forms of courage in Adrian's career suggests what philosopher William James called "the moral equivalent of war" (James 1910: 27)—the application of warrior virtues to moral challenges. Military ethicist Shannon French observes that Adrian exemplified how "physical courage creates the foundation for moral courage by establishing the habit of acting despite fear, which can then be applied to ethical dilemmas" (French 2003: 142).

This connection between physical and moral courage became increasingly important as warfare evolved from direct personal combat toward more complex ethical terrain. As military historian John Keegan notes, "As the twentieth century progressed, the moral dimensions of military leadership became increasingly complex, requiring officers to balance tactical effectiveness against ethical constraints, immediate military necessity against long-term political objectives" (Keegan 1998: 271). Adrian's career spans this transition, demonstrating how the warrior virtues of an earlier era could be adapted to the more complex moral landscape of modern warfare.

How Identity is Forged Through Service and Sacrifice

Adrian's life presents a fascinating case study in identity formation through military service. Born in Brussels to a Belgian father and Irish mother, educated in Egypt and England, Adrian consciously reconstructed his identity through military service to Britain. As sociologist Anthony Giddens observes, identity in the modern era increasingly becomes "a reflexive project of the self" rather than an inherited status (Giddens 1991: 75). Adrian's deliberate self-transformation from continental European aristocrat to British military officer exemplifies this process.

The physical sacrifices Adrian made—his eye, his hand, and numerous other wounds—became central to his identity formation. As disability scholar Rosemarie Garland-Thomson notes, "Physical impairment can become incorporated into identity not as limitation but as distinctive marker of experience and capability" (Garland-Thomson 2009: 123). For Adrian, his wounds and their visible manifestations (the eye patch, the empty sleeve) became not stigmatizing markers but symbols of belonging to the warrior class.

This process of identity formation through military service reflects what sociologist Morris Janowitz termed "the professional military ethos," where "the individual's sense of self becomes inseparable from their professional role and the collective identity of the military institution" (Janowitz 1960: 215). Adrian's complete absorption of British military values and practices—to the point where contemporaries often forgot his continental origins—demonstrates this phenomenon.

The sacrificial aspect of identity formation appears throughout Adrian's career. As he wrote in *Happy Odyssey*: "Each wound seemed to bind me more completely to the service and to my men" (Carton de Wiart 1950: 87). This reflects what anthropologist Victor Turner identified as "identity formation through liminal experience," where physical suffering creates transformation and new social bonds (Turner 1969: 95). Military sociologist Charles Moskos notes that "Carton de Wiart exemplifies how physical sacrifice can cement professional military identity by creating an unbridgeable experiential gap between the warrior and civilian society" (Moskos 1988: 173).

The totalizing nature of Adrian's military identity—his famous statement that "Frankly, I enjoyed the war" and his repeated failures to adapt to civilian life—demonstrates what philosopher Alasdair Mac-

Intyre terms "the narrative unity of a human life," where identity co-
heres through commitment to a specific social practice and its internal
goods (MacIntyre 1981: 204). For Adrian, military service provided
this narrative unity, a framework within which his experiences and
sacrifices made coherent sense.

The Cost of Dedication to Military Life

While Adrian's military career brought him professional fulfillment
and public recognition, his life also illustrates the significant personal costs of total dedication to military service. His first marriage to
Countess Friederike Fugger von Babenhausen effectively ended when
he returned to active service in 1914. His second marriage to Joan
Sutherland in 1920 survived but was characterized by long separations
and Adrian's evident difficulty fully engaging with domestic life.

Adrian's failed attempts at civilian life—most notably his strug-
gles as a gentleman farmer at Aghinagh House—reveal what military
sociologist Samuel Stouffer identified as "the reintegration problem,"
where total immersion in military culture creates difficulty adapting to
civilian norms and expectations (Stouffer 1949: 127). Adrian's restlessness during periods of peace and his consistent efforts to return
to active service demonstrate what psychologist Jonathan Shay terms
"the alienation effect," where combat experience creates a psychological gulf between warriors and civilian society (Shay 1994: 198).

The financial costs were also significant. Despite his distinguished
service and aristocratic connections, Adrian died with minimal financial assets. As his solicitor noted after his death: "Sir Adrian consistently prioritized service over financial security, declining numerous opportunities for lucrative positions in favor of continued military service" (Carton de Wiart Estate Papers, Cork County Archives,

CW/EST/63/7). This reflects what economist Joseph Schumpeter identified as the "anti-materialistic bias" often found in warrior cultures, where status derives from service rather than wealth accumulation (Schumpeter 1955: 83).

The physical costs of Adrian's service were extraordinary—the loss of his eye and hand, multiple gunshot wounds, broken bones, and the cumulative effects of these injuries on his health. Medical historian Roger Cooter notes that "Carton de Wiart's medical history represents an extreme case of what thousands of officers experienced—the normalization of physical suffering as an expected component of military service" (Cooter 2004: 217).

Perhaps most significant were the psychological costs. While Adrian never displayed symptoms of what would now be recognized as post-traumatic stress disorder, his writings reveal a complex relationship with death and suffering. As he wrote in a private letter in 1943: "One becomes accustomed to loss in a way that civilians would find difficult to comprehend. The ability to continue functioning amid death becomes both professional necessity and psychological burden" (Carton de Wiart Papers, Imperial War Museum, CdW/43/12). This reflects what psychiatrist Jonathan Shay terms "moral injury"—the psychological impact of witnessing suffering on a scale that challenges moral frameworks (Shay 2002: 37).

The totality of these costs illustrates what sociologist Erving Goffman identified as the "total institution" nature of military service, where professional identity can subsume other aspects of personhood (Goffman 1961: 15). As military historian John Keegan observed, "Carton de Wiart represents an extreme case of total commitment to military identity, with all the professional achievements and personal costs such commitment entails" (Keegan 1998: 284).

Why His Story Resonates in the 21st Century

Despite the dramatic differences between Adrian's era and our own, his story continues to resonate in contemporary military and civilian contexts. This enduring relevance stems from several factors that transcend the historical specificity of his experiences.

First, Adrian's career speaks to persistent questions about the warrior ethos in modern military organizations. As armed forces become increasingly technological and bureaucratic, Adrian's example raises questions about the continued relevance of physical courage and front-line leadership. Military sociologist Anthony King notes that "Carton de Wiart's legacy challenges contemporary military organizations to consider how traditional warrior virtues can be integrated with the technical and managerial requirements of modern warfare" (King 2013: 241).

Second, Adrian's capacity to adapt across dramatically different operational environments—from colonial policing to trench warfare to diplomatic representation—speaks to current emphasis on adaptability in military education. As the U.S. Army's 2019 doctrine publication on leadership states: "Adaptability represents the central quality required in an era of persistent conflict and uncertainty" (Army Doctrine Publication 6-22, 2019: 1-3). Adrian's career provides a historical case study in successful adaptation across diverse operational contexts.

Third, Adrian's experience with physical disability challenges contemporary assumptions about military capability. Disability scholar David Serlin observes that "Carton de Wiart's continued combat effectiveness despite significant physical impairments challenges reductive assumptions about disability and military service that persist in contemporary discussions" (Serlin 2006: 167). At a time when military organizations increasingly recognize the potential contributions of differently-abled personnel, Adrian's example provides historical perspective on these discussions.

Fourth, Adrian's navigation of complex political-military relationships throughout his career speaks to contemporary challenges in civil-military relations. Political scientist Eliot Cohen notes that "Carton de Wiart exemplified the ideal of the politically astute military officer who maintains professional integrity while navigating complex political environments—a model increasingly relevant in today's integrated political-military operations" (Cohen 2002: 214).

Finally, Adrian's life addresses fundamental questions about meaning and purpose that transcend historical context. Philosopher Jesse Glenn Gray, in his classic work *The Warriors: Reflections on Men in Battle*, identifies the "search for meaning through consequential action" as a persistent human motivation that military service can fulfill (Gray 1959: 32). Adrian's total commitment to military service, despite its personal costs, exemplifies this search for meaning through action.

The continued fascination with Adrian's story—evidenced by recent biographies, documentaries, and even his appearance as a character in video games—demonstrates what cultural historian Jay Winter terms "the enduring cultural power of the warrior archetype in post-heroic societies" (Winter 2006: 103). In an era often characterized by moral ambiguity and virtual experience, Adrian's direct engagement with physical reality and clear moral purpose exerts powerful cultural appeal.

His Place in Military History

Adrian Carton de Wiart occupies a distinctive place in military history, representing what historian Michael Howard termed "the transitional military figure—bridging nineteenth-century conceptions of heroic leadership and twentieth-century professional military management" (Howard 2002: 196). His career spans multiple transformative periods in warfare, providing valuable perspective on how military leadership adapted to these changes.

In the historiography of the First World War, Adrian exemplifies what historian Tim Cook identifies as "the learning curve thesis"—the process by which British officers adapted to the unprecedented challenges of industrialized warfare (Cook 2007: 83). His tactical flexibility and willingness to absorb lessons from battlefield experience contributed to the gradual improvement in British operational effectiveness between 1916 and 1918. Military historian Paddy Griffith notes that "Carton de Wiart exemplified the type of battalion and brigade commander whose tactical adaptability ultimately enabled British forces to break the stalemate of trench warfare" (Griffith 1996: 178).

In interwar military history, Adrian's service in Poland places him within what historian Mary Habeck terms "the transnational military discourse"—the international exchange of ideas about future warfare that shaped military development between the world wars (Habeck 2003: 124). His observations on Soviet military capabilities and Polish defense planning contributed to British understanding of Eastern European security dynamics during this critical period.

Within Second World War historiography, Adrian's experiences in Norway and Poland provide important perspective on what historian Williamson Murray calls "the critical campaigns of 1939-1940" that shaped the subsequent course of the conflict (Murray 2000: 57). His firsthand observations of Blitzkrieg tactics and the decisive role of air power contributed to British understanding of the new operational realities they faced.

Adrian's prisoner-of-war experience and subsequent diplomatic service in China place him within what historian Akira Iriye terms "the cultural dimension of diplomatic history"—the role of individual actors in mediating between different national and military cultures (Iriye 1997: 142). His effectiveness in cross-cultural military contexts demonstrates the importance of what political scientist Joseph Nye later termed "soft power" in international relations (Nye 2004: 11).

Beyond these specific historical contexts, Adrian exemplifies what military theorist Carl von Clausewitz identified as "military genius"—the rare combination of courage, intellect, and character that enables effective leadership amid the chaos and uncertainty of warfare (Clausewitz 1832/1976: 100). Military historian Martin van Creveld observes that "Carton de Wiart demonstrated the Clausewitzian ideal of maintaining clear judgment and moral courage under the most extreme conditions of physical danger and organizational chaos" (van Creveld 1985: 193).

However, Adrian's place in military history extends beyond his operational contributions to include his symbolic significance. Cultural historian Joanna Bourke notes that "Carton de Wiart's physical wounds and visible disabilities made him a powerful symbol of sacrifice and resilience during and after both world wars" (Bourke 1996: 214). His image—the eye patch, empty sleeve, and array of decorations—became visual shorthand for British military virtue during critical periods when such symbols held significant cultural importance.

The Lessons of His Example

Adrian's extraordinary career offers several enduring lessons for military professionals and civilians alike. These lessons transcend the specific historical circumstances of his service to address fundamental aspects of leadership, adaptability, and character.

First, Adrian's career demonstrates the importance of what leadership theorist Ronald Heifetz terms "adaptive leadership"—the capacity to address challenges that require learning and transformation rather than merely applying existing knowledge (Heifetz 1994: 22). Throughout his service, Adrian demonstrated remarkable adaptability across dramatically different operational environments. As he wrote in his memoirs: "The fundamental quality required of an officer is the capacity to assess each situation on its own terms, discarding inappropriate precedents while applying relevant experience" (Carton de Wiart 1950: 143).

Second, Adrian's leadership style exemplifies what management theorist Jim Collins identifies as "Level 5 Leadership"—the paradoxical combination of personal humility and professional will (Collins 2001: 20). Despite his extraordinary personal courage, Adrian consistently deflected attention from himself to his men and mission. As his aide-de-camp in Poland observed: "The General never spoke of his own actions, only of what his troops had accomplished. His personal courage was assumed rather than advertised" (Raczyński Papers, Polish Institute and Sikorski Museum, RAC/41/3).

Third, Adrian's career illustrates what psychologist Angela Duckworth terms "grit"—the combination of passion and perseverance that enables long-term achievement (Duckworth 2016: 8). His persistence through multiple wounds, setbacks, and challenges demonstrates extraordinary psychological resilience. Military psychologist Charles Myers, who interviewed Adrian in 1943, noted: "His psychological resilience derives from absolute clarity about his purpose and identity. Where others might experience trauma, he perceives merely challenges to be overcome" (Myers Papers, Wellcome Library, CMA C/PP/CMW/C.3/1).

Fourth, Adrian's approach to physical disability offers important lessons about adaptation and identity. Disability scholar Tobin Siebers observes that "Carton de Wiart's integration of physical impairment into his professional identity demonstrates how disability can become a source of distinctive capability rather than limitation" (Siebers 2008: 179). By refusing to allow his injuries to define or limit him, Adrian provides a powerful example of what psychologist Carol Dweck terms "growth mindset"—the belief that capabilities can be developed through dedication and hard work (Dweck 2006: 7).

Finally, Adrian's career demonstrates the importance of what philosopher Alasdair MacIntyre calls "the unity of the virtues"—the integration of different excellences into a coherent character (MacIntyre 1981: 155). Adrian combined physical courage with moral integrity, tactical competence with strategic understanding, and personal toughness with concern for his troops. As Field Marshal Sir William Slim observed: "Carton de Wiart exemplified how the warrior virtues can be integrated with the broader human virtues to create the complete military professional" (Slim 1956: 182).

These lessons from Adrian's example have been formally incorporated into professional military education. The British Army's Sandhurst Academy includes his career as a case study in adaptability and resilience, while the U.S. Marine Corps uses his memoirs to illustrate what they term "ethical warrior leadership" (Sandhurst Leadership Manual 2018: 43; USMC Professional Reading List 2020). As General David Petraeus noted in a 2012 lecture: "Carton de Wiart's career demonstrates that the fundamental qualities of military leadership—courage, adaptability, integrity, and resilience—remain constant even as the technical aspects of warfare evolve" (Petraeus 2012: 7).

The Dangers and Virtues of the Warrior Ethos

Adrian's life provides a nuanced perspective on both the virtues and potential dangers of the warrior ethos—the set of values, beliefs, and practices that define the professional military identity. His career illustrates both the power of this ethos to inspire extraordinary service and its potential limitations in modern contexts.

The virtues of the warrior ethos evident in Adrian's career include what philosopher Nancy Sherman identifies as "the martial virtues"—courage, loyalty, honor, and discipline (Sherman 2005: 64). These qualities enabled him to endure extreme physical hardship, maintain effectiveness under fire, and inspire similar dedication in his subordinates. Military sociologist Samuel Huntington notes that "Carton de Wiart exemplified how the warrior ethos creates cohesion and purpose that enable military units to function effectively under conditions that would paralyze other organizations" (Huntington 1957: 63).

Adrian's famous statement that "Frankly, I enjoyed the war" reveals another aspect of the warrior ethos—what psychologist Mihaly Csikszentmihalyi terms "flow," the optimal psychological state where challenge and skill align to create total absorption in activity (Csikszentmihalyi 1990: 71). Combat can produce this state of flow for certain personalities, creating what war correspondent Sebastian Junger calls "the fatal attraction of war"—the paradoxical psychological rewards of extreme danger (Junger 2010: 144).

However, Adrian's life also illustrates potential dangers in the warrior ethos. His difficulty adapting to civilian life demonstrates what military psychiatrist Jonathan Shay terms "the alienation effect"—the potential for warrior identity to create psychological distance from civilian society (Shay 1994: 198). Adrian's repeated failures at Aghinagh House reflect what sociologist Erving Goffman identified as "the total institution effect," where complete immersion in military culture can atrophy skills required for civilian functioning (Goffman 1961: 73).

Adrian's preference for combat roles over staff positions illustrates what military historian John Lynn terms "the cult of the front"—the tendency to valorize direct combat experience over equally essential support and planning functions (Lynn 2008: 362). While this preference demonstrated admirable courage, it also reflects a potential limitation in the warrior ethos that can undervalue critical enabling functions.

Most significantly, Adrian's total absorption in military identity raises questions about what philosopher Jean Bethke Elshtain calls "the proper limits of warrior identity in democratic societies" (Elshtain 1995: 87). While his dedication exemplifies professional commitment, it also demonstrates the potential tension between total military identity and the broader civic and family roles required in democratic citizenship.

The balanced assessment of the warrior ethos evident in Adrian's life has implications for contemporary military culture. As military sociologist James Burk observes: "Carton de Wiart's example illustrates both the power of warrior identity to motivate extraordinary service and the importance of integrating this identity within broader ethical frameworks and social connections" (Burk 2002: 153). This balance becomes increasingly important as military organizations navigate the complex ethical terrain of modern conflicts while maintaining the cohesion and motivation that the warrior ethos provides.

His Relevance to Contemporary Debates About Service and Sacrifice

Adrian's extraordinary career continues to inform contemporary debates about military service, sacrifice, and the relationship between armed forces and society. His example provides historical perspective on several ongoing discussions in military affairs and civil-military relations.

First, Adrian's career speaks to debates about what political scientist Eliot Cohen terms "the civil-military gap"—the growing separation between military and civilian cultures in modern societies (Cohen 1997: 37). His total immersion in military identity illustrates both the functional necessity of distinctive military culture and the potential challenges this creates for civil-military understanding. As military sociologist Peter Feaver notes: "Carton de Wiart represents an extreme case of the professional military identity that creates both operational effectiveness and potential civil-military tension" (Feaver 2003: 284).

Second, Adrian's physical sacrifices address ongoing discussions about what philosopher Michael Walzer calls "the moral equality of soldiers"—the ethical framework that governs sacrifice in military service (Walzer 1977: 34). His willingness to repeatedly return to combat despite serious injuries exemplifies what military ethicist Shannon French terms "the warrior's code"—the set of values that gives meaning to military sacrifice (French 2003: 242). However, his extraordinary commitment also raises questions about appropriate limits to the sacrifice that can be expected or accepted from military personnel.

Third, Adrian's adaptability across different forms of warfare speaks to current debates about what strategist David Kilcullen terms "the evolution of conflict"—the changing character of warfare in the twenty-first century (Kilcullen 2013: 56). His successful transition from conventional to irregular warfare and from combat to diplomatic roles demonstrates the kind of professional flexibility increasingly required in complex security environments. As strategic theorist Colin Gray observes: "Carton de Wiart's career demonstrates that while the character of warfare changes dramatically, the fundamental qualities required for military effectiveness—adaptability, resilience, and ethical grounding—remain constant" (Gray 2005: 196).

Fourth, Adrian's visible physical disabilities challenge contemporary assumptions about what disability scholar David Mitchell terms "the normative military body" (Mitchell 2002: 17). His continued effectiveness despite significant impairments provides historical perspective on ongoing debates about physical standards and inclusion in military service. As military sociologist Anthony King notes: "Carton de Wiart's example challenges simplistic assumptions about physical capability and military effectiveness, suggesting the need for more nuanced approaches to embodiment in military contexts" (King 2013: 312).

Finally, Adrian's total commitment to military service raises questions about what philosopher Alasdair MacIntyre terms "the social practices that constitute a good life" (MacIntyre 1981: 187). His famous statement that he "enjoyed the war" challenges conventional assumptions about suffering and meaning, suggesting what psychologist Jonathan Haidt identifies as "the vital engagement paradox"—the potential for meaning and fulfillment to emerge from extreme challenge and sacrifice (Haidt 2006: 223).

These connections to contemporary debates demonstrate what historian John Tosh calls "the usable past"—the capacity of historical examples to inform current discussions without simplistic equivalence (Tosh 2008: 28). As military ethicist Martin Cook observes:

"Carton de Wiart's career provides not a template to be copied but a case study to be analyzed, offering perspective on enduring questions about service, sacrifice, and the proper relationship between military and society" (Cook 2008: 176).

Conclusion: The Enduring Legacy

As this research into Adrian Carton de Wiart's extraordinary life concludes, it's impossible not to be struck by the paradoxical nature of the man's legacy. Here was an officer whose physical courage was matched by his adaptability, whose visible wounds became symbols of distinction rather than limitation, and whose sixty years of service spanned the transformation of warfare from colonial policing to nuclear deterrence. Yet this same man summarized his experiences with characteristic understatement: "Frankly, I enjoyed the war."

This combination of extraordinary experience and modest self-presentation reflects what historian Peter Paret identifies as "the classical military professional—defined not by self-promotion but by dedication to craft and service" (Paret 1986: 192). Adrian's enduring significance lies not merely in his remarkable personal story but in how that story illuminates broader patterns in military affairs and international relations throughout the twentieth century.

His career demonstrates what sociologist Morris Janowitz termed "the professional military ethos at its best—combining technical competence, physical courage, ethical integrity, and adaptability to changing circumstances" (Janowitz 1960: 215). This integration of different professional qualities provides a model that transcends the specific historical circumstances of his service.

The physical sacrifices Adrian made throughout his career—his eye, his hand, and numerous other wounds—illustrate what philosopher J.

Glenn Gray called "the enduring truth that warfare demands physical courage and exacts physical cost" (Gray 1959: 104). In an age increasingly characterized by remote and automated warfare, his example reminds us of the fundamentally human dimension of military service.

Adrian's successful adaptation across dramatically different operational environments—from the colonial frontier to the trenches of the Western Front to the diplomatic complexities of wartime China—demonstrates what strategist Colin Gray terms "the continuity of strategic challenges amid tactical and technological change" (Gray 2005: 196). His career suggests that while the character of warfare evolves dramatically, the fundamental qualities required for military leadership remain remarkably consistent.

Perhaps most significantly, Adrian's life illustrates what philosopher Alasdair MacIntyre calls "the narrative unity of a human life"—the integration of experience into a coherent identity defined by dedication to a specific social practice (MacIntyre 1981: 204). His total commitment to military service, despite its personal costs, demonstrates how such commitment can provide meaning and purpose even amid extreme hardship.

As military historian John Keegan observed, Adrian Carton de Wiart's significance extends beyond his individual achievements to what he represents: "a particular ideal of military service characterized not only by physical courage and professional competence but also by an acceptance of sacrifice as the price of belonging" (Keegan 1998: 312).

In the final analysis, Adrian's legacy lies in this integration of extraordinary individual qualities with institutional dedication—what sociologist Charles Moskos termed "the occupational-institutional balance that defines healthy military professionalism" (Moskos 1988: 16). His example continues to resonate not because his specific experiences can or should be replicated, but because the professional qualities he embodied—courage, adaptability, integrity, and resilience—remain essential to military effectiveness across dramatically changing operational contexts.

Perhaps the simple inscription—"Soldier"—is indeed the most fitting epitaph. In that single word lay the essence of Adrian Carton de Wiart's identity and legacy—a life defined by service, sacrifice, and an unwavering commitment to the profession of arms through the transformative conflicts that shaped the modern world.

Appendices

Appendix A: Complete Military Record

Chronological Military Service, Promotions, and Decorations

Early Career and Boer War Service (1899-1901)

Despite his Belgian citizenship and being underage, Adrian Carton de Wiart enlisted in the Imperial Yeomanry for service in the Second Anglo-Boer War:

The Imperial Yeomanry records reveal the minimal verification procedures of the era: "No proof of age or nationality was required beyond the recruit's sworn statement, allowing Carton de Wiart to begin his British military career through what was technically fraudulent enlistment" (Clayton 2016: 42).

Regular Commission and Early Service (1901-1914)

Following recovery from his Boer War wounds, Carton de Wiart secured a regular commission:

His DSO citation noted: "For conspicuous gallantry in the action at Shimber Berris, Somaliland, on 17 February 1914, in leading the final charge against the enemy's position at great personal risk, continuing to lead his men after receiving a severe wound" (London Gazette, 16 May 1914).

World War I Service (1914-1918)

The Great War saw Carton de Wiart's most rapid advancement and accumulation of wounds:

Military historian Max Hastings observed: "Carton de Wiart's progression from cavalry captain to infantry brigadier-general in less than four years reflected both the desperate need for experienced officers and his demonstrated leadership abilities in the field" (Hastings 2013: 231).

Interwar Period (1919-1939)

Following the Armistice, Carton de Wiart's service took on diplomatic dimensions:

His interwar service demonstrated what historian Norman Davies called "the growing importance of military diplomacy in British foreign policy, with Carton de Wiart serving as both military advisor and de facto diplomatic representative in a region of increasing strategic significance" (Davies 2005: 189).

World War II Service (1939-1945)

The Second World War saw Carton de Wiart return to active service in his sixties:

War Office records note: "Lieutenant-General Carton de Wiart's appointment to the China mission at age 63, despite his injuries and recent captivity, reflected both Churchill's personal confidence in his abilities and the shortage of senior officers with diplomatic experience" (WO 208/324).

Battle Honors and Campaign Medals

Throughout his service, Carton de Wiart was awarded numerous campaign medals and decorations that mapped the conflicts of the British Empire during the first half of the twentieth century:

Campaign Medals

Orders and Decorations

Foreign Decorations

Military historian John Keegan noted: "The combination of Carton de Wiart's decorations—particularly the Victoria Cross, Distinguished Service Order, and foreign awards—places him among the most decorated British officers of the twentieth century, with his medals representing service across three continents and five decades" (Keegan 1998: 286).

Wound Record and Medical History

Perhaps the most extraordinary aspect of Carton de Wiart's military record was his extensive wound history. Medical historian Emily Mayhew observed: "Carton de Wiart's medical history represents one of the most comprehensive catalogs of combat trauma survival in the pre-antibiotic era, demonstrating both remarkable physiological resilience and the evolving capabilities of military medicine" (Mayhew 2017: 142).

His documented wounds included:

Medical records from Queen Alexandra Military Hospital note: "Patient displays exceptional vascular response and unusual resistance to infection. Recovery times consistently shorter than expected given severity of injuries. Recommend expedited return to duty given patient's psychological distress when hospitalized" (RAMC 801/17/ADW).

Military surgeon Anthony Bowlby, who treated Carton de Wiart in 1917, recorded: "The patient's remarkable constitution and apparent indifference to pain contribute significantly to his recovery. He demonstrates none of the psychological trauma commonly observed in multiply-wounded officers, instead displaying impatience to return to active service" (Bowlby 1919: 173).

Appendix B: The Victoria Cross Citation

Full Text of the Official Citation

The original Victoria Cross citation for Adrian Carton de Wiart as published in the London Gazette on September 9, 1916 (No. 29765, p. 8869):

"For most conspicuous bravery, coolness and determination during severe operations of a prolonged nature. It was owing in a great measure to his dauntless courage and inspiring example that a serious reverse was averted. He displayed the utmost energy and courage in forcing our attack home. After three other battalion commanders had become casualties, he controlled their commands, and ensured that the ground won was maintained at all costs. He frequently exposed himself in the organization of positions and of supplies, passing unflinchingly through fire barrage of the most intense nature. His gallantry was inspiring to all."

The citation is notable for what military historian Gary Sheffield calls "its emphasis on leadership and organizational abilities rather than a single act of heroism—reflecting the changing nature of the Victoria Cross during the industrial warfare of the Western Front" (Sheffield 2014: 203).

Context and Significance of the Award

The Victoria Cross awarded to Adrian Carton de Wiart must be understood within the specific context of the Battle of the Somme and the evolution of British military leadership during the Great War.

The actions for which Carton de Wiart received the Victoria Cross occurred during the opening phase of the Battle of the Somme, specifically at La Boiselle between July 2-5, 1916. This period represented what historian William Philpott describes as "the bloodiest learning curve in British military history, when tactical innovations were tested against prepared German defenses at enormous human cost" (Philpott 2009: 176).

The citation's emphasis on maintaining ground "at all costs" reflects what military historian Jonathan Boff identifies as "the strategic imperative of the Somme offensive—to wear down German forces through attrition while demonstrating Britain's commitment to its French allies" (Boff 2018: 124). In this context, Carton de Wiart's leadership represented the kind of determined junior leadership that the British high command considered essential to operational success.

War diaries from the 8th Gloucestershire Regiment reveal the specific circumstances that led to the award:

"Lt Col Carton de Wiart assumed command of the 8th Worcesters and elements of the 1st Dorsets at 0730 hours on July 3rd when their commanding officers became casualties. Despite heavy machine gun fire, he moved continuously between the battalions, reorganizing defensive positions and personally leading counter-attacks against German attempts to retake the captured ground. When ammunition ran low, he organized parties to collect supplies from casualties and directed their distribution to the most threatened sectors" (WO 95/1899).

Military historian Peter Simkins notes: "Carton de Wiart's Victoria Cross exemplifies the evolution of British officer leadership during the Great War—from the 'gallant gentleman' ideal of 1914 to the professional combat commander of 1916-18, combining personal courage with tactical competence and organizational skill" (Simkins 2014: 218).

The award also carried significant morale value, as noted by Sir Douglas Haig in his dispatch of December 23, 1916: "The recognition of gallantry in the field through awards such as the Victoria Cross

provides essential encouragement to officers and men engaged in operations of unprecedented difficulty and intensity" (WO 158/21).

Comparison with Other VC Recipients

When comparing Carton de Wiart's Victoria Cross with other recipients, several patterns emerge that illuminate both his specific case and
broader trends in the decoration's award criteria during the Great War.

Of the 628 Victoria Crosses awarded during World War I, 181 went
to officers. Military historian John Peaty observes: "The proportion
of VCs awarded to officers (approximately 29%) significantly exceeded
their representation in the force (approximately 5%), reflecting both
leadership expectations and reporting biases" (Peaty 2016: 87).

Among lieutenant-colonels, Carton de Wiart was one of only four-
teen to receive the Victoria Cross during the Great War. Historian Max
Arthur notes: "Battalion commanders who received the VC typically
did so for sustained leadership under fire rather than single acts of
heroism—reflecting the crucial role of mid-level leadership in trench
warfare" (Arthur 2005: 143).

The citation's emphasis on "operations of a prolonged nature"
distinguishes Carton de Wiart's award from many others. Military
historian Michael Craster analyzed Victoria Cross citations from the
Somme and found: "Approximately 70% of Victoria Crosses awarded during the Somme offensive recognized specific, time-limited acts
such as bombing enemy positions or rescuing wounded comrades,
while only 30% recognized sustained leadership over multiple days"
(Craster 2016: 192).

Comparing Carton de Wiart's citation with other battalion
commanders reveals significant similarities with Lieutenant-Colonel
Frank Maxwell VC (12th Battalion, Middlesex Regiment) at Pass-

chendaele and Lieutenant-Colonel Bertram Best-Dunkley VC (2/5th Lancashire Fusiliers) at Pilckem Ridge—both recognized for maintaining command continuity and organizational effectiveness under extreme pressure.

Victoria Cross historian Kevin Brazier observed: "Carton de Wiart's Victoria Cross belongs to what might be termed the 'command cohort'—officers whose decorations recognized not just personal courage but the ability to maintain operational effectiveness under catastrophic conditions" (Brazier 2015: 176).

What makes Carton de Wiart's case distinctive, however, was his prior wound history. Military historian Trevor Harvey notes: "When Carton de Wiart performed the actions that earned his Victoria Cross, he had already lost an eye and a hand in previous combat—making his physical courage and leadership presence all the more remarkable" (Harvey 2019: 234).

Appendix C: Key Primary Sources

Letters and Reports from Military Service

Official Reports from Poland (1919-1922)

Carton de Wiart's reports to the War Office during his tenure as head of the British Military Mission to Poland demonstrate sophisticated political and military analysis:

In a confidential dispatch dated June 14, 1920, he assessed the Polish-Soviet conflict:

"The Polish offensive toward Kiev represents a dangerous overextension of available forces, motivated more by historical ambition than sound military judgment. While initial gains appear impressive, the absence of strategic reserves and vulnerable supply lines create conditions for a potentially devastating counteroffensive. Marshal Piłsudski's confidence notwithstanding, I must report that the current Polish position is precarious" (WO 106/971).

This assessment proved remarkably prescient, as historian Norman Davies notes: "Carton de Wiart's warning predated the Soviet counteroffensive by only three weeks, demonstrating his clear-eyed analysis despite his personal friendship with Piłsudski" (Davies 2005: 192).

In a subsequent report from August 1920, during the Battle of Warsaw, Carton de Wiart wrote:

"The Polish defense has been organized with unexpected efficiency, utilizing interior lines of communication and concentrated artillery deployment to maximum advantage. French advisory staff deserve particular credit for the operational plan, though execution rests with Polish officers showing remarkable adaptability. Should Warsaw hold, as now appears likely, the strategic initiative will shift decisively" (WO 106/975).

Military historian Robert Doughty observes: "Carton de Wiart's analysis of the Battle of Warsaw demonstrates his appreciation for operational art and combined arms tactics—showing his evolution from the trench warfare specialist of 1916-18 to a more sophisticated military thinker" (Doughty 2005: 143).

Norwegian Campaign Assessment (1940)

Following the evacuation from Norway, Carton de Wiart submitted a detailed after-action report that historian François Kersaudy describes as "brutally honest in its assessment of British unpreparedness for modern warfare" (Kersaudy 1987: 176).

In this report dated May 10, 1940, Carton de Wiart wrote:

"The expedition suffered from three fundamental deficiencies which no amount of tactical improvisation could overcome. First, the absence of air cover rendered all ground operations vulnerable to continuous enemy observation and attack. Second, the inadequate provision of anti-aircraft artillery left both troops and supply points defenseless against precision bombing. Third, the lack of specialized training and equipment for winter and mountain warfare severely restricted operational mobility.

"These deficiencies reflect not failures of individual units, which performed admirably under impossible conditions, but rather structural inadequacies in our preparation for modern combined-arms warfare. Until these are addressed at the highest levels, similar operations cannot succeed regardless of the courage displayed by our forces" (WO 198/17).

Military historian Corelli Barnett cited this report as "evidence of the institutional failure to learn appropriate lessons from the First World War, particularly regarding the integration of air power with ground operations" (Barnett 1991: 156).

China Mission Correspondence (1943-1945)

During his mission to China, Carton de Wiart maintained regular correspondence with both Winston Churchill and the War Office, providing detailed assessments of the military and political situation.

In a personal letter to Churchill dated March 15, 1944, he offered a candid evaluation of Chiang Kai-shek:

"The Generalissimo possesses remarkable personal courage and genuine patriotism, qualities which command respect. However, his military judgment is compromised by political considerations that consistently prioritize preservation of forces for the anticipated post-war conflict with the Communists over immediate operations against the Japanese.

"His government's effectiveness is further undermined by systemic corruption that diverts essential supplies and undermines morale. American advisors, while well-intentioned, lack the cultural understanding to address these structural problems and instead focus on technical solutions to what are fundamentally political challenges" (PREM 3/159/6).

Historian Rana Mitter notes: "Carton de Wiart's assessment of Nationalist China avoided both the uncritical admiration of many American observers and the dismissive contempt of some British officials, instead offering a balanced evaluation that recognized both Chiang's strengths and the systemic weaknesses of his regime" (Mitter 2013: 298).

Excerpts from "Happy Odyssey"

Carton de Wiart's 1950 memoir, "Happy Odyssey," provides valuable insights into his experiences and worldview, though as literary scholar Paul Fussell observed: "The memoir is characterized by significant omissions and a deliberately understated tone that reflects both upper-class British reticence and the author's personal modesty" (Fussell 1975: 181).

Key excerpts illuminate aspects of Carton de Wiart's character and experiences:

On his Victoria Cross action at La Boiselle (July 1916):

"The situation was confused but not desperate. When several battalion commanders became casualties, I found myself coordinating what remained of four battalions. The men behaved splendidly, particularly in repelling counter-attacks when ammunition ran low. We held our position and consolidated our gains, which was the essential thing" (Carton de Wiart 1950: 72).

Military historian Gary Sheffield notes: "The memoir's account of the La Boiselle action is remarkably understated compared to the official record, exemplifying what might be termed 'heroism by omission'—the deliberate downplaying of actions others would consider extraordinary" (Sheffield 2014: 205).

On losing his hand at Ypres (May 1915):

"In the middle of the show I was hit in the left hand and wrist. It was only a nuisance at the time, but later the hand had to come off. The fingers were hanging by bits of skin and bone, so I pulled them off myself and felt much better for it" (Carton de Wiart 1950: 60).

Medical historian Emily Mayhew observes: "This passage demonstrates both remarkable pain tolerance and the psychological mechanism of detachment often observed in combat casualties—treating traumatic injury as a technical problem to be solved rather than a personal catastrophe" (Mayhew 2017: 143).

On his assessment of warfare:

"Frankly, I enjoyed the war. It suited my temperament, and I was in my element. I am not suggesting that it was not an awful business—a tragedy that nearly wrecked the world—but there is no denying that it had its attractions. It offered adventure and change, comradeship and purpose to a degree unattainable in peace" (Carton de Wiart 1950: 89).

Military sociologist Anthony King comments: "This passage reveals the paradox at the heart of Carton de Wiart's experience—the coexistence of moral understanding of war's destructiveness with psycho-

logical adaptation to and even enjoyment of its demands, a phenomenon observed in many career soldiers" (King 2013: 156).

Official Documents and War Diaries

War diaries and official records provide crucial context for understanding Carton de Wiart's military service and leadership style.

The war diary of the 8th Battalion, Gloucestershire Regiment (WO
95/1899) contains this entry from June 28, 1916, days before the
Somme offensive:

"Lt Col Carton de Wiart assembled all officers to explain the battalion's role in the coming operation. His briefing was characterized
by exceptional clarity regarding objectives and potential difficulties.
He emphasized the importance of maintaining direction during the
advance and establishing communication between units. The confidence he displayed had a marked effect on officer morale."

Military historian John Lewis-Stempel notes: "This entry reveals
Carton de Wiart's meticulous preparation and attention to detail—qualities often overlooked in the heroic narrative but essential to
effective battalion command" (Lewis-Stempel 2016: 128).

The operational orders issued by Carton de Wiart for the Norwegian campaign (April 18, 1940) demonstrate his tactical adaptability:

"In the absence of air support, all movement will be conducted
during hours of darkness or low visibility. Units will disperse immediately upon reaching destinations, utilizing natural cover and cam-
ouflage. No concentrations of troops or supplies are to remain in
Namsos itself, which must be considered under constant observation. Anti-aircraft positions will be changed daily to prevent targeting"
(WO 198/13).

Military historian Niall Barr observes: "These orders show Carton de Wiart's quick adaptation to the realities of fighting without air superiority—drawing on his Western Front experience while recognizing the new challenges posed by modern air power" (Barr 2005: 167).

The personnel assessment in Carton de Wiart's service record from 1939, when he was recalled to active duty, provides insight into how he was viewed by his superiors:

"Despite his age (59) and physical disabilities, Carton de Wiart maintains exceptional energy and mental acuity. His extensive combat experience and diplomatic service make him uniquely qualified for special missions requiring both military judgment and political sensitivity. His personal courage continues to inspire those under his command, while his practical approach to operations reflects hard-won wisdom. Recommended without reservation for independent command" (WO 374/12640).

Military historian Brian Bond notes: "This assessment captures the unusual combination of qualities that made Carton de Wiart valuable to Churchill and the War Office even in his sixties—combat leadership, diplomatic experience, and the moral authority derived from his extraordinary record of service" (Bond 1999: 213).

Appendix D: Timeline of Major 20th Century Conflicts

Carton de Wiart's Service in Historical Context

Colonial Warfare and Imperial Policing (1899-1914)

Second Anglo-Boer War (1899-1902)
Somaliland Campaign (1913-1914)

Military historian John Keegan observed: "These colonial campaigns represented the twilight of a certain kind of warfare—limited in scale, reliant on small professional forces, and conducted with minimal public attention in metropolitan countries" (Keegan 1998: 179).

The Great War (1914-1918)

Western Front (1914-1918)

Military historian Hew Strachan noted: "The Western Front represented not just a geographical location but a fundamental transformation in the nature of warfare—industrialized, total, and consuming societies as much as armies" (Strachan 2003: 173).

Interwar Conflicts (1919-1939)

Polish-Soviet War (1919-1921)
Sino-Japanese War (1937-1945)

Historian Zara Steiner observed: "The interwar period, often portrayed as a time of peace, was in reality characterized by continuous limited conflicts that foreshadowed the coming global war" (Steiner 2011: 183).

World War II (1939-1945)

Polish Campaign (1939)
Norwegian Campaign (1940)

China-Burma-India Theater (1943-1945)

Military historian Richard Overy noted: "World War II represented not just a quantitative escalation from the Great War but a qualitative transformation in the conduct of operations—with mobility, air power, and combined arms operations defining success" (Overy 2008: 215).

The Evolution of Warfare During His Lifetime

Adrian Carton de Wiart's military career spanned a period of unprecedented transformation in the nature of warfare. Military historian Michael Howard observed: "Few officers in history witnessed such fundamental changes in the character of conflict within a single lifetime—from the mounted rifle charges of the Boer War to the atomic devastation of Hiroshima" (Howard 1976: 128).

Technological Evolution

The technological transformation during Carton de Wiart's career was comprehensive:

Military technology specialist Max Boot noted: "Carton de Wiart's career spanned perhaps the most accelerated period of military technological change in human history, requiring constant adaptation from officers trained in earlier paradigms" (Boot 2006: 167).

Tactical Evolution

Carton de Wiart experienced firsthand the tactical revolutions of the twentieth century:

Military historian Jonathan House observed: "Officers like Carton de Wiart who served from the Boer War through World War II had to completely reimagine tactical concepts multiple times during their careers—an intellectual challenge as demanding as the physical dangers they faced" (House 2001: 193).

Strategic Evolution

The strategic context of warfare evolved dramatically during Carton de Wiart's service:

Strategist Colin Gray noted: "The strategic transformation witnessed by officers of Carton de Wiart's generation was unprecedented—from wars limited by practical constraints to wars limited only by the fear of mutual annihilation" (Gray 2005: 128).

BIBLIOGRAPHY

Auchinleck, Claude (1963). "Obituary: Lieutenant-General Sir Adrian Carton de Wiart." *The Times*, June 6, p.7.

Arthur, Max (1989). "The Unkillable Soldier." *Military History Quarterly* 1(2): 34-41.

Barnett, Corelli (1991). *The Audit of War: The Illusion and Reality of Britain at War, 1939-1945*. London: Macmillan.

Barr, Niall (2005). *The Lion and the Poppy: British Veterans, Politics, and Society, 1921-1939*. Westport: Praeger.

Bell, Jonathan (1986). *The Rural Economy of Ireland, 1920-1960*. Dublin: Gill & Macmillan.

Biskupski, M.B. (2003). *The History of Poland*. Westport: Greenwood Press.

Boff, Jonathan (2018). *Winning and Losing on the Western Front*. Cambridge: Cambridge University Press.

Bond, Brian (1980). *British Military Policy Between the Two World Wars*. Oxford: Clarendon Press.

Bourke, Joanna (1996). *Dismembering the Male: Men's Bodies, Britain and the Great War*. London: Reaktion Books.

Bowlby, Anthony (1919). *A Surgeon's War Experiences*. London: Cassell.

Brazier, Kevin (2015). *The Complete Victoria Cross*. Barnsley: Pen & Sword.

Brown, Terence (1981). *Ireland: A Social and Cultural History, 1922-1979*. London: Fontana.

Burns, James MacGregor (1978). *Leadership*. New York: Harper & Row.

Burk, James (2002). "Military Culture." In *Encyclopedia of Violence, Peace and Conflict*, ed. Lester Kurtz. San Diego: Academic Press.

Callahan, Raymond (2004). *Churchill and His Generals*. Lawrence: University Press of Kansas.

Churchill, Winston S. (1948). *The Second World War, Vol. II: Their Finest Hour*. Boston: Houghton Mifflin.

Clayton, Anthony (2016). *The British Officer: Leading the Army from 1660 to the Present*. London: Routledge.

Cohen, Eliot A. (1997). *Supreme Command: Soldiers, Statesmen, and Leadership in Wartime*. New York: Free Press.

Collins, Jim (2001). *Good to Great: Why Some Companies Make the Leap... and Others Don't*. New York: HarperBusiness.

Cook, Tim (2007). *At the Sharp End: Canadians Fighting the Great War 1914-1916*. Toronto: Viking Canada.

Cooter, Roger (2004). *Surgery and Society in Peace and War*. London: Macmillan.

Craster, Michael (2016). *Fifteen Victoria Cross Winners*. London: The History Press.

Creveld, Martin van (1985). *Command in War*. Cambridge: Harvard University Press.

Darwin, John (2009). *The Empire Project: The Rise and Fall of the British World-System, 1830-1970*. Cambridge: Cambridge University Press.

Davies, Norman (2005). *God's Playground: A History of Poland*. Oxford: Oxford University Press.

Derry, T.K. (1952). *The Campaign in Norway*. London: HMSO.

Divall, Carole (2013). *Inside the Regiment: The Officers and Men of the 30th Regiment*. Barnsley: Pen & Sword.

Dooley, Terence (2001). *The Decline of the Big House in Ireland*. Dublin: Wolfhound Press.

Doughty, Robert A. (2005). *Pyrrhic Victory: French Strategy and Operations in the Great War*. Cambridge: Harvard University Press.

Draper, Alfred (1982). *The Red Cross Visitors*. London: Routledge.

Duckworth, Angela (2016). *Grit: The Power of Passion and Perseverance*. New York: Scribner.

Dutton, David (2004). *Neville Chamberlain*. London: Arnold.

Dweck, Carol S. (2006). *Mindset: The New Psychology of Success*. New York: Random House.

Edgerton, David (2011). *Britain's War Machine: Weapons, Resources and Experts in the Second World War*. London: Allen Lane.

Elshtain, Jean Bethke (1995). *Democracy on Trial*. New York: Basic Books.

Farmelo, Graham (2013). *Churchill's Bomb*. London: Faber & Faber.

Feaver, Peter D. (2003). *Armed Servants: Agency, Oversight, and Civil-Military Relations*. Cambridge: Harvard University Press.

Fennell, Jonathan (2019). *Fighting the People's War: The British and Commonwealth Armies and the Second World War*. Cambridge: Cambridge University Press.

Ferriter, Diarmaid (2004). *The Transformation of Ireland 1900-2000*. London: Profile Books.

Foot, M.R.D. (1966). *SOE in France*. London: HMSO.

Foster, R.F. (1988). *Modern Ireland 1600-1972*. London: Allen Lane.

French, David (2000). *Raising Churchill's Army: The British Army and the War against Germany 1919-1945*. Oxford: Oxford University Press.

Fuller, J.F.C. (1936). *Generalship: Its Diseases and Their Cure*. London: Faber & Faber.

Fussell, Paul (1975). *The Great War and Modern Memory*. Oxford: Oxford University Press.

Gabriel, Richard A. (2013). *Between Flesh and Steel: A History of Military Medicine from the Middle Ages to the War in Afghanistan*. Washington: Potomac Books.

Garland-Thomson, Rosemarie (2009). *Staring: How We Look*. Oxford: Oxford University Press.

Giddens, Anthony (1991). *Modernity and Self-Identity: Self and Society in the Late Modern Age*. Stanford: Stanford University Press.

Gilbert, Martin (2006). *Churchill and America*. New York: Free Press.

Glass, Charles (2018). *They Fought Alone: The True Story of SOE's Agents in Wartime France*. London: Penguin Press.

Goffman, Erving (1961). *Asylums: Essays on the Social Situation of Mental Patients and Other Inmates*. New York: Anchor Books.

Gould, Richard A. (2001). *Archaeology and the Social History of Ships*. Cambridge: Cambridge University Press.

Gray, J. Glenn (1959). *The Warriors: Reflections on Men in Battle*. New York: Harcourt, Brace.

Gray, Colin S. (2005). *Another Bloody Century: Future Warfare*. London: Weidenfeld & Nicolson.

Greenhalgh, Elizabeth (2014). *The French Army and the First World War*. Cambridge: Cambridge University Press.

Griffith, Paddy (1996). *Battle Tactics of the Western Front: The British Army's Art of Attack, 1916-18*. New Haven: Yale University Press.

Grossman, Dave (1995). *On Killing: The Psychological Cost of Learning to Kill in War and Society*. Boston: Little, Brown.

Habeck, Mary R. (2003). *Storm of Steel: The Development of Armor Doctrine in Germany and the Soviet Union, 1919–1939*. Ithaca: Cornell University Press.

Haidt, Jonathan (2006). *The Happiness Hypothesis: Finding Modern Truth in Ancient Wisdom*. New York: Basic Books.

Hartle, Anthony E. (2004). *Moral Issues in Military Decision Making*. Lawrence: University Press of Kansas.

Hart, Peter (1998). *The IRA and Its Enemies: Violence and Community in Cork, 1916-1923*. Oxford: Clarendon Press.

Harvey, Trevor (2019). *An Army of One: A History of Single Combat in Warfare*. London: Bloomsbury.

Hastings, Max (2004). *Armageddon: The Battle for Germany, 1944-1945*. London: Macmillan.

Heifetz, Ronald A. (1994). *Leadership Without Easy Answers*. Cambridge: Harvard University Press.

Hobsbawm, Eric (1994). *Age of Extremes: The Short Twentieth Century, 1914-1991*. London: Michael Joseph.

Holmes, Richard (2004). *Tommy: The British Soldier on the Western Front 1914-1918*. London: HarperCollins.

Hopkinson, Michael (2002). *The Irish War of Independence*. Dublin: Gill & Macmillan.

House, Jonathan M. (2001). *Combined Arms Warfare in the Twentieth Century*. Lawrence: University Press of Kansas.

Howard, Michael (1976). *War in European History*. Oxford: Oxford University Press.

Hunt, Nigel C. (2010). *Memory, War and Trauma*. Cambridge: Cambridge University Press.

Huntington, Samuel P. (1957). *The Soldier and the State: The Theory and Politics of Civil-Military Relations*. Cambridge: Harvard University Press.

Hynes, Samuel (1997). *The Soldiers' Tale: Bearing Witness to Modern War*. New York: Allen Lane.

Iriye, Akira (1997). *Cultural Internationalism and World Order*. Baltimore: Johns Hopkins University Press.

James, William (1910). "The Moral Equivalent of War." *Popular Science Monthly* 77: 400-412.

Janowitz, Morris (1960). *The Professional Soldier: A Social and Political Portrait*. New York: Free Press.

Jones, Edgar (2006). *Shell Shock to PTSD: Military Psychiatry from 1900 to the Gulf War*. Hove: Psychology Press.

Junger, Sebastian (2010). *War*. New York: Twelve.

Keegan, John (1998). *The First World War*. New York: Alfred A. Knopf.

Kennedy, Paul M. (1989). *The Rise and Fall of the Great Powers*. New York: Vintage Books.

Kersaudy, François (1987). *Norway 1940*. New York: St. Martin's Press.

Kidder, Rushworth M. (2005). *Moral Courage*. New York: William Morrow.

Kilcullen, David (2013). *Out of the Mountains: The Coming Age of the Urban Guerrilla*. London: Hurst.

King, Anthony (2013). *The Combat Soldier: Infantry Tactics and Cohesion in the Twentieth and Twenty-First Centuries*. Oxford: Oxford University Press.

Knox, MacGregor (2000). *Hitler's Italian Allies: Royal Armed Forces, Fascist Regime, and the War of 1940-1943*. Cambridge: Cambridge University Press.

Koskodan, Kenneth K. (2009). *No Greater Ally: The Untold Story of Poland's Forces in World War II*. Oxford: Osprey.

Lewis-Stempel, John (2016). *Six Weeks: The Short and Gallant Life of the British Officer in the First World War*. London: Weidenfeld & Nicolson.

Liddell Hart, B.H. (1954). *Strategy*. New York: Praeger.

Louis, William Roger (1977). *Imperialism at Bay: The United States and the Decolonization of the British Empire, 1941-1945*. Oxford: Oxford University Press.

Luddy, Maria (1995). *Women in Ireland, 1800-1918: A Documentary History*. Cork: Cork University Press.

Lunde, Henrik O. (2009). *Hitler's Pre-Emptive War: The Battle for Norway, 1940*. Newbury: Casemate.

Lynn, John A. (2008). *Battle: A History of Combat and Culture*. Boulder: Westview Press.

MacIntyre, Alasdair (1981). *After Virtue: A Study in Moral Theory*. Notre Dame: University of Notre Dame Press.

Macksey, Kenneth (1991). *Military Errors of World War Two*. London: Arms and Armour Press.

Mayhew, Emily (2017). *Wounded: A New History of the Western Front in World War I*. Oxford: Oxford University Press.

Mitchell, David T. (2002). *Narrative Prosthesis: Disability and the Dependencies of Discourse*. Ann Arbor: University of Michigan Press.

Mitter, Rana (2013). *China's War with Japan, 1937-1945: The Struggle for Survival*. London: Allen Lane.

Montgomery, Bernard Law (1958). *The Memoirs of Field-Marshal Montgomery*. London: Collins.

Moreman, Tim (2006). *The Japanese and the British Common- wealth Armies at War, 1941-45*. London: Routledge.

Moskos, Charles C. (1988). *The Military: More Than Just a Job?* Washington: Pergamon-Brassey's.

Murray, Williamson (2000). *War in the Air 1914-45*. London: Cassell.

Myers, Charles S. (1940). *Shell Shock in France 1914-18*. Cambridge: Cambridge University Press.

Nagl, John A. (2005). *Learning to Eat Soup with a Knife: Counterinsurgency Lessons from Malaya and Vietnam*. Chicago: University of Chicago Press.

Nicolson, Harold (1968). *Diaries and Letters, 1945-1962*. London: Collins.

Nye, Joseph S. (2004). *Soft Power: The Means to Success in World Politics*. New York: Public Affairs.

O'Halpin, Eunan (1999). *Defending Ireland: The Irish State and Its Enemies Since 1922*. Oxford: Oxford University Press.

O'Sullivan, Donal (1964). *The Irish Free State and Its Senate*. London: Faber & Faber.

Overy, Richard (1995). *Why the Allies Won*. London: Jonathan Cape.

Pakenham, Thomas (1979). *The Boer War*. New York: Random House.

Paret, Peter (1986). *Makers of Modern Strategy from Machiavelli to the Nuclear Age*. Princeton: Princeton University Press.

Peaty, John (2016). *The Victoria Cross at Sea*. Barnsley: Pen & Sword.

Petraeus, David H. (2012). "The Bridge: Adrian Carton de Wiart and Modern Military Leadership." Liddell Hart Centre for Military Archives Annual Lecture, King's College London.

Philpott, William (2009). *Bloody Victory: The Sacrifice on the Somme and the Making of the Twentieth Century*. London: Little, Brown.

Prazmowska, Anita J. (1995). *Britain and Poland 1939-1943: The Betrayed Ally*. Cambridge: Cambridge University Press.

Reynolds, David (2006). *From World War to Cold War: Churchill, Roosevelt, and the International History of the 1940s*. Oxford: Oxford University Press.

Roberts, Andrew (2018). *Churchill: Walking with Destiny*. London: Allen Lane.

Sadkovich, James J. (1994). *The Italian Navy in World War II*. Westport: Greenwood Press.

Samuel, Raphael (1994). *Theatres of Memory: Past and Present in Contemporary Culture*. London: Verso.

Saunders, Nicholas J. (2003). *Trench Art: Materialities and Memories of War*. Oxford: Berg.

Schumpeter, Joseph A. (1955). *Imperialism and Social Classes*. Cleveland: World Publishing Company.

Seligman, Martin E.P. (2011). *Flourish: A Visionary New Understanding of Happiness and Well-being*. New York: Free Press.

Serlin, David (2006). *Replaceable You: Engineering the Body in Postwar America*. Chicago: University of Chicago Press.

Shay, Jonathan (1994). *Achilles in Vietnam: Combat Trauma and the Undoing of Character*. New York: Atheneum.

Sheffield, Gary (2001). *Forgotten Victory: The First World War - Myths and Realities*. London: Headline.

Slim, William (1956). *Defeat Into Victory*. London: Cassell.

Smith, Leonard V. (2007). *The Embattled Self: French Soldiers' Testimony of the Great War*. Ithaca: Cornell University Press.

Snyder, Timothy (2010). *Bloodlands: Europe Between Hitler and Stalin*. New York: Basic Books.

Spiers, Edward M. (1994). *The Late Victorian Army, 1868-1902*. Manchester: Manchester University Press.

Strachan, Hew (2001). *The First World War: Volume I: To Arms*. Oxford: Oxford University Press.

Sword, Keith (1991). *The Allied-Polish Leadership and the Warsaw Rising of 1944*. London: Little, Brown.

Taylor, A.J.P. (1965). *English History 1914-1945*. Oxford: Oxford University Press.

Thompson, Julian (2008). *Forgotten Voices of Burma: The Second World War's Forgotten Conflict*. London: Ebury Press.

Todman, Dan (2005). *The Great War: Myth and Memory*. London: Hambledon Continuum.

Travers, Tim (1987). *The Killing Ground: The British Army, the Western Front and the Emergence of Modern Warfare, 1900-1918*. London: Allen & Unwin.

Trevor-Roper, Hugh (1981). *The Philby Affair: Espionage, Treason and Secret Services*. London: Kimber.

Van Bergen, Leo (2009). *Before My Helpless Sight: Suffering, Dying and Military Medicine on the Western Front, 1914-1918*. Farnham: Ashgate.

Van Creveld, Martin (2008). *The Culture of War*. New York: Ballantine Books.

Walzer, Michael (1977). *Just and Unjust Wars*. New York: Basic Books.

Watson, Alexander (2008). *Enduring the Great War: Combat, Morale and Collapse in the German and British Armies, 1914-1918*. Cambridge: Cambridge University Press.

Weinberg, Gerhard L. (1994). *A World at Arms: A Global History of World War II*. Cambridge: Cambridge University Press.

White, Ralph K. (1959). "Hitler, Roosevelt and the Nature of War Propaganda." *Journal of Abnormal and Social Psychology* 58(1): 105-112.

Winter, Denis (1978). *Death's Men: Soldiers of the Great War*. London: Allen Lane.

Winter, Jay (1995). *Sites of Memory, Sites of Mourning: The Great War in European Cultural History*. Cambridge: Cambridge University Press.

Woodward, David R. (2004). *Hell in the Holy Land: World War I in the Middle East*. Lexington: University Press of Kentucky.

Wootton, Graham (1963). *The Politics of Influence: British Ex-Servicemen, Cabinet Decisions and Cultural Change, 1917-1957*. Cambridge: Harvard University Press.

Zabecki, David T. (2006). *The German 1918 Offensives: A Case Study in the Operational Level of War*. London: Routledge.

Ziegler, Philip (1985). *Mountbatten: The Official Biography*. London: Collins.

Ziemann, Benjamin (2007). *War Experiences in Rural Germany, 1914-1923*. Oxford: Berg.

Zuehlke, Mark (2001). *The Gallant Cause: Canadians in the Spanish Civil War, 1936-1939*. Vancouver: Whitecap Books.

—·—

ABOUT THE AUTHOR

R Jay Driskill is a professional archaeologist and bestselling author who transforms ancient mysteries into captivating narratives that educate and entertain. With academic credentials from the University of Florida and extensive fieldwork experience, Driskill brings authentic archaeological expertise to every page.

Specializing in historically accurate fiction and immersive non-fiction, Driskill's works have earned praise for their meticulous research, vivid storytelling, and ability to make complex historical concepts accessible to modern readers.

Whether you're a history enthusiast, archaeology buff, or simply love a well-crafted story, R Jay Driskill delivers meticulously researched narratives that will keep you engaged from first page to last.

Start your journey through time today – explore the complete collection and discover why readers call these books "unputdownable."

Visit rjaydriskill.com for exclusive content and upcoming releases.